Weight Loss Meal Prep Cookbook for Beginners

1000 Easy Recipes and Weekly Plans to Preserve Your Time and Promote Weight Loss Naturally

Nigal Methe

© Copyright 2021 Nigal Methe - All Rights Reserved.

In no way is it legal to reproduce, duplicate, or transmit any part of this document by either electronic means or in printed format. Recording of this publication is strictly prohibited, and any storage of this material is not allowed unless with written permission from the publisher. All rights reserved.

The information provided herein is stated to be truthful and consistent, in that any liability, regarding inattention or otherwise, by any usage or abuse of any policies, processes, or directions contained within is the solitary and complete responsibility of the recipient reader. Under no circumstances will any legal liability or blame be held against the publisher for any reparation, damages, or monetary loss due to the information herein, either directly or indirectly.

Respective authors own all copyrights not held by the publisher.

Legal Notice:

This book is copyright protected. This is only for personal use. You cannot amend, distribute, sell, use, quote or paraphrase any part of the content within this book without the consent of the author or copyright owner. Legal action will be pursued if this is breached.

Disclaimer Notice:

Please note the information contained within this document is for educational and entertainment purposes only. Every attempt has been made to provide accurate, up-to-date and reliable, complete information. No warranties of any kind are expressed or implied. Readers acknowledge that the author is not engaging in the rendering of legal, financial, medical or professional advice.

By reading this document, the reader agrees that under no circumstances are we responsible for any losses, direct or indirect, which are incurred as a result of the use of information contained within this document, including, but not limited to, errors, omissions, or inaccuracies.

Table of Contents

Introduction 12
Chapter 1: Breakfast Recipes 13

- Baked Breakfast Frittata 13
- Easy Asparagus Quiche 13
- Zucchini Egg Casserole................. 13
- Sausage Egg Omelet 14
- Sausage Breakfast Casserole 14
- Sausage Ricotta Cheese Casserole 15
- Easy Cheese Quiche...................... 15
- Easy Cheese Egg Bake 15
- Zucchini Bacon Bake 16
- Broccoli Egg Bake......................... 16
- Baked Breakfast Egg..................... 16
- Chicken Cheese Quiche 17
- Cheese Mushrooms Egg Bake 17
- Ranch Breakfast Quiche 18
- Healthy Veggie Frittata 18
- Turkey Cheese Frittata 18
- Jalapeno Breakfast Casserole....... 19
- Cauliflower Casserole 19
- Healthy Veggie Casserole 20
- Cauliflower Breakfast Casserole...20
- Mushroom Kale Muffins 20
- Egg Ham Muffins 21
- Greek Breakfast Muffins 21
- Easy Cheese Omelet 22
- Cheese Herb Egg Cups 22
- Healthy Spinach Muffins..............22
- Cheese Ham Baked Omelet 23
- Cheese Egg Cups...........................23
- Cheese Bacon Chaffle 23
- Banan Breakfast Bread 24
- Healthy Zucchini Chaffle..............24
- Breakfast Cheese Tomato Quiche.24
- Coconut Chaffle 25
- Healthy Tuna Waffles 25
- Delicious Cheese Bacon Quiche ...25
- Quick & Easy Frittata 26
- Sausage Zucchini Casserole..........26
- Cauliflower Chaffle 27
- Healthy Tofu Scramble.................27
- Spinach Egg Scramble 27
- Kale Sausage Muffins 28
- Nutritious Chicken Muffins......... 28
- Easy Bacon Muffins 28
- Italian Spinach Frittata 29
- Mexican Frittata 29
- Scrambled Egg 30
- Spinach Tomato Breakfast Bake . 30
- Spinach Tofu Scramble................ 30
- Tasty Breakfast Waffles 31
- Easy Broccoli Omelet.................... 31
- Asparagus Frittata 32
- Spinach Kale Egg Bake 32

Simple Asparagus Omelet 32
Spinach Tomato Chicken Egg Muffin 33
Spicy Scrambled Egg 33
Healthy Pumpkin Pancake 33

Tasty Broccoli Bread 34
Spicy Jalapeno Muffins 34
Vegetable Ham Egg Muffins 35
Cheesy Zucchini Quiche 35

Chapter 2: Poultry 36

Italian Baked Pesto Chicken 36
Chicken Cheese Casserole 36
Parmesan Chicken Tenders 36
Delicious Chicken Cacciatore 37
Cheesy Chicken Casserole 37
Perfect Ranch Chicken 38
Cajun Air Fried Chicken 38
Balsamic Chicken 38
Chicken Broccoli Casserole 39
Creamy Chicken Marsala 39
Lemon Pepper Chicken 39
Mediterranean Chicken 40
Air Fryer Chicken Wings 40
Delicious Baked Chicken Fajitas .. 41
Meatballs 41
Coconut Chicken Curry 41
Turkey Meatloaf 42
Italian Chicken 42
Turkey Patties 42
Creamy Garlic Butter Chicken 43
Zesty Chicken Soup 43
Flavorful Chicken Casserole 44
Taco Chicken Chaffle 44

Balsamic Chicken Thighs 44
Yummy Chicken Tenders 45
Chicken Cacciatore Stew 45
Tasty Chicken Fajita 46
Stir Fry Chicken 46
Dried Herb Chicken 46
Chicken Skewers 47
BBQ Chicken Chaffle 47
Chicken Chaffle............................. 47
Tasty Chicken Stew 48
Creamy Coconut Chicken Curry .. 48
Turkey Breast with Veggie 49
Turkey Bacon Burgers 49
Spicy Chicken Breasts................... 49
Spinach Turkey Burgers 50
Paprika Lemon Chicken 50
Flavorful Chili Lime Chicken........ 50
Taco Chicken Drumsticks 51
Tasty Chicken Kebabs................... 51
Spicy Chili Chicken 52
Grilled Chicken Breast.................. 52
Juicy Garlic Chicken 52
Chicken with Olives & Artichokes 53

Flavorful Chicken Skewers 53
Greek Chicken 54
Cheesy Chicken Casserole 54
Cajun Chicken Stew 54
Meatballs 55
Tasty Chicken Curry 55
Tomato Olive Capers Chicken 56
Roasted Pepper Artichoke Chicken 56
Chicken Shawarma 56
Easy Chicken Kebabs 57
Pesto Chicken 57
Chicken with Mushrooms 58
Rosemary Turkey Breast 58
Salsa Chicken 58

Chapter 3: Vegetarian 59

Cheesy Cauliflower Mashed 59
Simple Pumpkin Casserole 59
Delicious Cauliflower Rice 59
Green Beans with Jicama 60
Roasted Garlic Mushrooms 60
Sauteed Mushrooms & Green Beans 60
Spinach Mushroom Cauliflower Rice 61
Flavors Zucchini in Sauce 61
Roasted Asparagus 62
Spinach Cheese Squares 62
Healthy Broccoli Casserole 62
Roasted Brussels Sprouts 63
Crispy Brussels Sprouts 63
Lemon Garlic Broccoli 63
Broccoli Mushroom Stir Fry 64
Cabbage Chaffle 64
Broccoli Chaffle 64
Dill Zucchini Chaffle 65
Grilled Cauliflower Wedges 65
Zucchini Chaffle 65
Mac and Cheese 66
Roasted Cauliflower 66
Tasty Brussel Sprouts Skewers 67
Italian Sauteed Mushrooms 67
Eggplant & Zucchini 67
Cauliflower Soup 68
Tomato Basil Soup 68
Pesto Zucchini Noodles 69
Grilled Zucchini 69
Parmesan Asparagus 69
Eggplant Curry 70
Easy Roasted Artichoke Hearts 70
Spinach Broccoli Curry 70
Ratatouille 71
Zucchini Spinach Soup 71
Carrot Tomato Soup 72
Creamy Pumpkin Soup 72
Stir Fried Eggplant 72

Cheesy Zucchini Casserole 73	Healthy Zucchini Garlic Noodles . 75
Roasted Vegetables 73	Zucchini Stir Fry 75
Creamy Asparagus Soup 73	Tofu Stir Fry 76
Broccoli Soup 74	Zucchini with Herbs 76
Roasted Herb Zucchini 74	Curried Squash Coconut Soup 76
Asian Zucchini Noodles 74	Healthy Pumpkin Soup 77

Chapter 4: Meat Recipes 78

Easy Ranch Pork Chops 78	Meatballs 85
Flavorful Beef Chili 78	Beef Stew 85
Mexican Beef 78	Rosemary Beef Tips 86
Easy Beef Stroganoff 79	Montreal Steak Tips 86
Healthy Beef Stroganoff 79	Beef Kebabs 87
Keto Butter Beef 79	Delicious Beef Kebabs 87
Crispy Crusted Pork Chops 80	Meatballs 87
Hearty Taco Soup 80	Easy Steak Fajitas 88
Beef Fajitas 80	Simple Spice Pork Chops 88
Beef & Broccoli 81	Curried Pork Chops 88
Easy Pulled Pork 81	Salsa Pork Chops 89
Juicy Pork Tenderloin 82	Lemon Pepper Pork Tenderloin .. 89
Meatballs 82	Grilled Lamb Chops 89
Lemon Pepper Pork Chops 82	Grilled Steak Kababs 90
Meatballs 82	Lamb Chops 90
Simple Steak with Mushrooms 83	Lamb Roast 90
Meatloaf 83	Flank Steak 91
Easy & Tasty Steak 84	Lamb Kebabs 91
Meatballs 84	Lamb Patties 92
Cheesy Burger Patties 84	Beef Kofta 92
Burger Patties 84	Herb Beef Patties 92
Simple Sirloin Steak 85	Tasty Pork Kabobs 93

- Meatballs 93
- Classic Pork Cacciatore 94
- Meatballs 94
- Greek Pork Chops 94
- Italian Pork Roast 95
- Simple Pork Carnitas 95
- Meatloaf 95
- Pork Roast 96
- Tasty Burger Patties 96
- Cabbage Skillet 97
- Italian Shredded Beef 97
- Meatballs 97
- Rosemary Pork Chops 98
- Meatloaf 98
- Rosemary Dijon Pork Chops 99
- Italian Beef Chuck Roast 99
- Smoked Tenderloin 99
- Minced Pork 100
- Spicy Pepper Beef 100
- Greek Beef Roast 100
- Meatloaf 101
- Beef Ribs 101
- Rosemary Lamb Roast 102
- Steak Bites 102
- Apple Cider Pork Chops 102
- Beef Barbacoa 103
- Lamb Curry 103
- Beef Mushroom Stew 103
- Meatloaf 104
- Chili Chuck Roast 104
- Tasty Ground Beef 105
- Juicy & Tender Chuck Roast 105
- Zucchini Lamb Curry 105
- Easy Pork Soup 106
- Herb Pork Chops 106
- Beef Chili 107

Chapter 5: Fish & Seafood 108

- Simple Cajun Salmon 108
- Tasty Crab Cakes 108
- White Fish Fillets 108
- Spicy Air Fryer Shrimp 109
- Paprika Herb Salmon 109
- Quick Cajun Shrimp 109
- Garlic Tomato Shrimp 109
- Easy Salmon Patties 110
- Rosemary Garlic Shrimp 110
- Lemon Pepper Fish Fillets 110
- Slow Cook Shrimp Scampi 111
- Delicious Crab Cakes 111
- Tuna Chaffle 112
- Tasty Shrimp Fajitas 112
- Cajun Scallops 112
- Flavorful Blackened Shrimp 112
- Blackened Mahi-Mahi Fish Fillets 113
- Tuna Patties 113
- Baked Basa Fillets 114

Parmesan Garlic Shrimp 114
Cajun Salmon 114
Baked Tilapia Fish Fillets 115
Baked Halibut 115
Grilled Lemon Scallops 115
Baked Swordfish Fillets 116
Lemon Cod 116
Lemon Butter Tilapia 117
Cajun Catfish Fillets 117
Grilled Salmon 117
Lemon Herb Salmon 118
Grilled Mahi Mahi Fish Fillets 118
Spicy Grilled Shrimp 118
Grilled Cajun Shrimp 119
Lemon Garlic Grilled Halibut 119
Spicy Tuna Cakes 120
Greek Tilapia 120
Parmesan Cod Fillets 120
Greek Baked Salmon 121
Rosemary Basil Salmon 121
Healthy Fish Stew 122

Lemon Garlic Baked Shrimp 122
Garlic Herb Red Snapper Fillet .. 122
Lemon Paprika Shrimp 123
Nutritious Crab Stew 123
Crab Cake Waffles 124
Baked White Fish Fillets 124
Feta Mint Tuna Patties 124
Broiled Tilapia 125
Asian Coconut Shrimp 125
Flavorful Sauteed Shrimp 125
Delicious Salmon Waffles 126
Shrimp Olive Stir Fry 126
Salmon with Baby Carrots 127
Tomato Lemon Cod Fillets 127
Shrimp Soup 127
Delicious Fish Stew 128
Pesto Fish Fillets 128
Sauteed Lemon Garlic Scallops .. 128
Spicy Garlic Shrimp 129
Lemon Garlic Prawns 129

Chapter 6: Salad Recipes 130

Southern Chicken Salad 130
Easy Avocado Egg Salad 130
Keto Italian Salad 130
Nutritious Chicken Avocado Salad
.... 131
Delicious Tuna Salad 131
Cucumber Feta Cheese Salad 131

Flavorful Deviled Egg Salad 132
Cauliflower Egg Salad 132
Healthy Mediterranean Salad 133
Quick & Easy Greek Salad 133
Tuna Avocado Salad 133
Delicious Asian Chicken Salad ... 134
Shrimp Avocado Salad 134

Quick Pepperoni Avocado Salad 134
Flavorful Asian Cucumber Salad 135
Tasty Buffalo Chicken Salad....... 135
Bacon Broccoli Salad 135
Flavors Salmon Salad 136
Chipotle Chicken Salad 136
Turkey Salad 137
Cauliflower Broccoli Salad 137
Caprese Chicken Salad 137
Classic Chicken Salad 138
Lobster Salad 138
Healthy Shrimp Salad 138
Easy Loaded Cauliflower Salad .. 139
Healthy Greek Salad 139
Healthy Greek Cucumber Salad .140
Spinach Egg Bacon Salad 140
Easy Bacon Ranch Chicken Salad 140
Dill Cucumber Salad 141
Nutritious Tuna Salad 141
Feta Avocado Cucumber Salad... 141
Egg Bacon Salad 141
Delicious Antipasto Salad........... 142
Cauliflower Shrimp Salad........... 142
Cucumber Cabbage Salad........... 143
Zucchini Noodle Salad................ 143
BLT Salad.................................... 143
Avocado Salmon Salad 144

Chapter 7: Snack & Appetizers 145

Broccoli Nuggets......................... 145
Spicy Jalapeno Poppers.............. 145
Bacon Cheese Dip 145
Roasted Mix Nuts 146
Delicious Avocado Deviled Eggs 146
Roasted Pepper Dip.................... 146
Macadamia Hummus 147
Flavors Chive Dip 147
Chicken Nuggets......................... 147
Turkey Meatballs........................ 147
Cilantro Lime Dip 148
Meatballs 148
Mediterranean Dip..................... 148
Spicy Walnuts............................. 149
Herb Mushrooms........................ 149
Spicy Brussels Sprouts................ 149
Air Fryer Tofu 150
Cauliflower Bites......................... 150
Crab Dip...................................... 150
Meatballs.....................................151
Broccoli Fritters 151
Vegan Queso 151
Kale Spread................................. 152
Spicy Cucumber Salsa................. 152
Guacamole 152
Rosemary Parmesan Tomatoes.. 153
Zucchini Fritters 153
Cauliflower Hummus 153

Healthy Carrot Fries 154
Chicken Jalapeno Poppers 154
Jalapeno Poppers 154
Cajun Broccoli Fritters 155
Toasted Pecans 155
Ranch Dip 155
Tasty Cauliflower Hummus 156
Feta Jalapeno Poppers 156
Tasty Spicy Almonds 156
Cauliflower Skewers 157
Cheese Bacon Jalapeno Poppers 157
Parmesan Spinach Dip 157
Italian Roasted Pepper Dip 158
Yummy Chicken Dip 158
Spicy Guacamole 159
Garlic Zucchini Dip 159

Chapter 8: Desserts 160

Lemon Melon Pops 160
Lemon Cheesecake Mousse 160
Delicious Brownie Bites 160
Chocolate Chaffle 161
Blueberry Muffins 161
Lemon Strawberry Granita 161
Silky Chocolate Mousse 162
Avocado Coconut Pops 162
Cinnamon Protein Bars 162
Lemon Yogurt Muffins 163
Peanut Butter Chaffle 163
Vanilla Blackberry Yogurt 163
Vanilla Coconut Bars 163
Pumpkin Cheese Ice Bombs 164
Chocolate Ice Cream 164
Vanilla Almond Ice Bombs 164
Delicious Chocolate Fudge 165
Choco Cheese Fat Bombs 165
Fudge Bars 165
Strawberry Ice Cream 166
Whipped Cream & Fresh Berries 166
Almond Peanut Butter Bars 166
Chocolate Cake 167
Pecan Carrot Cake 167
Peanut Butter Chocolate Fudge .. 168
Chocolate Frosty 168
Berry Cheesecake Ice Bombs 168
Raspberry Cheese Bites 168
Delicious Lemon Cake 169
Butter Cake 169
Vanilla Custard 170
Almond Peanut Butter Fat Bombs 170
Smooth Peanut Butter Mousse ... 170
Blackberry Ice Cream 170
Vanilla Pumpkin Ice Cream 171
Coffee Fat Bombs 171
Berry Yogurt 171
Delicious Lemon Mousse 172
Cocoa Butter Raspberry Candy .. 172

Coconut Butter Fat Bombs......... 172
Coconut Butter Pops................... 173
Choco Peppermint Mousse 173
Almond Butter Fat Bombs 173
Raspberry Cheese Fat Bombs 174
Chocolate Custard 174
Mint Ice Cream 174
Berry Sorbet................................ 175
Raspberry Coconut Pudding 175
Delicious Strawberry Yogurt 175
Lemon Ricotta Cheesecake......... 175

Chapter 9: 21-Day Meal Plan..177

Conclusion 180

Introduction

People have different motivations for changing their eating habits. Some want to lose weight, others want to learn how to control their hunger, and some just want to stay healthy. Luckily for you, this book can help you meet these goals, no matter which category you fall into. In this book, I've provided plenty of mouth-watering recipes, as well as meal plans and an exercise regimen that offers the guidance to lose weight and keep your body healthy while you do it. The meal plan is designed to give you structure, ensure you stay in your calorie range, and give you a clear road map on your road to weight loss.

From this Weight Loss Meal Prep Cookbook, I want you to learn how to eat low-calorie while also taking care of your health. Let's go!

Chapter 1: Breakfast Recipes
Baked Breakfast Frittata

Preparation Time: 10 minutes; Cooking Time: 35 minutes; Serve: 12

Ingredients:
- 12 eggs
- 1 tsp garlic powder
- 2 1/2 cups mushrooms, chopped
- 1 cup cheddar cheese, shredded
- 1 red bell pepper, chopped
- 1 small onion, chopped
- 1 cup ham, chopped
- 1 1/2 cups asparagus, chopped
- Pepper
- Salt

Directions:
1. Preheat the oven to 375 F. Grease 9*13-inch baking pan.
2. Add asparagus, mushrooms, cheese, bell pepper, onion, and ham into the prepared pan.
3. In a bowl, whisk eggs with garlic powder, pepper, and salt.
4. Pour egg mixture over vegetables and stir gently.
5. Bake for 25-35 minutes or until frittata is set.
6. Slice and serve.

Nutritional Value (Amount per Serving):
Calories 132; Fat 8.6 g; Carbohydrates 3.5 g; Sugar 1.8 g; Protein 10.8 g; Cholesterol 180 mg

Easy Asparagus Quiche

Preparation Time: 10 minutes; Cooking Time: 45 minutes; Serve: 8

Ingredients:
- 10 eggs
- 2 lbs asparagus, trimmed and remove ends
- 3 tbsp olive oil
- Pepper
- Salt

Directions:
1. Preheat the oven to 425 F.
2. Arrange asparagus on the baking sheet. Drizzle 1 tablespoon olive oil over asparagus.
3. Roast asparagus in preheated oven for 15 minutes.
4. In a mixing bowl, whisk eggs with remaining oil, pepper, and salt.
5. Transfer roasted asparagus in a quiche pan. Pour egg mixture over asparagus.
6. Bake at 350 F for 30 minutes or until egg sets.
7. Slice and serve.

Nutritional Value (Amount per Serving):
Calories 146; Fat 10.9 g; Carbohydrates 4.8 g; Sugar 2.6 g; Protein 9.4 g; Cholesterol 205 mg

Zucchini Egg Casserole

Preparation Time: 10 minutes; Cooking Time: 30 minutes; Serve: 8

Ingredients:
- 10 eggs
- 3 cherry tomatoes, halved
- 1/2 cup mushrooms, sliced
- 1/3 cup ham, chopped
- 1 small zucchini, sliced into rounds
- 1/2 cup spinach
- 2/3 cup heavy cream
- Pepper
- Salt

Directions:
1. Preheat the oven to 350 F. Grease 9*13-inch pan and set aside.
2. In a large bowl, whisk eggs with heavy cream, pepper, and salt. Stir in tomatoes, mushrooms, ham, zucchini, and spinach.
3. Pour egg mixture in prepared pan and bake for 30-35 minutes.
4. Serve and enjoy.

Nutritional Value (Amount per Serving):
Calories 134; Fat 9.8 g; Carbohydrates 3.4 g; Sugar 2 g; Protein 8.8 g; Cholesterol 222 mg

Sausage Egg Omelet

Preparation Time: 10 minutes; Cooking Time: 23 minutes; Serve: 12

Ingredients:
- 7 eggs
- 1 tsp mustard
- 2 cups cheddar cheese, shredded
- 3/4 cup heavy whipping cream
- 1/4 onion, chopped
- 1/2 green bell pepper, chopped
- 1 lb breakfast sausage
- 1/4 tsp pepper
- 1/2 tsp salt

Directions:
1. Preheat the oven to 350 F. Grease 9*13-inch casserole dish and set aside.
2. Brown the sausage in a pan. Add onion and bell pepper and cook until onion is softened. Remove pan from heat.
3. In a bowl, whisk eggs with mustard, 1 3/4 cups of cheese, cream, pepper, and salt.
4. Spread sausage mixture into the prepared casserole. Pour egg mixture on top of the sausage mixture and top with remaining cheese.
5. Bake for 20-23 minutes.
6. Serve and enjoy.

Nutritional Value (Amount per Serving):
Calories 271; Fat 22.4 g; Carbohydrates 1.4 g; Sugar 0.7 g; Protein 15.6 g; Cholesterol 157 mg

Sausage Breakfast Casserole

Preparation Time: 10 minutes; Cooking Time: 40 minutes; Serve: 8

Ingredients:
- 12 eggs
- 1 tbsp hot sauce
- 3/4 cup heavy whipping cream
- 2 cups cheddar cheese, shredded
- 12 oz breakfast sausage
- Pepper
- Salt

Directions:
1. Preheat the oven to 350 F. Grease 9*13-inch casserole dish.
2. Heat a large pan over medium-high heat.
3. Add sausage to the pan and break with a wooden spoon and cook for 5-7 minutes or until meat is no longer pink.
4. Transfer cooked sausage into the prepared dish and spread evenly.
5. In a large bowl, whisk eggs with hot sauce, cream, cheese, pepper, and salt.
6. Pour egg mixture over sausage and bake for 30-40 minutes.
7. Serve and enjoy.

Nutritional Value (Amount per Serving):

Calories 391; Fat 32.2 g; Carbohydrates 1.2 g; Sugar 0.7 g; Protein 23.8 g; Cholesterol 326 mg

Sausage Ricotta Cheese Casserole

Preparation Time: 10 minutes; Cooking Time: 55 minutes; Serve: 12
Ingredients:
- 10 eggs
- 2 1/2 lbs Italian sausage
- 1 tbsp fresh basil, chopped
- 12 cherry tomatoes, halved
- 16 oz ricotta cheese, cut into cubes
- 4 oz cream cheese
- 1 tsp salt

Directions:
1. Preheat the oven to 400 F.
2. Add sausage into the casserole dish and bake for 20 minutes. Once done, drain sausage well and break in small pieces using a masher.
3. In a bowl, whisk eggs with cream cheese until smooth and pour over sausage. Season with salt. Sprinkle ricotta cheese cubes, tomatoes, and basil on top.
4. Bake for 35-40 minutes more.
5. Serve and enjoy.

Nutritional Value (Amount per Serving):
Calories 480; Fat 37 g; Carbohydrates 7.3 g; Sugar 3.7 g; Protein 29.1 g; Cholesterol 238 mg

Easy Cheese Quiche

Preparation Time: 10 minutes; Cooking Time: 45 minutes; Serve: 6
Ingredients:
- 12 eggs
- 12 tbsp butter, melted
- 4 oz cream cheese, softened
- 8 oz cheddar cheese, grated
- Pepper
- Salt

Directions:
1. Spread cheddar cheese into the 9-5-inch pie pan.
2. Add eggs, cream cheese, butter, pepper, and salt into the blender and blend until well combined.
3. Pour egg mixture over cheese in pie pan and bake at 325 F for 45 minutes.
4. Slice and serve.

Nutritional Value (Amount per Serving):
Calories 548; Fat 50.9 g; Carbohydrates 1.7 g; Sugar 0.9 g; Protein 22.2 g; Cholesterol 449 mg

Easy Cheese Egg Bake

Preparation Time: 10 minutes; Cooking Time: 30 minutes; Serve: 4
Ingredients:
- 4 eggs
- 1/3 cup half and half
- 4 oz cream cheese
- Pinch of salt

Directions:
1. Preheat the oven to 350 F.
2. Add eggs, half and half, cream cheese, and salt into the blender and blend until smooth.
3. Pour egg mixture into the greased baking dish and bake for 30 minutes.
4. Serve and enjoy.

Nutritional Value (Amount per Serving):
Calories 188; Fat 16.6 g; Carbohydrates 2 g; Sugar 0.4 g; Protein 8.3 g; Cholesterol 202 mg

Zucchini Bacon Bake

Preparation Time: 10 minutes; Cooking Time: 30 minutes; Serve: 8
Ingredients:
- 8 egg whites
- 3 tbsp bacon, crumbled
- 1/4 cup unsweetened almond milk
- 3 wedges Swiss cheese
- 1/2 cup cottage cheese
- 2 cups shredded zucchini
- 1/2 tsp salt

Directions:
1. Preheat the oven to 350 F. Grease 8*8-inch casserole dish.
2. Add shredded zucchini into the prepared dish.
3. Add egg, bacon, milk, Swiss cheese, cottage cheese, and salt into the blender and blend until smooth.
4. Pour blended egg mixture over shredded zucchini.
5. Bake in preheated oven for 30 minutes.
6. Serve and enjoy.

Nutritional Value (Amount per Serving):
Calories 114; Fat 6.4 g; Carbohydrates 2.4 g; Sugar 0.9 g; Protein 11.4 g; Cholesterol 19 mg

Broccoli Egg Bake

Preparation Time: 10 minutes; Cooking Time: 30 minutes; Serve: 6
Ingredients:
- 12 eggs
- 2 cups broccoli florets, chopped
- 1/2 cup cheddar cheese, shredded
- 3/4 tsp onion powder
- 1/2 cup unsweetened coconut milk
- Pepper
- Salt

Directions:
1. Preheat the oven to 350 F. Grease 9*13-inch baking dish.
2. In a bowl, whisk eggs with cheese, onion powder, milk, pepper, and salt. Stir in broccoli.
3. Pour egg mixture into the prepared dish and bake for 30 minutes.
4. Slice and serve.

Nutritional Value (Amount per Serving):
Calories 221; Fat 16.7 g; Carbohydrates 4.2 g; Sugar 2 g; Protein 14.8 g; Cholesterol 337 mg

Baked Breakfast Egg

Preparation Time: 10 minutes; Cooking Time: 15 minutes; Serve: 1
Ingredients:
- 2 eggs
- 2 tbsp half and half
- 1 tbsp parmesan cheese, grated
- 2 tbsp cheddar cheese, shredded
- Pepper
- Salt

Directions:
1. Grease 8-ounce ramekin and set aside.

2. In a small bowl, whisk eggs and a half and half. Stir in cheddar cheese, parmesan cheese, pepper, and salt.
3. Pour egg mixture into the prepared ramekin and bake at 400 F for 15 minutes.
4. Serve and enjoy.

Nutritional Value (Amount per Serving):
Calories 269; Fat 20 g; Carbohydrates 2.7 g; Sugar 0.8 g; Protein 20.2 g; Cholesterol 364 mg

Chicken Cheese Quiche

Preparation Time: 10 minutes; Cooking Time: 45 minutes; Serve: 4
Ingredients:
- 8 eggs
- 1/2 tsp oregano
- 1/4 tsp onion powder
- 1/4 tsp garlic powder
- 1/4 cup mozzarella cheese, shredded
- 5 oz cooked chicken breast, chopped
- 1/4 tsp pepper
- 1/2 tsp salt

Directions:
1. Preheat the oven to 350 F.
2. In a bowl, whisk eggs with oregano, onion powder, pepper, and salt. Stir in cheese and chicken.
3. Pour egg mixture in pie pan and bake for 35-45 minutes.
4. Slice and serve.

Nutritional Value (Amount per Serving):
Calories 173; Fat 10 g; Carbohydrates 1.2 g; Sugar 0.8 g; Protein 19.2 g; Cholesterol 351 mg

Cheese Mushrooms Egg Bake

Preparation Time: 10 minutes; Cooking Time: 25 minutes; Serve: 4
Ingredients:
- 6 eggs
- 8 oz mushrooms, sliced
- 1/3 cup shallot, minced
- 2 tbsp olive oil
- 1/2 cup mozzarella cheese, shredded
- 3/4 cup unsweetened coconut milk
- 2 tbsp fresh thyme, chopped
- Pepper
- Salt

Directions:
1. Grease four ramekins and set aside.
2. Heat oil in a pan over medium-high heat.
3. Add shallot and sauté for 3 minutes. Add mushrooms and sauté for 5 minutes.
4. Add thyme stir well and remove the pan from heat.
5. In a bowl, whisk eggs with milk, pepper, and salt. Add cheese and mushroom mixture and stir well.
6. Pour egg mixture into the prepared ramekins.
7. Bake at 400 F for 25 minutes.
8. Serve and enjoy.

Nutritional Value (Amount per Serving):
Calories 213; Fat 15 g; Carbohydrates 7.9 g; Sugar 3.6 g; Protein 13 g; Cholesterol 251 mg

Ranch Breakfast Quiche

Preparation Time: 10 minutes; Cooking Time: 55 minutes; Serve: 6

Ingredients:
- 8 eggs
- 1 cup sour cream
- 1 tbsp ranch seasoning
- 1 1/2 cups cheddar cheese, shredded
- 1 lb ground Italian sausage

Directions:
1. Preheat the oven to 350 F.
2. Brown the sausage in an oven-safe skillet and drain well.
3. In a bowl, whisk eggs with ranch seasoning, and sour cream. Stir in cheddar cheese.
4. Pour egg mixture over sausage in skillet. Cover skillet with foil.
5. Bake for 30 minutes. Remove foil and bake for 25 minutes more.
6. Serve and enjoy.

Nutritional Value (Amount per Serving):
Calories 511; Fat 40.6 g; Carbohydrates 3.8 g; Sugar 2 g; Protein 29 g; Cholesterol 318 mg

Healthy Veggie Frittata

Preparation Time: 10 minutes; Cooking Time: 20 minutes; Serve: 2

Ingredients:
- 4 eggs
- 1 cup bell peppers, chopped
- 1 cup zucchini, chopped
- 1 cup mushrooms, sliced
- 2 tbsp unsweetened coconut milk
- 1 tbsp olive oil
- 1 cup cheddar cheese
- 1/2 cup onion, chopped
- Pepper
- Salt

Directions:
1. Preheat the oven to 350 F.
2. Grease baking dish and set aside.
3. Heat oil in a pan over medium heat.
4. Add onion, bell peppers, zucchini, and mushrooms, and sauté for 5 minutes.
5. Remove pan from heat and set aside to cool.
6. In a bowl, whisk eggs with milk, pepper, and salt. Add sautéed vegetables and cheese and stir well.
7. Pour egg mixture into the prepared baking dish and bake for 20 minutes.
8. Serve and enjoy.

Nutritional Value (Amount per Serving):
Calories 565; Fat 46.4 g; Carbohydrates 11.1 g; Sugar 6.6 g; Protein 32.6 g; Cholesterol 112 mg

Turkey Cheese Frittata

Preparation Time: 10 minutes; Cooking Time: 25 minutes; Serve: 8

Ingredients:
- 8 eggs
- 8 oz turkey deli meat
- 2 tbsp cheddar cheese, shredded
- 2 tbsp parmesan cheese, shredded
- 1/2 tsp oregano
- 1/2 tsp thyme
- 1/4 tsp pepper
- 1/4 tsp salt

Directions:
1. Preheat the oven to 350 F.

2. Line an 8-inch skillet with the turkey deli meat.
3. In a bowl, whisk eggs with oregano, thyme, pepper, and salt. Pour egg mixture over meat.
4. Sprinkle parmesan cheese and cheddar cheese on top.
5. Bake for 20-25 minutes.
6. Serve and enjoy.

Nutritional Value (Amount per Serving):
Calories 108; Fat 6 g; Carbohydrates 1.2 g; Sugar 0.4 g; Protein 11.8 g; Cholesterol 178 mg

Jalapeno Breakfast Casserole

Preparation Time: 10 minutes; Cooking Time: 30 minutes; Serve: 10
Ingredients:
- 12 eggs
- 2 jalapeno peppers, sliced
- 4 oz cream cheese, cut into cubes
- 1 cup cheddar cheese, shredded
- 1/2 cup bacon, cooked and chopped
- 1 cup heavy whipping cream
- 1/2 tsp pepper
- 1/4 tsp salt

Directions:
1. Preheat the oven to 350 F. Grease 9*13-inch baking pan and set aside.
2. In a large bowl, whisk eggs with cream cheese, cream, pepper, and salt and pour into the prepared pan.
3. Sprinkle jalapeno slices, bacon, and 3/4 cup cheddar cheese evenly over egg mixture.
4. Bake for 25-30 minutes. Remove pan from oven and top with remaining cheese and bake for 5 minutes more.
5. Serve and enjoy.

Nutritional Value (Amount per Serving):
Calories 209; Fat 17.8 g; Carbohydrates 1.5 g; Sugar 0.6 g; Protein 11 g; Cholesterol 238 mg

Cauliflower Casserole

Preparation Time: 10 minutes; Cooking Time: 30 minutes; Serve: 8
Ingredients:
- 1 egg
- 1/2 cup scallions, chopped
- 1 cup bacon, crumbled
- 1 1/2 cups cheddar cheese, shredded
- 1/4 cup heavy cream
- 1/3 cup butter, softened
- 8 oz cream cheese, softened
- 20 oz frozen cauliflower, steamed and drain well
- 1 tsp salt

Directions:
1. Preheat the oven to 400 F. Grease 8*8-inch baking dish and set aside.
2. Add cauliflower, cream cheese, butter, heavy cream, egg, and salt into the food processor and process until smooth.
3. Add 1/2 cheddar cheese, scallions, and bacon into the cauliflower mixture and stir everything well.
4. Pour cauliflower mixture into the prepared baking dish and spread well.
5. Top with remaining cheddar cheese and bacon and bake for 30 minutes.
6. Serve and enjoy.

Nutritional Value (Amount per Serving):
Calories 599; Fat 50.3 g; Carbohydrates 6.2 g; Sugar 2.1 g; Protein 30.8 g; Cholesterol 162 mg

Healthy Veggie Casserole

Preparation Time: 10 minutes; Cooking Time: 40 minutes; Serve: 12

Ingredients:
- 10 eggs
- 1 cup cheddar cheese, shredded
- 2 tbsp hot sauce
- 2 bell peppers, diced
- 1/2 onion, diced
- 2 cups broccoli, chopped
- 10 oz mushrooms, sliced
- 2 tbsp garlic, minced
- 1 tbsp olive oil
- 1 tsp pepper
- 1 tsp salt

Directions:
1. Preheat the oven to 375 F. Grease 9*13-inch baking dish and set aside.
2. Heat oil in a pan over medium heat.
3. Add onion, mushrooms, and garlic and sauté for 4 minutes.
4. Turn off the heat. Add broccoli and bell peppers and stir well and set aside.
5. In a bowl, whisk eggs with hot sauce, pepper, and salt.
6. Add sautéed veggies into the prepared baking dish. Pour egg mixture over veggies and top with shredded cheddar cheese.
7. Bake in preheated oven for 35-40 minutes.
8. Slice and serve.

Nutritional Value (Amount per Serving):
Calories 122; Fat 8.1 g; Carbohydrates 4.7 g; Sugar 2.2 g; Protein 8.5 g; Cholesterol 146 mg

Cauliflower Breakfast Casserole

Preparation Time: 10 minutes; Cooking Time: 45 minutes; Serve: 6

Ingredients:
- 10 eggs
- 4 cups cauliflower rice
- 12 oz bacon, cooked and crumbled
- 1/2 cup heavy whipping cream
- 1 tsp paprika
- 8 oz cheddar cheese, shredded
- 1/4 tsp pepper
- 1 tsp salt

Directions:
1. Preheat the oven to 350 F. Grease 2-quart casserole dish.
2. Spread cauliflower rice into the prepared dish and top with half cheddar cheese.
3. In a bowl, whisk eggs with cream, paprika, pepper, and salt and pour over cauliflower. Top with remaining cheese and bacon.
4. Bake for 45 minutes.
5. Serve and enjoy.

Nutritional Value (Amount per Serving):
Calories 637; Fat 48.5 g; Carbohydrates 6.9 g; Sugar 3.5 g; Protein 42.5 g; Cholesterol 389 mg

Mushroom Kale Muffins

Preparation Time: 10 minutes; Cooking Time: 15 minutes; Serve: 8

Ingredients:
- 6 eggs
- 1 cup mushrooms, diced

- 1 cup kale, chopped
- 1 tsp olive oil
- 2 tbsp onion, minced
- 1/2 cup Swiss cheese, shredded
- Pepper
- Salt

Directions:
1. Preheat the oven to 350 F.
2. Heat olive oil in a pan over medium-high heat. Add mushrooms and sauté for 2-3 minutes.
3. Add onion and kale and sauté for 2 minutes. Remove pan from heat and set aside to cool.
4. In a bowl, whisk eggs with pepper and salt.
5. Add sautéed mushroom kale mixture and shredded cheese and stir well.
6. Pour egg mixture into the silicone muffin molds and bake for 15 minutes.
7. Serve and enjoy.

Nutritional Value (Amount per Serving):
Calories 85; Fat 5.8 g; Carbohydrates 2 g; Sugar 0.6 g; Protein 6.5 g; Cholesterol 129 mg

Egg Ham Muffins

Preparation Time: 10 minutes; Cooking Time: 25 minutes; Serve: 6
Ingredients:
- 6 eggs
- 6 tbsp cheddar cheese, shredded
- 1/4 tsp garlic powder
- 1 green onion, sliced
- 4 oz ham, cubed
- 1/2 cup unsweetened almond milk
- Pepper
- Salt

Directions:
1. Preheat the oven to 350 F.
2. In a large bowl, whisk eggs with milk, garlic powder, pepper, and salt. Stir in green onion, ham, and cheese.
3. Pour egg mixture into the six silicone muffin molds.
4. Bake for 25 minutes.
5. Serve and enjoy.

Nutritional Value (Amount per Serving):
Calories 169; Fat 13.1 g; Carbohydrates 2.5 g; Sugar 1.1 g; Protein 11 g; Cholesterol 182 mg

Greek Breakfast Muffins

Preparation Time: 10 minutes; Cooking Time: 15 minutes; Serve: 6
Ingredients:
- 2 eggs
- 1/4 cup tomatoes, diced
- 1/2 cup unsweetened coconut milk
- 4 egg whites
- 1/4 cup feta cheese, crumbled
- 1 tbsp fresh parsley, chopped
- 1/4 cup olives, diced
- 1/4 cup onion, diced
- Pepper
- Salt

Directions:
1. Preheat the oven to 350 F.
2. In a bowl, whisk eggs with milk, pepper, and salt. Add remaining ingredients and stir everything well.
3. Pour egg mixture into the six silicone muffin molds.
4. Bake for 15 minutes.

5. Serve and enjoy.

Nutritional Value (Amount per Serving):
Calories 69; Fat 3.9 g; Carbohydrates 2.7 g; Sugar 1.9 g; Protein 6 g; Cholesterol 62 mg

Easy Cheese Omelet

Preparation Time: 10 minutes; Cooking Time: 25 minutes; Serve: 6

Ingredients:
- 8 eggs
- 1/4 cup cheddar cheese, shredded
- 2 tbsp green onions, chopped
- 1/4 tsp garlic powder
- 1/2 cup unsweetened coconut milk
- 1/2 cup half and half
- Pepper
- Salt

Directions:
1. Preheat the oven to 350 F.
2. Grease an 8-inch baking dish and set aside.
3. In a bowl, whisk eggs with milk, half and half, garlic powder, pepper, and salt. Stir in green onion and cheddar cheese.
4. Pour egg mixture into the prepared baking dish and bake for 25 minutes.
5. Serve and enjoy.

Nutritional Value (Amount per Serving):
Calories 140; Fat 10.1 g; Carbohydrates 2.6 g; Sugar 1.5 g; Protein 9.9 g; Cholesterol 232 mg

Cheese Herb Egg Cups

Preparation Time: 10 minutes; Cooking Time: 20 minutes; Serve: 6

Ingredients:
- 6 eggs
- 1/2 tbsp fresh dill, chopped
- 1 tbsp fresh parsley, chopped
- 1/2 tbsp chives, chopped
- 1/2 tbsp fresh basil, chopped
- 1/4 cup mozzarella cheese, grated
- Pepper
- Salt

Directions:
1. Preheat the oven to 350 F.
2. In a bowl, whisk eggs with pepper and salt. Add remaining ingredients and stir well.
3. Pour egg mixture into the silicone muffin molds and bake for 20 minutes.
4. Serve and enjoy.

Nutritional Value (Amount per Serving):
Calories 67; Fat 4.6 g; Carbohydrates 0.6 g; Sugar 0.4 g; Protein 6 g; Cholesterol 164 mg

Healthy Spinach Muffins

Preparation Time: 10 minutes; Cooking Time: 15 minutes; Serve: 6

Ingredients:
- 5 eggs
- 1 cup spinach, chopped
- 1/4 tsp garlic powder
- 1/4 tsp onion powder
- 1 bacon slice, cooked and crumbled
- 1/2 cup mushrooms, chopped
- Pepper
- Salt

Directions:
1. In a bowl, whisk eggs with garlic powder, onion powder, pepper, and salt. Stir in spinach, mushrooms, and bacon.

2. Pour egg mixture into the 6 silicone muffin molds.
3. Bake at 400 F for 15 minutes.
4. Serve and enjoy.

Nutritional Value (Amount per Serving):
Calories 73; Fat 5 g; Carbohydrates 0.9 g; Sugar 0.5 g; Protein 6.1 g; Cholesterol 140 mg

Cheese Ham Baked Omelet

Preparation Time: 10 minutes; Cooking Time: 40 minutes; Serve: 4

Ingredients:
- 8 eggs
- 2.5 oz cooked ham, diced
- 1 cup unsweetened coconut milk
- 1/2 tsp garlic powder
- 1 tbsp onion, minced
- 1/2 cup mozzarella cheese, shredded
- 1/3 cup cheddar cheese, shredded
- Pepper
- Salt

Directions:
1. Preheat the oven to 350 F. Grease 8-inch baking dish and set aside.
2. In a bowl, whisk eggs with milk, garlic powder, pepper, and salt.
3. Add onion, mozzarella cheese, cheddar cheese, and ham and stir well.
4. Pour egg mixture into the prepared baking dish and bake for 40 minutes.
5. Serve and enjoy.

Nutritional Value (Amount per Serving):
Calories 343; Fat 28.3 g; Carbohydrates 5.4 g; Sugar 2.9 g; Protein 18.8 g; Cholesterol 349 mg

Cheese Egg Cups

Preparation Time: 10 minutes; Cooking Time: 15 minutes; Serve: 12

Ingredients:
- 3 eggs, lightly beaten
- 2 tbsp green chilies, diced
- 2 tbsp cottage cheese
- 1 tbsp unsweetened coconut milk
- 2 tbsp cheddar cheese, shredded
- Pepper
- Salt

Directions:
1. Preheat the oven to 350 F.
2. Spray mini muffin pan with cooking spray and set aside.
3. In a bowl, whisk eggs with milk, pepper, and salt. Add cheddar cheese, green chilies, and cottage cheese and stir well.
4. Pour egg mixture in a prepared muffin pan and bake for 15 minutes.
5. Serve and enjoy.

Nutritional Value (Amount per Serving):
Calories 25; Fat 1.6 g; Carbohydrates 0.5 g; Sugar 0.3 g; Protein 2.1 g; Cholesterol 42 mg

Cheese Bacon Chaffle

Preparation Time: 10 minutes; Cooking Time: 12 minutes; Serve: 4

Ingredients:
- 2 eggs, lightly beaten
- 3/4 cup cheddar cheese, shredded
- 2 bacon slices, cooked and chopped
- 1/4 tsp garlic powder

- 1/4 tsp onion powder

Directions:
1. Heat waffle maker and lightly grease.
2. In a bowl, whisk eggs with garlic powder, onion powder, bacon, and cheese.
3. Pour 1/4 of the batter in the hot waffle maker and cook for 3 minutes or until cooked.
4. Serve and enjoy.

Nutritional Value (Amount per Serving):
Calories 169; Fat 13.2 g; Carbohydrates 0.8 g; Sugar 0.4 g; Protein 11.6 g; Cholesterol 115 mg

Banan Breakfast Bread

Preparation Time: 10 minutes; Cooking Time: 50 minutes; Serve: 10

Ingredients:
- 3 eggs, lightly beaten
- 3 bananas, mashed
- 2 cups almond flour
- 1/2 cup walnuts, chopped
- 4 tbsp olive oil
- 1 tsp baking soda

Directions:
1. Preheat the oven to 350F. Grease loaf pan and set aside.
2. Add all ingredients into the food processor and process until just combined.
3. Pour batter into the prepared loaf pan and bake for 50 minutes.
4. Once done then let it cool for 10 minutes.
5. Slice and serve.

Nutritional Value (Amount per Serving):
Calories 142; Fat 1.3 g; Carbohydrates 5.5 g; Sugar 3.3 g; Protein 3.6 g; Cholesterol 0 mg

Healthy Zucchini Chaffle

Preparation Time: 10 minutes; Cooking Time: 8 minutes; Serve: 4

Ingredients:
- 4 eggs
- 1/4 tsp garlic powder
- 1 tsp onion powder
- 2 tbsp spring onion, sliced
- 3 bacon slices, cooked & diced
- 1 zucchini, grated
- 1 1/4 cups mozzarella cheese, shredded
- 1/2 cup almond flour
- 1/4 tsp baking powder
- Pepper
- Salt

Directions:
1. In a mixing bowl, whisk eggs. Add spring onion, baking powder, garlic powder, onion powder, bacon, zucchini, pepper, and salt and stir to combine.
2. Add shredded cheese and almond flour and stir well.
3. A heat waffle iron.
4. Pour 1/4 of egg mixture in a hot waffle iron and cook until golden brown.
5. Serve and enjoy.

Nutritional Value (Amount per Serving):
Calories 197; Fat 13.7 g; Carbohydrates 4.2 g; Sugar 1.6 g; Protein 14.8 g; Cholesterol 184 mg

Breakfast Cheese Tomato Quiche

Preparation Time: 10 minutes; Cooking Time: 45 minutes; Serve: 6

Ingredients:
- 6 eggs
- 1 cup tomatoes, chopped
- 3/4 cup cheddar cheese, grated
- 1 cup unsweetened coconut milk
- Pepper
- Salt

Directions:
1. Preheat the oven to 350 F.
2. Grease an 8-inch baking dish and set aside.
3. In a bowl, whisk eggs with cheese, coconut milk, pepper, and salt. Stir in tomatoes.
4. Pour egg mixture into the prepared baking dish and bake for 45 minutes.
5. Serve and enjoy.

Nutritional Value (Amount per Serving):
Calories 217; Fat 18.7 g; Carbohydrates 3.9 g; Sugar 2.5 g; Protein 10.2 g; Cholesterol 179 mg

Coconut Chaffle

Preparation Time: 10 minutes; Cooking Time: 8 minutes; Serve: 2

Ingredients:
- 2 tbsp coconut flour
- 1/4 cup mozzarella cheese, shredded
- 1 tbsp cream cheese
- 2 1/2 tbsp water
- 1 tbsp flaxseed meal
- Pinch of salt

Directions:
1. Heat waffle maker and lightly grease.
2. In a bowl, mix together all ingredients.
3. Pour half of the batter in the hot waffle maker and cook for 4-5 minutes.
4. Serve and enjoy.

Nutritional Value (Amount per Serving):
Calories 76; Fat 4.5 g; Carbohydrates 5.3 g; Sugar 0.6 g; Protein 3 g; Cholesterol 7 mg

Healthy Tuna Waffles

Preparation Time: 10 minutes; Cooking Time: 8 minutes; Serve: 4

Ingredients:
- 10 oz can tuna, drained
- 1 tbsp olive oil
- 1 tbsp fresh lemon juice
- 1/2 cup sunflower seed flour
- 1 tbsp chives, chopped
- 2 eggs, lightly beaten
- 1 tbsp paleo mayonnaise
- 1/4 tsp salt

Directions:
1. In a bowl, mix together tuna, sunflower seed flour, chives, eggs, oil, lemon juice, mayonnaise, and salt.
2. Heat waffle maker.
3. Make four even shape patties from the mixture.
4. Place two patties onto the hot waffle maker. Cover and cook for 4 minutes.
5. Serve and enjoy.

Nutritional Value (Amount per Serving):
Calories 111; Fat 8.4 g; Carbohydrates 3.2 g; Sugar 0.3 g; Protein 6.7 g; Cholesterol 83 mg

Delicious Cheese Bacon Quiche

Preparation Time: 10 minutes; Cooking Time: 30 minutes; Serve: 4

Ingredients:
- 6 eggs
- 1/2 cup onion, chopped
- 1/8 tsp cayenne
- 1/8 tsp nutmeg
- 8 oz cheddar cheese, grated
- 1 tbsp olive oil
- 4 bacon slices, cooked and chopped
- 3/4 cup unsweetened coconut milk
- 1/2 tsp garlic, minced
- Pepper
- Salt

Directions:
1. Preheat the oven to 350 F. Grease 8-inch baking dish and set aside.
2. Heat oil in a pan over medium heat. Add onion and sauté for 5 minutes.
3. Add garlic and sauté for 30 seconds. Remove pan from heat and set aside to cool.
4. In a bowl, whisk eggs with milk, pepper, and salt. Stir in sautéed onion garlic, cayenne, nutmeg, bacon, and cheese.
5. Pour egg mixture into the prepared baking dish and bake for 25 minutes.
6. Serve and enjoy.

Nutritional Value (Amount per Serving):
Calories 485; Fat 37.8 g; Carbohydrates 5.3 g; Sugar 3.5 g; Protein 31.2 g; Cholesterol 330 mg

Quick & Easy Frittata

Preparation Time: 10 minutes; Cooking Time: 15 minutes; Serve: 4

Ingredients:
- 6 eggs, lightly beaten
- 2 tsp olive oil
- 1 tsp fresh oregano, chopped
- 1/2 cup green onion, chopped
- 1 bell pepper, chopped
- Pepper
- Salt

Directions:
1. Preheat the oven to 350 F.
2. Whisk eggs in a bowl until well combined.
3. Heat oil in a 10-inch skillet over medium heat. Add bell pepper and sauté for 2 minutes.
4. Add green onion and sauté for a minute. Season with pepper and salt.
5. Pour egg mixture into the pan and cook over medium-low heat for 8 minutes.
6. Place pan in the oven and bake for 5 minutes. Sprinkle oregano on top.
7. Slice and serve.

Nutritional Value (Amount per Serving):
Calories 129; Fat 9 g; Carbohydrates 3.9 g; Sugar 2.3 g; Protein 8.9 g; Cholesterol 246 mg

Sausage Zucchini Casserole

Preparation Time: 10 minutes; Cooking Time: 50 minutes; Serve: 8

Ingredients:
- 12 eggs
- 2 small zucchinis, shredded
- 1 lb ground Italian sausage
- 3 tomatoes, sliced
- 3 tbsp coconut flour
- 1/4 cup coconut milk
- 1/4 tsp pepper
- 1/2 tsp salt

Directions:
1. Preheat the oven to 350 F. Grease casserole dish and set aside.
2. Cook Italian sausage in a pan until lightly brown. Transfer sausage to a large bowl.

3. Add coconut flour, milk, eggs, zucchini, pepper, and salt. Stir to mix.
4. Add eggs and whisk until combined.
5. Transfer bowl mixture into the prepared casserole dish and top with tomato slices.
6. Bake for 45-50 minutes.
7. Serve and enjoy.

Nutritional Value (Amount per Serving):
Calories 308; Fat 22 g; Carbohydrates 6.5 g; Sugar 3.7 g; Protein 19.8 g; Cholesterol 286 mg

Cauliflower Chaffle

Preparation Time: 10 minutes; Cooking Time: 10 minutes; Serve: 2
Ingredients:
- 1 egg, lightly beaten
- 1/2 cup cauliflower rice
- 1/4 cup Mexican cheese, shredded
- 1 tbsp almond flour
- Pepper
- Salt

Directions:
1. Heat waffle maker and lightly grease.
2. Add all ingredients into the mixing bowl and mix until well combined.
3. Pour 1/2 of the batter in the hot waffle maker and cook for 4-5 minutes.
4. Serve and enjoy.

Nutritional Value (Amount per Serving):
Calories 170; Fat 13.7 g; Carbohydrates 5.3 g; Sugar 1.7 g; Protein 9.4 g; Cholesterol 93 mg

Healthy Tofu Scramble

Preparation Time: 10 minutes; Cooking Time: 10 minutes; Serve: 2
Ingredients:
- 8 oz extra-firm tofu, mash with a fork
- 1 tsp Dijon mustard
- 1/2 tsp paprika
- 1/2 tsp turmeric
- 1/3 cup unsweetened coconut milk
- 1/4 tsp onion powder
- 1/2 tsp garlic powder
- 2 tbsp nutritional yeast
- 1 tbsp butter
- 1/4 tsp salt

Directions:
1. In a bowl, mix together nutritional yeast, onion powder, garlic powder, mustard, paprika, turmeric, and salt. Add coconut milk and whisk well.
2. Melt butter in a pan over medium heat.
3. Add tofu and stir until lightly browned.
4. Add the nutritional yeast mixture and stir everything well and cook until tofu absorbed all the liquid.
5. Serve and enjoy.

Nutritional Value (Amount per Serving):
Calories 162; Fat 9.6 g; Carbohydrates 7.9 g; Sugar 2.6 g; Protein 14.5 g; Cholesterol 5 mg

Spinach Egg Scramble

Preparation Time: 10 minutes; Cooking Time: 10 minutes; Serve: 2
Ingredients:
- 4 eggs
- 1 tbsp olive oil

- 3 tomatoes, chopped
- 1 1/2 cups baby spinach, chopped
- 1/3 cup basil, chopped
- Pepper
- Salt

Directions:
1. Heat oil in a pan over medium heat. Add tomatoes and cook until softened.
2. Meanwhile, in a bowl, whisk eggs with basil, pepper, and salt.
3. Add spinach to the pan and cook until wilted.
4. Pour egg mixture to the pan and cook until eggs are set.
5. Serve and enjoy.

Nutritional Value (Amount per Serving):
Calories 225; Fat 16.2 g; Carbohydrates 8.8 g; Sugar 5.6 g; Protein 13.5 g; Cholesterol 327 mg

Kale Sausage Muffins

Preparation Time: 10 minutes; Cooking Time: 35 minutes; Serve: 12
Ingredients:
- 10 eggs
- 1 cup unsweetened coconut milk
- 1/4 cup sausage, sliced
- 1/4 cup kale, chopped
- 1/4 cup sun-dried tomatoes, chopped
- Pepper
- Salt

Directions:
1. Preheat the oven to 350 F. Spray a muffin tray with cooking spray and set aside.
2. In a large bowl, add all ingredients and whisk until well combined.
3. Pour egg mixture into the prepared tray and bake for 30-35 minutes.
4. Serve and enjoy.

Nutritional Value (Amount per Serving):
Calories 102; Fat 8.6 g; Carbohydrates 1.7 g; Sugar 1.1 g; Protein 5.3 g; Cholesterol 137 mg

Nutritious Chicken Muffins

Preparation Time: 10 minutes; Cooking Time: 15 minutes; Serve: 12
Ingredients:
- 10 eggs
- 1 cup chicken, cooked and chopped
- 1/3 cup green onions, chopped
- 1/4 tsp pepper
- 1 tsp sea salt

Directions:
1. Preheat the oven to 400 F. Spray a muffin tray with cooking spray and set aside.
2. In a large bowl, whisk eggs with pepper and salt. Add remaining ingredients and stir well.
3. Pour egg mixture into the prepared muffin tray and bake for 15 minutes.
4. Serve and enjoy.

Nutritional Value (Amount per Serving):
Calories 71; Fat 4 g; Carbohydrates 0.5 g; Sugar 0.3 g; Protein 8 g; Cholesterol 145 mg

Easy Bacon Muffins

Preparation Time: 10 minutes; Cooking Time: 25 minutes; Serve: 12
Ingredients:
- 12 eggs, lightly beaten
- 2 tbsp fresh parsley, chopped
- 1/2 tsp dry mustard powder
- 1/3 cup unsweetened coconut milk

- 2 green onion, chopped
- 8 bacon slices, cooked and crumbled
- Pepper
- Salt

Directions:
1. Preheat the oven to 375 F. Spray a muffin tray with cooking spray and set aside.
2. In a bowl, whisk eggs with coconut milk, mustard, pepper, and salt until well combined.
3. Add bacon, green onion, and parsley and whisk well.
4. Pour egg mixture into the muffin tray and bake for 20-25 minutes.
5. Serve and enjoy.

Nutritional Value (Amount per Serving):
Calories 149; Fat 11.3 g; Carbohydrates 1.2 g; Sugar 0.6 g; Protein 10.5 g; Cholesterol 178 mg

Italian Spinach Frittata

Preparation Time: 10 minutes; Cooking Time: 17 minutes; Serve: 6

Ingredients:
- 8 eggs
- 1 tbsp olive oil
- 2 cups spinach, chopped
- 1 tbsp Italian seasoning, crushed
- 1/4 cup onion, diced
- 1 1/2 cup mushrooms, sliced
- Pepper
- Salt

Directions:
1. Preheat the oven to 350 F.
2. Heat oil in the oven-safe pan over medium-high heat. Add onion and mushrooms and sauté for 5 minutes.
3. Add spinach and cook for 2 minutes.
4. In a bowl, whisk eggs with Italian seasoning, pepper, and salt.
5. Transfer pan mixture to the egg mixture and stir well.
6. Return egg mixture into the oven-safe pan and bake in preheated oven for 10 minutes.
7. Serve and enjoy.

Nutritional Value (Amount per Serving):
Calories 119; Fat 9 g; Carbohydrates 2.1 g; Sugar 1.2 g; Protein 8.3 g; Cholesterol 220 mg

Mexican Frittata

Preparation Time: 10 minutes; Cooking Time: 20 minutes; Serve: 6

Ingredients:
- 8 eggs, scrambled
- 1/2 cup salsa
- 2 tsp taco seasoning
- 1/2 lb ground beef
- 1/2 cup cheddar cheese, grated
- 3 scallions, chopped
- 1/3 lb tomatoes, sliced
- 1 small green pepper, chopped
- 1 tbsp olive oil
- 1/4 tsp salt

Directions:
1. Preheat the oven to 375 F.
2. Heat oil in a pan over medium heat.
3. Add ground beef and sauté until brown. Add salsa and taco seasoning and stir well to coat.
4. Remove meat from the pan and place on a plate.

5. Add green pepper to the pan and cook for few minutes until crisp.
6. Return meat to the pan. Add scallions and tomato.
7. Add scrambled eggs on top and sprinkle with grated cheese.
8. Bake for 20-25 minutes.
9. Serve and enjoy.

Nutritional Value (Amount per Serving):
Calories 229; Fat 13.8 g; Carbohydrates 4.5 g; Sugar 2.3 g; Protein 22.1 g; Cholesterol 262 mg

Scrambled Egg

Preparation Time: 10 minutes; Cooking Time: 5 minutes; Serve: 2
Ingredients:
- 2 eggs, lightly beaten
- 1/2 tomato, chopped
- 2 tbsp fresh basil, chopped
- 1 tbsp olive oil
- Pepper
- Salt

Directions:
1. Heat oil in a pan over medium heat.
2. Add tomatoes and cook until softened.
3. Whisk eggs with basil, pepper, and salt.
4. Pour egg mixture to the pan and cook until eggs are set.
5. Serve and enjoy.

Nutritional Value (Amount per Serving):
Calories 126; Fat 11.4 g; Carbohydrates 1 g; Sugar 0.8 g; Protein 5.8 g; Cholesterol 164 mg

Spinach Tomato Breakfast Bake

Preparation Time: 10 minutes; Cooking Time: 45 minutes; Serve: 6
Ingredients:
- 10 eggs
- 2 large tomatoes, sliced
- 1 tbsp olive oil
- 10 bacon sliced, cooked and crumbled
- 2 tbsp chives, chopped
- 3 cups baby spinach, chopped
- 1/2 tsp salt

Directions:
1. Preheat the oven to 350 F. Grease 9-inch baking dish and set aside.
2. Heat oil in a pan over medium heat.
3. Add spinach and cook until spinach wilted.
4. Whisk eggs and salt in mixing bowl.
5. Add spinach and chives and whisk well.
6. Pour egg mixture into the prepared baking dish. Top with bacon and tomatoes.
7. Bake for 40-45 minutes.
8. Serve and enjoy.

Nutritional Value (Amount per Serving):
Calories 197; Fat 12.9 g; Carbohydrates 3.5 g; Sugar 2.2 g; Protein 15.2 g; Cholesterol 278 mg

Spinach Tofu Scramble

Preparation Time: 10 minutes; Cooking Time: 7 minutes; Serve: 2
Ingredients:

- 1/2 block firm tofu, crumbled
- 1 cup spinach
- 1 tbsp olive oil
- 1 medium tomato, chopped
- 1/4 cup zucchini, chopped
- 1/4 tsp ground cumin
- 1 tbsp turmeric
- Pepper
- Salt

Directions:
1. Heat oil in a pan over medium heat.
2. Add tomato, zucchini, and spinach and sauté for 2 minutes.
3. Add tofu, cumin, turmeric, pepper, and salt, and sauté for 4-5 minutes.
4. Serve and enjoy.

Nutritional Value (Amount per Serving):
Calories 107; Fat 8.6 g; Carbohydrates 6.3 g; Sugar 2.2 g; Protein 3.6 g; Cholesterol 0 mg

Tasty Breakfast Waffles

Preparation Time: 10 minutes; Cooking Time: 20 minutes; Serve: 1
Ingredients:
- 2/3 cup egg whites
- 1/4 tsp baking powder
- 1/4 cup coconut flour
- 12 tsp vanilla
- 1/4 cup unsweetened almond milk
- 1/4 tsp cinnamon
- 1 tbsp swerve
- Pinch of salt

Directions:
1. In a large bowl, mix together dry ingredients and set aside.
2. In a separate bowl, whisk egg whites with vanilla, and almond milk.
3. Pour egg mixture into the dry ingredients and mix until a thick batter is formed.
4. Heat waffle iron and spray with cooking spray.
5. Once waffle iron is hot then pour the batter and cook until waffle is lightly golden brown.
6. Serve and enjoy.

Nutritional Value (Amount per Serving):
Calories 122; Fat 8 g; Carbohydrates 4 g; Sugar 2 g; Protein 8 g; Cholesterol 0 mg

Easy Broccoli Omelet

Preparation Time: 10 minutes; Cooking Time: 10 minutes; Serve: 2
Ingredients:
- 4 eggs
- 1 cup broccoli, chopped and cooked
- 1 tbsp fresh parsley, chopped
- 1 tbsp olive oil
- 1/4 tsp pepper
- 1/2 tsp salt

Directions:
1. In a bowl, whisk eggs with pepper, and salt.
2. Heat olive oil in a pan over medium heat.
3. Add broccoli and egg mixture into the pan and cook until set.
4. Flip omelet to the other side and cook until lightly golden brown.
5. Garnish with parsley and serve.

Nutritional Value (Amount per Serving):
Calories 203; Fat 15.9 g; Carbohydrates 4 g; Sugar 1.5 g; Protein 12.4 g; Cholesterol 327 mg

Asparagus Frittata

Preparation Time: 10 minutes; Cooking Time: 15 minutes; Serve: 4
Ingredients:
- 6 eggs
- 10 asparagus, chopped
- 1/4 cup half and half
- 2 tsp butter
- 3 mushrooms, sliced
- 1 cup mozzarella cheese, shredded
- 1 tsp pepper
- 1 tsp salt

Directions:
1. Melt butter in oven safe skillet over medium heat.
2. Add mushrooms and sauté for 5 minutes. Add asparagus and sauté for 2 minutes.
3. Meanwhile, in a bowl, whisk eggs with half and half, pepper, and salt and pour over asparagus. Cook over medium heat until set.
4. Sprinkle cheese on top and transfer pan to the oven and cook at 350 F for 5 minutes.
5. Slice and serve.

Nutritional Value (Amount per Serving):
Calories 163; Fat 11.6 g; Carbohydrates 3.7 g; Sugar 1.5 g; Protein 12.1 g; Cholesterol 260 mg

Spinach Kale Egg Bake

Preparation Time: 10 minutes; Cooking Time: 35 minutes; Serve: 6
Ingredients:
- 12 eggs, beaten
- 4 tbsp butter, sliced
- 1 cup kale
- 1 cup spinach
- 2 cups of cottage cheese
- 1 tomato, sliced
- 1/3 cup green onions, sliced
- Pepper
- Salt

Directions:
1. Preheat the oven to 350 F. Grease casserole dish.
2. Add vegetables to the casserole dish.
3. In a bowl, whisk together eggs, cheese, pepper, and salt.
4. Pour egg mixture over vegetables. Place tomato slices and top with butter slices.
5. Bake for 35 minutes.
6. Slice and serve.

Nutritional Value (Amount per Serving):
Calories 276; Fat 19.6 g; Carbohydrates 4.7 g; Sugar 1.3 g; Protein 20.6 g; Cholesterol 358 mg

Simple Asparagus Omelet

Preparation Time: 10 minutes; Cooking Time: 10 minutes; Serve: 1
Ingredients:
- 2 large eggs, lightly beaten
- 1/3 cup asparagus, chopped
- 1 tbsp onion, chopped
- 1 tbsp parsley, chopped
- 1/2 oz cheddar cheese, shredded
- 1 tbsp butter
- Pepper
- Salt

Directions:
1. Melt butter in a pan over medium heat.
2. Add asparagus and onion and sauté until onion is softened.

3. Add beaten eggs and stir gently to scramble, and then form into a flat surface.
4. Sprinkle the shredded cheese and parsley and fold the eggs over.
5. Transfer omelet on a serving plate. Season with pepper and salt.
6. Serve and enjoy.

Nutritional Value (Amount per Serving):
Calories 316; Fat 26.3 g; Carbohydrates 3.9 g; Sugar 2.1 g; Protein 17.4 g; Cholesterol 417 mg

Spinach Tomato Chicken Egg Muffin

Preparation Time: 10 minutes; Cooking Time: 30 minutes; Serve: 3
Ingredients:
- 6 large eggs
- 1/4 cup tomatoes, chopped
- 1/4 cup spinach, chopped
- 1/2 cup chicken breast, cooked and shredded
- 1/4 tsp garlic powder
- 1/2 tsp black pepper
- 1/4 cup unsweetened almond milk
- 1/8 tsp salt

Directions:
1. Preheat the oven to 350 F. Spray muffin tray with cooking spray and set aside.
2. In a large bowl, whisk together eggs, garlic powder, pepper, almond milk, pepper, and salt.
3. Pour egg mixture into the prepared muffin tray and top with chicken, tomatoes, and spinach.
4. Bake for 25-30 minutes.
5. Serve and enjoy.

Nutritional Value (Amount per Serving):
Calories 170; Fat 10.7 g; Carbohydrates 2 g; Sugar 1.2 g; Protein 16.5 g; Cholesterol 383 mg

Spicy Scrambled Egg

Preparation Time: 10 minutes; Cooking Time: 10 minutes; Serve: 2
Ingredients:
- 4 eggs
- 1 Serrano chili pepper, chopped
- 2 tbsp scallions, sliced
- 1/4 tsp pepper
- 2 tbsp cilantro, chopped
- 1/3 cup heavy cream
- 1 tomato, diced
- 3 tbsp butter
- 1/2 tsp salt

Directions:
1. Melt butter in a pan over medium heat.
2. Add tomato and chili pepper and sauté for 2 minutes.
3. In a bowl, whisk eggs with cilantro, cream, pepper, and salt.
4. Pour egg mixture into the pan and stir until egg is set.
5. Top with scallions and serve.

Nutritional Value (Amount per Serving):
Calories 358; Fat 33.5 g; Carbohydrates 3.6 g; Sugar 1.7 g; Protein 12.1 g; Cholesterol 401 mg

Healthy Pumpkin Pancake

Preparation Time: 10 minutes; Cooking Time: 10 minutes; Serve: 4
Ingredients:

- 4 eggs
- 1/2 tsp cinnamon
- 1/2 cup pumpkin puree
- 1 cup almond flour
- 2 tbsp butter
- 2 tsp liquid stevia
- 1 tsp baking powder

Directions:
1. In a bowl, whisk together almond flour, stevia, baking powder, cinnamon, pumpkin puree, and eggs until well combined.
2. Melt a half tablespoon of butter in a pan over medium heat.
3. Pour spoonful batter into the melted butter and make a round pancake.
4. Cook pancakes until lightly browned from both sides.
5. Serve and enjoy.

Nutritional Value (Amount per Serving):
Calories 166; Fat 13.7 g; Carbohydrates 5.1 g; Sugar 1.6 g; Protein 7.5 g; Cholesterol 179 mg

Tasty Broccoli Bread

Preparation Time: 10 minutes; Cooking Time: 30 minutes; Serve: 10
Ingredients:
- 5 eggs, lightly beaten
- 3/4 cup broccoli, chopped
- 1 cup cheddar cheese, shredded
- 2 tsp baking powder, gluten-free
- 3 1/2 tbsp coconut flour
- 1 tsp salt

Directions:
1. Preheat the oven to 350 F. Grease loaf pan and set aside.
2. In a bowl, add all ingredients and whisk until well combined.
3. Pour mixture into the prepared loaf pan.
4. Bake for 30-35 minutes.
5. Slice and serve.

Nutritional Value (Amount per Serving):
Calories 101; Fat 6.7 g; Carbohydrates 4 g; Sugar 0.7 g; Protein 6.5 g; Cholesterol 94 mg

Spicy Jalapeno Muffins

Preparation Time: 10 minutes; Cooking Time: 20 minutes; Serve: 12
Ingredients:
- 9 eggs
- 8 bacon slices, cooked and chopped
- 3/4 cup heavy cream
- 1 jalapeno pepper, sliced
- 9 oz cheddar cheese, shredded
- Pepper
- Salt

Directions:
1. Preheat the oven to 350 F. Grease 12 cups muffin tray and add cooked bacon slices to each muffin cup.
2. In a bowl, whisk eggs with shredded cheese, cream, pepper, and salt.
3. Pour egg mixture into the prepared muffin cups evenly.
4. Add sliced jalapeno into each muffin cup.
5. Bake for 15-20 minutes.
6. Serve and enjoy.

Nutritional Value (Amount per Serving):
Calories 228; Fat 18.4 g; Carbohydrates 1 g; Sugar 0.4 g; Protein 14.3 g; Cholesterol 169 mg

Vegetable Ham Egg Muffins

Preparation Time: 10 minutes; Cooking Time: 25 minutes; Serve: 6
Ingredients:
- 12 eggs
- 1/4 cup bell pepper, diced
- 1/4 tsp garlic powder
- 1 cup ham, diced and cooked
- 2 tbsp onion, chopped
- 1/2 cup fresh spinach, shredded
- 1 cup cheddar cheese, shredded
- 1/4 cup mushrooms, chopped and sautéed
- 1/4 tsp pepper
- 1/2 tsp salt

Directions:
1. Preheat the oven to 350 F. Grease 12 cup muffin pan and set aside.
2. In a large bowl, beat eggs until just combined. Add remaining ingredients and mix well.
3. Pour egg mixture into the prepared muffin tray and bake for 20-25 minutes.
4. Serve and enjoy.

Nutritional Value (Amount per Serving):
Calories 243; Fat 17 g; Carbohydrates 2.8 g; Sugar 1.3 g; Protein 19.8 g; Cholesterol 360 mg

Cheesy Zucchini Quiche

Preparation Time: 10 minutes; Cooking Time: 40 minutes; Serve: 6
Ingredients:
- 8 eggs
- 1 cup cheddar cheese, shredded
- 1 cup zucchini, shredded and squeezed
- 1 cup ham, cooked and diced
- 1/2 tsp dry mustard
- 1/2 cup heavy cream
- Pepper
- Salt

Directions:
1. Preheat the oven to 375 F. Grease 9-inch pie dish.
2. Combine ham, cheddar cheese, and zucchini in a pie dish.
3. In a bowl, whisk together eggs, heavy cream, and seasoning. Pour egg mixture over ham mixture.
4. Bake for 40 minutes.
5. Serve and enjoy.

Nutritional Value (Amount per Serving):
Calories 235; Fat 17.8 g; Carbohydrates 2.6 g; Sugar 0.9 g; Protein 16.3 g; Cholesterol 265 mg

Chapter 2: Poultry
Italian Baked Pesto Chicken

Preparation Time: 10 minutes; Cooking Time: 45 minutes; Serve: 4
Ingredients:
- 4 chicken breasts, sliced into 8 pieces
- 8 oz mozzarella cheese, shredded
- 3 tbsp basil pesto
- 1/4 tsp pepper
- 1/2 tsp salt

Directions:
1. Preheat the oven to 350 F.
2. Spray baking dish with cooking spray.
3. Place chicken in a prepared baking dish in a single layer and season with pepper and salt.
4. Spread pesto and cheese on top of chicken.
5. Bake for 35-45 minutes.
6. Serve and enjoy.

Nutritional Value (Amount per Serving):
Calories 438; Fat 20.8 g; Carbohydrates 2.1 g; Sugar 0 g; Protein 58.3 g; Cholesterol 160 mg

Chicken Cheese Casserole

Preparation Time: 10 minutes; Cooking Time: 35 minutes; Serve: 8
Ingredients:
- 2 1/2 lbs cooked chicken, cubed
- 2 oz mozzarella cheese, shredded
- 4 bacon slices, cooked and crumbled
- 1 cup parmesan cheese, grated
- 12 oz frozen spinach, thawed and drained
- 2 tsp dried onion, minced
- 2 tsp garlic powder
- 4 oz mayonnaise
- 4 oz sour cream
- 8 oz cream cheese, softened

Directions:
1. Preheat the oven to 350 F. Grease 9*13-inch baking dish and set aside.
2. Add chicken and remaining ingredients into the mixing bowl and mix until just combined.
3. Dump chicken mixture into the prepared baking dish and bake for 35 minutes.
4. Serve and enjoy.

Nutritional Value (Amount per Serving):
Calories 523; Fat 30 g; Carbohydrates 7.7 g; Sugar 1.4 g; Protein 54.7 g; Cholesterol 173 mg

Parmesan Chicken Tenders

Preparation Time: 10 minutes; Cooking Time: 30 minutes; Serve: 8
Ingredients:
- 2 1/2 lbs chicken tenderloins
- 1 tsp garlic powder
- 3/4 cup parmesan cheese, shredded
- 3/4 cup mayonnaise
- 1/2 tsp salt

Directions:
1. Preheat the oven to 400 F. Line baking sheet with parchment paper and set aside.

2. In a bowl, mix together mayonnaise, garlic powder, 1/4 cup cheese, and salt. Add chicken and stir to coat.
3. Arrange chicken on a prepared baking sheet and top with remaining cheese.
4. Bake for 25-30 minutes.
5. Serve and enjoy.

Nutritional Value (Amount per Serving):
Calories 278; Fat 12.8 g; Carbohydrates 6.3 g; Sugar 1.5 g; Protein 36 g; Cholesterol 82 mg

Delicious Chicken Cacciatore

Preparation Time: 10 minutes; Cooking Time: 3 hours; Serve: 8
Ingredients:
- 3 lbs chicken thighs, skinless and boneless
- 1 tsp dried basil
- 2 tsp dried parsley
- 1 tsp dried oregano
- 3 garlic cloves, sliced
- 2 small onions, sliced
- 1 sweet pepper, sliced
- 28 oz can whole tomatoes, peeled
- 1 tsp salt

Directions:
1. Add all ingredients into the slow cooker and stir well.
2. Cover and cook on high for 3 hours.
3. Stir well and serve.

Nutritional Value (Amount per Serving):
Calories 358; Fat 12.7 g; Carbohydrates 7.5 g; Sugar 4.1 g; Protein 50.5 g; Cholesterol 151 mg

Cheesy Chicken Casserole

Preparation Time: 10 minutes; Cooking Time: 3 hours; Serve: 8
Ingredients:
- 3 cups cooked chicken, shredded
- 4 oz cream cheese, cubed
- 1 tsp poultry seasoning
- 1 egg, lightly beaten
- 1/2 cup chicken broth
- 1/2 cup parmesan cheese, shredded
- 2 cups cheddar cheese, shredded
- 1 cup mushrooms, sliced
- 1 tbsp garlic, minced
- 2 tbsp dried onion, minced
- 2 tbsp butter
- Pepper
- Salt

Directions:
1. Melt butter in a pan over medium heat.
2. Add onion, garlic, and mushrooms and saute for 3-5 minutes.
3. Transfer sauteed onion mixture into the slow cooker. Add cabbage, egg, poultry seasoning, broth, parmesan, chicken, 1 1/2 cups cheddar cheese, pepper, and salt and stir to combine.
4. Top with remaining cheddar cheese and cream cheese.
5. Cover and cook on high for 3 hours.
6. Serve and enjoy.

Nutritional Value (Amount per Serving):
Calories 303; Fat 20.8 g; Carbohydrates 2.1 g; Sugar 0.5 g; Protein 26.7 g; Cholesterol 118 mg

Perfect Ranch Chicken

Preparation Time: 10 minutes; Cooking Time: 8 hours; Serve: 8
Ingredients:
- 1 1/2 lbs chicken breast
- 8 jarred pepperoncini peppers
- 1 oz ranch seasoning mix
- 4 oz cream cheese
- 1 tbsp butter

Directions:
1. Add all ingredients into the slow cooker and stir well.
2. Cover and cook for 8 hours.
3. Stir everything well and shred chicken and peppers using a fork.
4. Serve and enjoy.

Nutritional Value (Amount per Serving):
Calories 178; Fat 8.5 g; Carbohydrates 3.4 g; Sugar 1 g; Protein 19.4 g; Cholesterol 74 mg

Cajun Air Fried Chicken

Preparation Time: 10 minutes; Cooking Time: 25 minutes; Serve: 4
Ingredients:
- 4 small chicken thighs
- 1 1/2 tbsp Cajun seasoning
- 1 egg, lightly beaten
- 1/2 cup almond flour
- Salt

Directions:
1. Preheat the oven to 390 F.
2. In a shallow dish, mix together almond flour, Cajun seasoning, and salt.
3. Add egg in a separate shallow dish.
4. Coat chicken with flour then dip in egg and again coat with flour mixture.
5. Place coated chicken in the air fryer basket and cook for 25 minutes.
6. Serve and enjoy.

Nutritional Value (Amount per Serving):
Calories 321; Fat 11.9 g; Carbohydrates 5.8 g; Sugar 0.3 g; Protein 44.4 g; Cholesterol 171 mg

Balsamic Chicken

Preparation Time: 10 minutes; Cooking Time: 15 minutes; Serve: 4
Ingredients:
- 2 lbs chicken tenders
- 10 basil leaves, chopped
- 2 sun-dried tomatoes, cut into strips
- 1/3 cup balsamic vinegar
- 1 tbsp olive oil
- 1/2 tsp pepper
- 1 tsp salt

Directions:
1. Heat oil in a large pan over medium heat.
2. Add chicken to the pan and season with pepper and salt and cook for 4 minutes on each side. Remove chicken from pan and set aside.
3. Turn heat to medium-high and add sundried tomatoes and vinegar to the pan and cook until vinegar reduced by half.
4. Return chicken to the pan and coat well with vinegar. Transfer chicken to a serving dish and top with basil.
5. Serve and enjoy.

Nutritional Value (Amount per Serving):
Calories 477; Fat 20.5 g; Carbohydrates 2.8 g; Sugar 1.7 g; Protein 66.2 g; Cholesterol 202 mg

Chicken Broccoli Casserole

Preparation Time: 10 minutes; Cooking Time: 35 minutes; Serve: 8
Ingredients:
- 1 1/2 lbs cooked chicken, cubed
- 8 oz cheddar cheese, shredded
- 4 oz mayonnaise
- 4 oz sour cream
- 8 oz cream cheese, softened
- 1/2 tbsp dried dill
- 1/2 tbsp garlic powder
- 1 tbsp dried parsley
- 6 tbsp bacon, crumbled
- 1 tbsp dried onion, minced
- 1 lb fresh broccoli florets, steamed and drained
- 1/2 tsp pepper
- 1/2 tsp salt

Directions:
1. Preheat the oven to 350 F. Grease 9*13-inch baking dish,
2. In a large bowl, combine cream cheese, spices, mayonnaise, and sour cream.
3. Add chicken, broccoli, 4 tablespoon bacon, and 3/4 of cheddar cheese and mix well.
4. Transfer chicken mixture into the prepared baking dish and spread well. Sprinkle remaining cheese and bacon on top.
5. Bake for 35 minutes.
6. Serve and enjoy.

Nutritional Value (Amount per Serving):
Calories 439; Fat 26.9 g; Carbohydrates 9.3 g; Sugar 2.3 g; Protein 39.4 g; Cholesterol 124 mg

Creamy Chicken Marsala

Preparation Time: 10 minutes; Cooking Time: 4 hours 30 minutes; Serve: 4
Ingredients:
- 4 chicken breasts, skinless and boneless
- 1/2 cup heavy whipping cream
- 1 cup dry marsala wine
- 8 oz mushrooms, sliced
- Pepper
- Salt

Directions:
1. Spray slow cooker from inside with cooking spray.
2. Add chicken into the slow cooker. Top with mushrooms and seasonings.
3. Pour wine over the chicken. Cover and cook on high for 4 hours.
4. Remove mushrooms and chicken from slow cooker and set aside.
5. Stir in cream and whisk until thickened.
6. Return chicken and mushrooms to slow cooker. Cover and cook for 30 minutes more.
7. Serve and enjoy.

Nutritional Value (Amount per Serving):
Calories 392; Fat 16.5 g; Carbohydrates 3.8 g; Sugar 1.4 g; Protein 44.4 g; Cholesterol 150 mg

Lemon Pepper Chicken

Preparation Time: 10 minutes; Cooking Time: 35 minutes; Serve: 4

Ingredients:
- 4 chicken thighs
- 1 tsp garlic powder
- 1 tbsp lemon pepper seasoning
- 2 tbsp fresh lemon juice
- 1/2 tsp paprika
- 1/2 tsp Italian seasoning
- 1/2 tsp onion powder
- 2 tbsp olive oil
- 1 tsp salt

Directions:
1. Preheat the oven to 400 F.
2. Add chicken in the bowl.
3. Mix together lemon juice and olive oil and pour over chicken.
4. Mix together paprika, Italian seasoning, onion powder, garlic powder, lemon pepper seasoning, and salt and rub all over the chicken.
5. Arrange chicken on a baking sheet and bake for 35 minutes.
6. Serve and enjoy.

Nutritional Value (Amount per Serving):
Calories 349; Fat 18.1 g; Carbohydrates 2.2 g; Sugar 0.5 g; Protein 42.7 g; Cholesterol 130 mg

Mediterranean Chicken

Preparation Time: 10 minutes; Cooking Time: 2 hours; Serve: 6

Ingredients:
- 2 1/2 lbs chicken thighs, skinless and boneless
- 1 tsp dried oregano
- 2 tsp dried garlic, minced
- 2 tbsp olive oil
- 3 tbsp fresh lemon juice
- 14 oz can artichokes
- 1/2 cup olives
- 1 cup roasted red peppers, drained and chopped
- 1/2 tsp pepper
- 1 tsp salt

Directions:
1. Add chicken into the slow cooker.
2. Pour remaining ingredients over chicken and stir to combine.
3. Cover and cook on high for 2 hours or until chicken is cooked.
4. Stir well and serve.

Nutritional Value (Amount per Serving):
Calories 149; Fat 9.3 g; Carbohydrates 9.4 g; Sugar 2.1 g; Protein 10.5 g; Cholesterol 0 mg

Air Fryer Chicken Wings

Preparation Time: 10 minutes; Cooking Time: 20 minutes; Serve: 2

Ingredients:
- 1 lb chicken wings
- 2 tbsp butter, melted
- 1 1/2 tbsp ranch seasoning
- 3 garlic cloves, minced

Directions:
1. Preheat the air fryer to 390 F.
2. In a bowl, mix together butter, garlic, ranch seasoning.
3. Add chicken wings and toss well. Cover and place in the refrigerator for 1 hour.
4. Arrange marinated chicken wings into the air fryer basket and cook for 10 minutes.
5. Turn chicken wings to the other side and air fry for 10 minutes more.
6. Serve and enjoy.

Nutritional Value (Amount per Serving):

Calories 562; Fat 28.4 g; Carbohydrates 1.5 g; Sugar 0.1 g; Protein 66 g; Cholesterol 232 mg

Delicious Baked Chicken Fajitas

Preparation Time: 10 minutes; Cooking Time: 35 minutes; Serve: 6
Ingredients:
- 2 lbs chicken thighs, skinless, boneless, and cut into strips
- 2 tbsp olive oil
- 2 tbsp fajita seasoning
- 1 large onion, sliced
- 1 red bell pepper, sliced
- 2 tsp salt

Directions:
1. Preheat the oven to 400 F.
2. Add all ingredients into the large mixing bowl and toss well.
3. Spread chicken mixture onto the baking sheet and bake for 35-40 minutes.
4. Serve and enjoy.

Nutritional Value (Amount per Serving):
Calories 354; Fat 16 g; Carbohydrates 5.9 g; Sugar 2.1 g; Protein 44.2 g; Cholesterol 135 mg

Meatballs

Preparation Time: 10 minutes; Cooking Time: 20 minutes; Serve: 4
Ingredients:
- 1 lb ground turkey
- 2 garlic cloves, minced
- 1/4 cup basil, chopped
- 3 tbsp scallions, chopped
- 1 egg, lightly beaten
- 1/2 cup almond flour
- 1/2 tsp red pepper, crushed
- 1 tbsp lemongrass, chopped
- 1 1/2 tbsp fish sauce

Directions:
1. Preheat the oven to 390 F.
2. Add all ingredients into a large bowl and mix until just combined.
3. Make small balls from meat mixture and place onto a parchment-lined baking sheet.
4. Bake for 20 minutes.
5. Serve and enjoy.

Nutritional Value (Amount per Serving):
Calories 169; Fat 15.4 g; Carbohydrates 3.4 g; Sugar 1.3 g; Protein 33.9 g; Cholesterol 157 mg

Coconut Chicken Curry

Preparation Time: 10 minutes; Cooking Time: 6 hours; Serve: 6
Ingredients:
- 1 lb chicken, cut into cubes
- 13 cups fresh spinach chopped
- 1 1/2 cup coconut cream
- 3/4 lb pumpkin, cut into cubes
- 2 tbsp curry paste
- 1 onion, sliced

Directions:
1. Add all ingredients except spinach into the slow cooker and stir well.
2. Cover and cook on low for 6 hours.
3. Just before 10 minutes of serving add spinach and stir until spinach is wilted.
4. Serve and enjoy.

Nutritional Value (Amount per Serving):
Calories 215; Fat 8.9 g; Carbohydrates 9.5 g; Sugar 2.7 g; Protein 23.5 g; Cholesterol 58 mg

Turkey Meatloaf

Preparation Time: 10 minutes; Cooking Time: 40 minutes; Serve: 8
Ingredients:
- 1 egg
- 2 oz BBQ sauce, sugar-free
- 1 tsp ground mustard
- 1 tsp chili powder
- 1 tsp garlic powder
- 1 tsp dried garlic, minced
- 1 tbsp dried onion, minced
- 1 cup cheddar cheese, shredded
- 2 lbs ground turkey meat
- 1 tsp salt

Directions:
1. Preheat the oven to 400 F. Grease 9*13-inch casserole dish.
2. In a mixing bowl, add all ingredients and mix until just combined.
3. Transfer meat mixture into the prepared casserole dish and bake for 30-40 minutes.
4. Slice and serve.

Nutritional Value (Amount per Serving):
Calories 232; Fat 12.5 g; Carbohydrates 3.6 g; Sugar 2.2 g; Protein 26.7 g; Cholesterol 101 mg

Italian Chicken

Preparation Time: 10 minutes; Cooking Time: 25 minutes; Serve: 4
Ingredients:
- 4 chicken breasts, skinless & boneless

For rub:
- 1 tsp onion powder
- 1 tsp basil
- 1 tsp oregano
- 1 tsp thyme
- 1 tbsp olive oil
- 1 tsp parsley
- Pepper
- Salt

Directions:
1. Preheat the air fryer to 390 F.
2. Brush chicken breast with olive oil.
3. In a small bowl, mix together all rub ingredients and rub all over the chicken.
4. Place chicken into the air fryer basket and cook for 25 minutes. Turn chicken halfway through.
5. Serve and enjoy.

Nutritional Value (Amount per Serving):
Calories 312; Fat 14.4 g; Carbohydrates 0.9 g; Sugar 0.2 g; Protein 42.4 g; Cholesterol 130 mg

Turkey Patties

Preparation Time: 10 minutes; Cooking Time: 22 minutes; Serve: 4
Ingredients:
- 1 lb ground turkey
- 4 oz feta cheese, crumbled
- 1 1/4 cup spinach, chopped
- 1 tsp Italian seasoning
- 1 tbsp olive oil
- 1 tbsp garlic paste
- Pepper
- Salt

Directions:
1. Preheat the air fryer to 390 F.
2. Add all ingredients into the mixing bowl and mix until well combined.
3. Make four equal shapes of patties from mixture and place into the air fryer basket and cook for 22 minutes. Turn patties halfway through.
4. Serve and enjoy.

Nutritional Value (Amount per Serving):
Calories 325; Fat 22.4 g; Carbohydrates 2.3 g; Sugar 1.3 g; Protein 35.5 g; Cholesterol 142 mg

Creamy Garlic Butter Chicken

Preparation Time: 10 minutes; Cooking Time: 6 hours; Serve: 4
Ingredients:
- 4 chicken breasts, boneless
- 6 garlic cloves, sliced
- 8 tbsp butter
- 1 tsp salt
- For sauce:
- 1/4 cup fresh parsley, chopped
- 3/4 cup chicken stock
- 8 oz cream cheese
- Pepper
- Salt

Directions:
1. Add chicken into the slow cooker. Add garlic and butter around the chicken. Season with salt.
2. Cover and cook on low for 6 hours.
3. Meanwhile, add the stock and cream cheese to a saucepan over medium heat. Cover and bring to simmer. Stir in parsley.
4. Pour sauce over chicken and season with pepper and salt.
5. Serve and enjoy.

Nutritional Value (Amount per Serving):
Calories 689; Fat 30.1 g; Carbohydrates 3.4 g; Sugar 0.3 g; Protein 47.3 g; Cholesterol 253 mg

Zesty Chicken Soup

Preparation Time: 10 minutes; Cooking Time: 10 minutes; Serve: 6
Ingredients:
- 2 chicken breast, boneless, skinless, & halves
- 8 oz cream cheese, softened
- 1 cup green salsa
- 2 cups chicken broth
- 28 oz can tomatoes, diced
- 2 tbsp taco seasoning
- 1/4 tsp salt

Directions:
1. Add chicken, tomatoes, broth, salsa, and taco seasoning into the instant pot and stir well.
2. Cover and cook on high pressure for 10 minutes.
3. Once done, allow to release pressure naturally for 10 minutes then release the remaining pressure manually. Open the lid.
4. Remove chicken from pot and shred using a fork.
5. Stir cream cheese into the instant pot soup mixture and whisk until melted.
6. Return shredded chicken to the instant pot and stir well.
7. Serve and enjoy.

Nutritional Value (Amount per Serving):

Calories 86; Fat 3.6 g; Carbohydrates 3.2 g; Sugar 1.3 g; Protein 9.6 g; Cholesterol 26 mg

Flavorful Chicken Casserole

Preparation Time: 10 minutes; Cooking Time: 35 minutes; Serve: 10
Ingredients:
- 2 lbs chicken breasts, cooked and diced
- 2/3 cup bacon, crumbled
- 8 oz cheddar cheese, shredded
- 1/2 cup sour cream
- 1/2 cup mayonnaise
- 6 oz cream cheese, softened
- 20 oz frozen cauliflower, thawed and drain well
- 1/8 tsp dried thyme
- 1/8 tsp dried rosemary
- 1/8 tsp chipotle powder
- 2 tsp paprika
- 2 tsp onion powder
- 2 tsp garlic powder
- 1/2 tsp pepper
- 1 tsp salt

Directions:
1. In a mixing bowl, mix together mayonnaise, cream, cheese, and all spices.
2. Add chicken, half bacon, cauliflower, and 3/4 of cheese and stir to combine.
3. Transfer chicken mixture in a casserole dish. Sprinkle remaining cheese and bacon on top.
4. Bake at 350 F for 35-40 minutes.
5. Serve and enjoy.

Nutritional Value (Amount per Serving):
Calories 465; Fat 30.9 g; Carbohydrates 8.3 g; Sugar 2.7 g; Protein 38.1 g; Cholesterol 141 mg

Taco Chicken Chaffle

Preparation Time: 10 minutes; Cooking Time: 8 minutes; Serve: 2
Ingredients:
- 1 egg
- 1/3 cup chicken, cooked and chopped
- 1/4 tsp taco seasoning
- 1/3 cup cheddar cheese, shredded

Directions:
1. A heat waffle iron.
2. In a medium bowl, whisk the egg with taco seasoning.
3. Add chicken and shredded cheese and mix until well combined.
4. Add half of the mixture into the hot waffle iron and cook for 4 minutes.
5. Serve and enjoy

Nutritional Value (Amount per Serving):
Calories 148; Fat 9.4 g; Carbohydrates 0.8 g; Sugar 0.3 g; Protein 14.5 g; Cholesterol 120 mg

Balsamic Chicken Thighs

Preparation Time: 10 minutes; Cooking Time: 4 hours; Serve: 8
Ingredients:
- 8 chicken thighs, skinless and boneless
- 1/2 cup balsamic vinegar
- 1 tbsp olive oil
- 1 tbsp garlic, minced
- 2 tsp dried onion
- 1/2 tsp pepper
- 1 tsp dried basil

- 1 tsp garlic powder
- 1/2 tsp salt

Directions:
1. Season chicken with garlic powder, pepper, and salt.
2. Add olive oil and chicken into the slow cooker.
3. Pour remaining ingredients over chicken.
4. Cover and cook on high for 4 hours.
5. Serve and enjoy.

Nutritional Value (Amount per Serving):
Calories 299; Fat 12.6 g; Carbohydrates 0.9 g; Sugar 0.2 g; Protein 42.4 g; Cholesterol 130 mg

Yummy Chicken Tenders

Preparation Time: 10 minutes; Cooking Time: 16 minutes; Serve: 4

Ingredients:
- 1 lb chicken tenders

For rub:
- 1/2 tbsp dried thyme
- 1 tbsp garlic powder
- 1 tbsp paprika
- 1/2 tbsp onion powder
- 1/2 tsp cayenne pepper
- Pepper
- Salt

Directions:
1. Preheat the oven to 370 F.
2. In a bowl, add all rub ingredients and mix well.
3. Add chicken tenders into the bowl and coat well with rub.
4. Place chicken tenders into the air fryer basket and air fry for 16 minutes. Turn chicken tenders halfway through.
5. Serve and enjoy.

Nutritional Value (Amount per Serving):
Calories 232; Fat 8.7 g; Carbohydrates 3.6 g; Sugar 1 g; Protein 33.6 g; Cholesterol 101 mg

Chicken Cacciatore Stew

Preparation Time: 10 minutes; Cooking Time: 8 hours; Serve: 8

Ingredients:
- 6 chicken thighs, skinless and boneless
- 1/4 cup fresh basil
- 1 bay leaf
- 1 tbsp dried oregano
- 10 oz mushrooms, sliced
- 1 bell pepper, sliced
- 1/2 onion, sliced
- 28 oz can tomatoes
- Pepper
- Salt

Directions:
1. Season chicken with pepper and salt.
2. Add chicken into the slow cooker.
3. Pour remaining ingredients over chicken. Cover and cook on low for 8 hours.
4. Discard bay leaves. Shred chicken using a fork.
5. Serve and enjoy.

Nutritional Value (Amount per Serving):
Calories 226; Fat 8.3 g; Carbohydrates 3.6 g; Sugar 1.8 g; Protein 33.1 g; Cholesterol 97 mg

Tasty Chicken Fajita

Preparation Time: 10 minutes; Cooking Time: 16 minutes; Serve: 4
Ingredients:
- 1 lb chicken breast, skinless, boneless, and sliced
- 2 tsp olive oil
- 1 onion, sliced
- 2 bell peppers, sliced
- 1/8 tsp cayenne
- 1 tsp cumin
- 2 tsp chili powder
- 1/2 tsp pepper
- 1 tsp salt

Directions:
1. Preheat the air fryer to 360 F.
2. In a large bowl, toss chicken with remaining ingredients.
3. Transfer chicken mixture into the air fryer basket and cook for 16 minutes. Stir chicken mixture halfway through.
4. Serve and enjoy.

Nutritional Value (Amount per Serving):
Calories 186; Fat 5.7 g; Carbohydrates 8.2 g; Sugar 4.3 g; Protein 25.2 g; Cholesterol 73 mg

Stir Fry Chicken

Preparation Time: 10 minutes; Cooking Time: 13 minutes; Serve: 6
Ingredients:
- 1 lb chicken thighs, boneless & cut into chunks
- 1 tbsp sesame seeds
- 1 tsp coconut amino
- 1 tsp sesame oil
- 2 cups broccoli florets
- 1 tbsp olive oil
- 1 garlic clove, minced
- 1/2 cup chicken broth
- 1/4 tsp red pepper flakes
- 1 tsp fresh ginger, minced
- 2 carrots, cut into strips
- 1 tsp salt

Directions:
1. Heat olive oil in a pan over high heat. Add chicken and sauté for 8 minutes.
2. Add carrots, ginger, garlic, broccoli, broth, red pepper flakes, and salt. Cover and cook for 5 minutes.
3. Remove pan from heat and stir in coconut amino, sesame seeds, and sesame oil.
4. Stir and serve.

Nutritional Value (Amount per Serving):
Calories 204; Fat 9.7 g; Carbohydrates 5 g; Sugar 1.6 g; Protein 23.6 g; Cholesterol 67 mg

Dried Herb Chicken

Preparation Time: 10 minutes; Cooking Time: 10 minutes; Serve: 2
Ingredients:
- 2 chicken breasts, boneless and skinless
- 1 tsp dried oregano
- 1 tsp dried basil
- 2 tsp garlic, minced
- 1 tsp dried thyme
- Pepper
- Salt

Directions:
1. Preheat the air fryer to 400 F.

2. In a small bowl, mix together garlic, thyme, oregano, basil, pepper, and salt and rub all over the chicken.
3. Place chicken into the air fryer basket and cook for 10 minutes.
4. Serve and enjoy.

Nutritional Value (Amount per Serving):
Calories 285; Fat 11 g; Carbohydrates 1.8 g; Sugar 0.1 g; Protein 42.6 g; Cholesterol 130 mg

Chicken Skewers

Preparation Time: 10 minutes; Cooking Time: 10 minutes; Serve: 4
Ingredients:
- 1 lb chicken breast, boneless, skinless, and cut into 3/4-inch cubes
- 1 tbsp rosemary, minced
- 1 tbsp oregano, minced
- 1/2 tsp red chili flakes, crushed
- 1 tbsp fresh lemon juice
- 2 cups green seedless grapes, rinsed
- 1 tsp lemon zest
- 2 garlic cloves, minced
- 1/4 cup olive oil
- 1/2 tsp salt

Directions:
1. Thread chicken pieces and grapes alternate onto the soaked wooden skewers and place skewers on the plate.
2. In a small bowl, mix together lemon juice, lemon zest, rosemary, oregano, chili flakes, garlic, oil, and salt and pour over chicken skewers.
3. Place chicken skewers into the refrigerator overnight.
4. Place marinated chicken skewers onto the hot grill and cook for 3-5 minutes on each side.
5. Serve and enjoy.

Nutritional Value (Amount per Serving):
Calories 255; Fat 15.8 g; Carbohydrates 3.9 g; Sugar 0.2 g; Protein 24.4 g; Cholesterol 73 mg

BBQ Chicken Chaffle

Preparation Time: 10 minutes; Cooking Time: 8 minutes; Serve: 2
Ingredients:
- 1 egg
- 1/2 cup cheddar cheese, shredded
- 1/3 cup chicken, cooked and diced
- 1 tbsp almond flour
- 1 tbsp BBQ sauce, sugar-free

Directions:
1. A heat waffle iron.
2. In a small bowl, mix together egg, cheese, chicken, BBQ sauce, and almond flour.
3. Add 1/2 of the mixture into hot waffle iron and cook for 4 minutes.
4. Serve and enjoy.

Nutritional Value (Amount per Serving):
Calories 398; Fat 29.9 g; Carbohydrates 11.4 g; Sugar 5.7 g; Protein 21.4 g; Cholesterol 151 mg

Chicken Chaffle

Preparation Time: 10 minutes; Cooking Time: 8 minutes; Serve: 2
Ingredients:
- 1 egg
- 1/4 cup broccoli, chopped

- 1/4 cup chicken, cooked and diced
- 1/4 tsp garlic powder
- 1/2 cup cheddar cheese, shredded

Directions:
1. A heat waffle iron.
2. In a small bowl, mix together egg, cheese, and garlic powder. Add chicken and broccoli and stir well.
3. Add 1/2 of the batter into hot waffle iron and cook for 4 minutes or until golden brown.
4. Serve and enjoy.

Nutritional Value (Amount per Serving):
Calories 177; Fat 12.1 g; Carbohydrates 1.5 g; Sugar 0.6 g; Protein 15.3 g; Cholesterol 125 mg

Tasty Chicken Stew

Preparation Time: 10 minutes; Cooking Time: 4 hours; Serve: 6
Ingredients:
- 1 1/2 lbs chicken breasts, boneless & cut into chunks
- 1 tsp thyme, dried
- 1 cup chicken stock
- 3 cups zucchini, diced
- 1 onion, diced
- 1 tsp basil, dried
- 1 tsp oregano, dried
- 8 oz mushrooms, sliced
- 6 oz tomato paste
- 1 tbsp garlic cloves, diced
- 1 cup bell pepper, diced
- Salt

Directions:
1. Add all ingredients into the crockpot and stir well.
2. Cover and cook on low for 4 hours.
3. Stir and serve.

Nutritional Value (Amount per Serving):
Calories 256; Fat 8.8 g; Carbohydrates 8.1 g; Sugar 4 g; Protein 35.6 g; Cholesterol 101 mg

Creamy Coconut Chicken Curry

Preparation Time: 10 minutes; Cooking Time: 30 minutes; Serve: 4
Ingredients:
- 1 lb chicken thighs, boneless
- 1 tbsp curry powder
- 3 oz green beans, chopped
- 1/2 lb broccoli, chopped
- 2 cans of coconut milk
- 3 tbsp olive oil
- 1 onion, chopped
- 1 tbsp ginger, grated
- 1 red chili pepper, chopped
- Pepper
- Salt

Directions:
1. Heat oil in a saucepan over medium heat.
2. Add ginger, chili pepper, and onion in a pan sauté for 5 minutes.
3. Add chicken and curry powder and cook for 10 minutes. Add green beans and broccoli and stir well.
4. Add coconut milk and stir well.
5. Turn heat to medium-low and simmer for 15 minutes.
6. Stir and serve.

Nutritional Value (Amount per Serving):

Calories 226; Fat 8.3 g; Carbohydrates 3.6 g; Sugar 1.8 g; Protein 33.1 g; Cholesterol 97 mg

Turkey Breast with Veggie

Preparation Time: 10 minutes; Cooking Time: 45 minutes; Serve: 4

Ingredients:
- 1 lb turkey breast, cut into 1-inch cubes
- 1 cup mushrooms, cleaned
- 1/2 lb Brussels sprouts, cut in half
- 1 tsp garlic powder
- 2 tbsp olive oil
- Pepper
- Salt

Directions:
1. Preheat the oven to 350 F.
2. In a small bowl, mix oil, garlic powder, pepper, and salt.
3. In a baking dish, mix together turkey, mushrooms, and Brussels sprouts. Pour oil mixture over turkey.
4. Cover dish with foil and bake for 45 minutes.
5. Serve and enjoy.

Nutritional Value (Amount per Serving):
Calories 190; Fat 8.3 g; Carbohydrates 10.2 g; Sugar 3.7 g; Protein 20.5 g; Cholesterol 10.2 mg

Turkey Bacon Burgers

Preparation Time: 10 minutes; Cooking Time: 8 minutes; Serve: 5

Ingredients:
- 1 lb ground turkey
- 1 cup cheddar cheese, shredded
- 1/4 cup BBQ sauce
- 1/2 tsp Garlic powder
- 1/3 cup bacon, chopped
- 1/3 cup green onions, chopped
- Pepper
- Salt

Directions:
1. Add ground turkey and remaining ingredients into the large bowl and mix until just combined.
2. Heat a grill to medium-high heat.
3. Make five equal shapes of patties from meat mixture and place on a hot grill and cook for 4 minutes on each side.
4. Serve and enjoy.

Nutritional Value (Amount per Serving):
Calories 290; Fat 17 g; Carbohydrates 5 g; Sugar 3.6 g; Protein 30.6 g; Cholesterol 116 mg

Spicy Chicken Breasts

Preparation Time: 10 minutes; Cooking Time: 12 minutes; Serve: 4

Ingredients:
- 4 chicken breasts
- 1 tsp ground cumin
- 1 tsp garlic powder
- 1/4 tsp black pepper
- 2 tbsp olive oil
- 1/2 tsp smoked paprika
- 1/2 tsp ground coriander
- 1/2 tsp sea salt

Directions:
1. Preheat the grill to medium-high heat.

2. In a small bowl, mix together garlic powder, oil, pepper, paprika, coriander, cumin, and salt and rub all over the chicken.
3. Place chicken on hot grill and cook for 4-6 minutes on each side.
4. Serve and enjoy.

Nutritional Value (Amount per Serving):
Calories 343; Fat 18 g; Carbohydrates 1 g; Sugar 0.2 g; Protein 42.5 g; Cholesterol 130 mg

Spinach Turkey Burgers

Preparation Time: 10 minutes; Cooking Time: 10 minutes; Serve: 4
Ingredients:
- 1 lb ground turkey
- 1 tsp oregano
- 1 tsp garlic powder
- 1/3 cup sun-dried tomatoes
- 1/2 cup feta cheese, crumbled
- 1 tbsp almond flour
- 1/4 tsp crushed red pepper
- 1 tsp parsley
- 1/2 cup baby spinach, chopped
- 1/2 tsp pepper
- 1/2 tsp sea salt

Directions:
1. Add all ingredients into the bowl and mix until just combined.
2. Make four equal shapes of patties from the mixture.
3. Preheat the grill to high heat.
4. Place patties on hot grill and cook for 3-5 minutes on each side.
5. Serve and enjoy.

Nutritional Value (Amount per Serving):
Calories 289; Fat 17.4 g; Carbohydrates 2.9 g; Sugar 1.4 g; Protein 34.5 g; Cholesterol 132 mg

Paprika Lemon Chicken

Preparation Time: 10 minutes; Cooking Time: 35 minutes; Serve: 4
Ingredients:
- 4 chicken breasts, skinless and boneless, cut into chunks
- 2 tbsp smoked paprika
- 3 tbsp olive oil
- 2 tsp garlic, minced
- 2 tbsp lemon juice
- Pepper
- Salt

Directions:
1. Preheat the oven to 350 F.
2. In a small bowl, mix together garlic, lemon juice, paprika, and olive oil.
3. Season chicken with pepper and salt.
4. Spread 1/3 bowl mixture on the bottom of the casserole dish.
5. Add seasoned chicken into the casserole dish and rub with fish sauce.
6. Pour remaining sauce over chicken and rub well.
7. Bake in preheated oven for 30-35 minutes.
8. Serve and enjoy.

Nutritional Value (Amount per Serving):
Calories 381; Fat 21.8 g; Carbohydrates 2.6 g; Sugar 0.5 g; Protein 42.9 g; Cholesterol 130 mg

Flavorful Chili Lime Chicken

Preparation Time: 10 minutes; Cooking Time: 10 minutes; Serve: 5

Ingredients:
- 2 lbs chicken thighs, skinless and boneless
- 2 tbsp garlic, minced
- 1/4 cup olive oil
- 1/4 cup fresh lime juice
- 2 tsp chili flakes
- 6 tbsp fresh cilantro, chopped
- 2 tbsp fresh ginger, minced
- 1/8 tsp black pepper
- 2 tsp salt

Directions:
1. Add all ingredients except chicken into the bowl and whisk until just combined.
2. Add chicken to the bowl and coat well, cover and place in the freezer for 4 hours.
3. Heat a grill to medium heat.
4. Place marinated chicken on hot grill and cook over medium heat for 3-5 minutes on each side.
5. Serve and enjoy.

Nutritional Value (Amount per Serving):
Calories 444; Fat 23 g; Carbohydrates 2.7 g; Sugar 0.1 g; Protein 53 g; Cholesterol 161 mg

Taco Chicken Drumsticks

Preparation Time: 10 minutes; Cooking Time: 30 minutes; Serve: 8

Ingredients:
- 2 lbs chicken legs
- 2 tbsp taco seasoning
- 2 tbsp olive oil

Directions:
1. Preheat the grill medium-high heat.
2. Brush chicken legs with oil and rub with taco seasoning.
3. Place chicken legs on hot grill and cook for 30 minutes.
4. Turn chicken legs every 10 minutes.
5. Serve and enjoy.

Nutritional Value (Amount per Serving):
Calories 245; Fat 11.9 g; Carbohydrates 0 g; Sugar 0 g; Protein 32.8 g; Cholesterol 101 mg

Tasty Chicken Kebabs

Preparation Time: 10 minutes; Cooking Time: 14 minutes; Serve: 6

Ingredients:
- 2 lbs chicken thighs, cut into pieces
- 3 garlic cloves, minced
- 1 tsp dried oregano
- 1 red bell pepper, cut into medium pieces
- 1 yellow bell pepper, cut into medium pieces
- 1 green bell pepper, cut into medium pieces
- 2 tbsp olive oil
- 2 tbsp soy sauce

Directions:
1. Add chicken and remaining ingredients into the bowl and mix well.
2. Cover bowl and place in the freezer overnight.
3. Preheat the grill to medium-high heat.
4. Thread marinated chicken pieces and bell pepper pieces onto the skewers.
5. Place skewers onto the hot grill and cooks for 7 minutes on each side.
6. Serve and enjoy.

Nutritional Value (Amount per Serving):

Calories 352; Fat 16 g; Carbohydrates 5.6 g; Sugar 3 g; Protein 44 g; Cholesterol 135 mg

Spicy Chili Chicken

Preparation Time: 10 minutes; Cooking Time: 6 hours; Serve: 5

Ingredients:
- 1 lb chicken breasts, skinless and boneless
- 14 oz can tomatoes, diced
- 2 cups of water
- 1 jalapeno pepper, chopped
- 1 poblano pepper, chopped
- 1/2 tsp paprika
- 1/2 tsp dried sage
- 1/2 tsp cumin
- 1 tsp dried oregano
- 12 oz can green chilies
- 1/2 cup dried chives
- 1 tsp sea salt

Directions:
1. Add all ingredients into the crockpot and stir well.
2. Cover and cook on low for 6 hours.
3. Remove chicken from crockpot and shred using a fork.
4. Return chicken to the crockpot and stir well.
5. Serve and enjoy.

Nutritional Value (Amount per Serving):
Calories 212; Fat 7.1 g; Carbohydrates 8.9 g; Sugar 3.4 g; Protein 27.9 g; Cholesterol 81 mg

Grilled Chicken Breast

Preparation Time: 10 minutes; Cooking Time: 10 minutes; Serve: 2

Ingredients:
- 2 chicken breasts, boneless
- 2 tbsp olive oil
- 1/4 tsp black pepper
- 1 tsp garlic powder
- 2 tbsp soy sauce

Directions:
1. Add chicken into the zip-lock bag.
2. In a small bowl, mix together olive oil, soy sauce, garlic powder, and pepper and pour over chicken.
3. Seal bag and place in the refrigerator overnight.
4. Heat the grill to medium-high heat.
5. Place marinated chicken onto the grill and cook for 5 minutes on each side.
6. Serve and enjoy.

Nutritional Value (Amount per Serving):
Calories 411; Fat 24 g; Carbohydrates 2.4 g; Sugar 0.6 g; Protein 43.5 g; Cholesterol 130 mg

Juicy Garlic Chicken

Preparation Time: 10 minutes; Cooking Time: 40 minutes; Serve: 6

Ingredients:
- 2 lbs chicken thighs, skinless and boneless
- 8 garlic cloves, sliced
- 2 tbsp olive oil
- 2 tbsp fresh parsley, chopped
- 1 fresh lemon juice
- Pepper
- Salt

Directions:

1. Preheat the oven to 450 F.
2. Place chicken on a baking sheet and season with pepper and salt.
3. Sprinkle parsley and garlic over the chicken and drizzle oil and lemon juice on top of chicken.
4. Bake for 30-40 minutes.
5. Serve and enjoy.

Nutritional Value (Amount per Serving):
Calories 336; Fat 16 g; Carbohydrates 1.6 g; Sugar 0.2 g; Protein 44.1 g; Cholesterol 135 mg

Chicken with Olives & Artichokes

Preparation Time: 10 minutes; Cooking Time: 8 hours; Serve: 6
Ingredients:
- 6 chicken thighs, skinless and boneless
- 10 oz frozen artichoke hearts
- 14 oz can tomatoes, diced
- 1/2 tsp garlic powder
- 1 tsp dried oregano
- 15 olives, pitted
- 3 tbsp fresh lemon juice
- 1 tsp dried basil
- Pepper
- Salt

Directions:
1. Season chicken with pepper and salt and place in the slow cooker.
2. Pour remaining ingredients over chicken.
3. Cover and cook on low for 8 hours.
4. Serve and enjoy.

Nutritional Value (Amount per Serving):
Calories 309; Fat 12.1 g; Carbohydrates 4.8 g; Sugar 2.5 g; Protein 43.2 g; Cholesterol 130 mg

Flavorful Chicken Skewers

Preparation Time: 10 minutes; Cooking Time: 20 minutes; Serve: 4
Ingredients:
- 1 1/2 lbs chicken breast, cut into 1-inch cubes

For marinade:
- 2 tbsp dried oregano
- 1/4 cup fresh mint leaves
- 5 garlic cloves
- 1/2 cup lemon juice
- 1 tbsp red wine vinegar
- 1/2 cup yogurt
- 2 tbsp fresh rosemary, chopped
- 1/4 tsp cayenne
- 1 cup olive oil
- Pepper
- Salt

Directions:
1. Add all marinade ingredients into the blender and blend until smooth.
2. Pour marinade in a large bowl.
3. Add chicken to the bowl and coat well. Cover bowl and place in the refrigerator for 1 hour.
4. Preheat the oven to 400 F.
5. Thread marinated chicken onto the skewers.
6. Place skewers on grill and bakes for 15-20 minutes.
7. Serve and enjoy.

Nutritional Value (Amount per Serving):

Calories 677; Fat 55.8 g; Carbohydrates 7.1 g; Sugar 3 g; Protein 38.8 g; Cholesterol 111 mg

Greek Chicken

Preparation Time: 10 minutes; Cooking Time: 6 hours; Serve: 4
Ingredients:
- 4 chicken breasts, skinless and boneless
- 1/4 cup fresh lemon juice
- 2 tsp dried oregano
- 1 tbsp garlic, minced
- 1/4 cup fresh parsley, chopped
- 1 cup chicken stock
- 3/4 tbsp lemon zest
- 1 tsp kosher salt

Directions:
1. Add all ingredients except parsley into the crockpot and mix well.
2. Cover and cook on low for 6 hours.
3. Garnish with parsley and serve.

Nutritional Value (Amount per Serving):
Calories 291; Fat 11.2 g; Carbohydrates 2.1 g; Sugar 0.6 g; Protein 42.9 g; Cholesterol 130 mg

Cheesy Chicken Casserole

Preparation Time: 10 minutes; Cooking Time: 40 minutes; Serve: 8
Ingredients:
- 2 lbs cooked chicken, shredded
- 6 oz cream cheese, softened
- 4 oz butter, melted
- 6 oz ham, cut into small pieces
- 5 oz Swiss cheese
- 1 oz fresh lemon juice
- 1 tbsp Dijon mustard
- 1/2 tsp salt

Directions:
1. Preheat the oven to 350 F.
2. Place chicken in the bottom of the baking dish then layers ham pieces on top.
3. Add butter, lemon juice, mustard, cream cheese, and salt into the blender and blend until smooth.
4. Spread butter mixture over chicken and ham mixture in the baking dish.
5. Arrange Swiss cheese slices on top and bake for 40 minutes.
6. Serve and enjoy.

Nutritional Value (Amount per Serving):
Calories 451; Fat 29.2 g; Carbohydrates 2.5 g; Sugar 0.4 g; Protein 43 g; Cholesterol 170 mg

Cajun Chicken Stew

Preparation Time: 10 minutes; Cooking Time: 4 hours; Serve: 8
Ingredients:
- 3 lbs chicken thighs, skinless and boneless
- 6 oz tomato paste
- 6 garlic cloves, chopped
- 2 cups green bell pepper, chopped
- 2 cups celery, chopped
- 2 cups onion, chopped
- 1 tsp dried thyme
- 2 bay leaves
- 2 tsp Cajun seasoning
- 1 cup chicken broth, low-sodium
- 15 oz tomatoes, chopped
- 2 tbsp olive oil
- 1/4 tsp ground black pepper

Directions:

1. Heat olive oil in a large pan over medium heat.
2. Add garlic, onion, bell pepper, and celery and sauté for 5-7 minutes. Add tomato paste and sauté for 2 minutes.
3. Transfer pan mixture into the slow cooker.
4. Add tomatoes, thyme, bay leaves, Cajun seasoning, chicken broth, and black pepper into the slow cooker and stir well.
5. Add chicken and stir well. Cover and cook on low for 4 hours.
6. Serve and enjoy.

Nutritional Value (Amount per Serving):
Calories 400; Fat 16.6 g; Carbohydrates 4.9 g; Sugar 4.9 g; Protein 51.4 g; Cholesterol 151 mg

Meatballs

Preparation Time: 10 minutes; Cooking Time: 25 minutes; Serve: 6
Ingredients:
- 1 egg, lightly beaten
- 1 lb ground turkey
- 1 tsp olive oil
- 2 tbsp chives, chopped
- 2 tbsp almond flour
- 1/2 tsp ground ginger
- 1/2 tsp salt

Directions:
1. Preheat the oven to 375 F.
2. In a large bowl, combine together turkey, chives, almond flour, olive oil, ginger, egg, and salt until just combined.
3. Make small even shape balls from meat mixture and place onto the baking sheet.
4. Bake meatballs for 23-25 minutes.
5. Serve and enjoy.

Nutritional Value (Amount per Serving):
Calories 219; Fat 14.5 g; Carbohydrates 2.2 g; Sugar 0.4 g; Protein 23.6 g; Cholesterol 104 mg

Tasty Chicken Curry

Preparation Time: 10 minutes; Cooking Time: 20 minutes; Serve: 6
Ingredients:
- 1 1/2 lbs chicken thighs, skinless, boneless, and cut into pieces
- 1 tbsp jalapeno pepper, minced
- 2 tbsp ginger, diced
- 2 tbsp olive oil
- 1/4 cup fresh cilantro, chopped
- 2 tbsp fresh lemon juice
- 2 tsp cayenne
- 1 tsp garam masala
- 2 tsp turmeric
- 1 cup tomatoes, chopped

Directions:
1. Heat olive oil in a pan over medium heat.
2. Add jalapenos and ginger to the pan and sauté for 2-3 minutes.
3. Add chicken and sear chicken from both sides.
4. Add tomatoes and stir well.
5. Add all spices and stir well and cook until chicken is completely cooked.
6. Add lemon juice and stir well.
7. Garnish with cilantro and serve.

Nutritional Value (Amount per Serving):

Calories 273; Fat 13.5 g; Carbohydrates 3.4 g; Sugar 1.1 g; Protein 33.4 g; Cholesterol 101 mg

Tomato Olive Capers Chicken

Preparation Time: 10 minutes; Cooking Time: 22 minutes; Serve: 4
Ingredients:
- 4 chicken breast, boneless and halves
- 15 olives, pitted and halved
- 2 cups cherry tomatoes
- 3 tbsp olive oil
- 3 tbsp capers, rinsed and drained
- Pepper
- Salt

Directions:
1. Preheat the oven to 475 F.
2. In a bowl, toss tomatoes, capers, olives with 2 tablespoons of oil. Set aside. Season chicken with pepper and salt.
3. Heat remaining oil in a pan over high heat.
4. Place chicken in the pan and cook for 4 minutes.
5. Turn chicken and top with tomato mixture.
6. Transfer pan to oven and roast chicken for 18 minutes.
7. Serve and enjoy.

Nutritional Value (Amount per Serving):
Calories 241; Fat 15 g; Carbohydrates 4.9 g; Sugar 2.4 g; Protein 22.3 g; Cholesterol 64 mg

Roasted Pepper Artichoke Chicken

Preparation Time: 10 minutes; Cooking Time: 2 hours; Serve: 6
Ingredients:
- 2 1/2 lbs chicken thighs, skinless and boneless
- 1 cup roasted red peppers, drained and cut into chunks
- 1 tsp dried oregano
- 14 oz can artichokes
- 1/2 cup olives
- 2 tsp dried garlic, minced
- 2 tbsp olive oil
- 3 tbsp lemon juice
- 1/2 tsp pepper
- 1 tsp salt

Directions:
1. Add chicken in the slow cooker.
2. Add remaining ingredients on top of the chicken and stir well to combine.
3. Cover and cook on high for 2 hours or until chicken is done.
4. Serve and enjoy.

Nutritional Value (Amount per Serving):
Calories 424; Fat 20 g; Carbohydrates 3.3 g; Sugar 1.5 g; Protein 55.2 g; Cholesterol 168 mg

Chicken Shawarma

Preparation Time: 10 minutes; Cooking Time: 3 hours; Serve: 5
Ingredients:
- 1 1/4 lbs chicken thigh, skinless and boneless
- 1 tsp cumin
- 2 tbsp garlic, minced
- 1/2 cup Greek yogurt
- 1/4 cup chicken stock
- 1/4 cup fresh lemon juice
- 1 1/2 tbsp tahini
- 1/4 tsp ground coriander
- 1/4 tsp cinnamon

- 1/2 tsp curry powder
- 1/2 tsp dried parsley
- 1 tsp paprika
- 1 tsp garlic powder
- 1 tbsp olive oil
- Pepper
- Salt

Directions:
1. Add chicken into the crockpot and season with pepper and salt.
2. Pour remaining ingredients over chicken.
3. Cover and cook on high for 3 hours.
4. Stir and serve.

Nutritional Value (Amount per Serving):
Calories 295; Fat 14.3 g; Carbohydrates 4.2 g; Sugar 1.4 g; Protein 36.2 g; Cholesterol 102 mg

Easy Chicken Kebabs

Preparation Time: 10 minutes; Cooking Time: 10 minutes; Serve: 4
Ingredients:
- 1 1/2 lbs chicken breast, skinless, boneless, and cut into 1-inch pieces
- 1 tsp dried oregano
- 1/2 tsp pepper
- 1 tbsp fresh lime juice
- 1 tbsp olive oil
- 1/2 tsp sea salt

Directions:
1. In a bowl, mix together lime juice, olive oil, oregano, pepper, and salt.
2. Add chicken to the bowl and coat well. Cover and place in the refrigerator overnight.
3. Heat grill over medium heat.
4. Thread marinated chicken onto the soaked wooden skewers.
5. Place chicken skewers onto the hot grill and cook for 8-10 minutes.
6. Serve and enjoy.

Nutritional Value (Amount per Serving):
Calories 228; Fat 7.8 g; Carbohydrates 1.3 g; Sugar 0.2 g; Protein 36.2 g; Cholesterol 109 mg

Pesto Chicken

Preparation Time: 10 minutes; Cooking Time: 25 minutes; Serve: 3
Ingredients:
- 1 lb chicken thighs, skinless, boneless, and cut into strips
- 1 lb asparagus, ends trimmed and cut in half
- 2 tbsp olive oil
- 1 1/2 cups cherry tomatoes, halved
- 1/4 cup basil pesto

Directions:
1. Heat olive oil in a pan over medium heat.
2. Add chicken to the hot olive oil and season with salt and cook for 5-8 minutes or until chicken is cooked.
3. Add pesto and asparagus and cook for 2-3 minutes or until asparagus cooked.
4. Remove pan from heat. Add tomatoes and stir well.
5. Serve and enjoy.

Nutritional Value (Amount per Serving):
Calories 408; Fat 20.7 g; Carbohydrates 7.3 g; Sugar 1.2 g; Protein 47 g; Cholesterol 135 mg

Chicken with Mushrooms

Preparation Time: 10 minutes; Cooking Time: 30 minutes; Serve: 4

Ingredients:
- 2 lbs chicken breasts, halved
- 8 oz mushrooms, sliced
- 1/2 cup mayonnaise
- 1/3 cup sun-dried tomatoes
- 1 tsp salt

Directions:
1. Preheat the oven to 400 F.
2. Grease baking dish with butter.
3. Place chicken breasts into the baking dish and top with sun-dried tomatoes, mushrooms, mayonnaise, and salt. Mix well.
4. Bake for 30 minutes.
5. Serve and enjoy.

Nutritional Value (Amount per Serving):
Calories 568; Fat 41.5 g; Carbohydrates 3.2 g; Sugar 2 g; Protein 68 g; Cholesterol 202 mg

Rosemary Turkey Breast

Preparation Time: 10 minutes; Cooking Time: 4 hours; Serve: 12

Ingredients:
- 6 lbs turkey breast, bone-in
- 4 fresh rosemary sprigs
- 1/2 cup water
- Pepper
- Salt

Directions:
1. Season turkey breast with pepper and salt and place in the crockpot.
2. Add water and rosemary on top of turkey breast.
3. Cover and cook on low for 4 hours.
4. Serve and enjoy.

Nutritional Value (Amount per Serving):
Calories 237; Fat 3.8 g; Carbohydrates 9.8 g; Sugar 8 g; Protein 38.7 g; Cholesterol 98 mg

Salsa Chicken

Preparation Time: 10 minutes; Cooking Time: 8 minutes; Serve: 4

Ingredients:
- 1 1/2 lbs chicken breasts, skinless and boneless
- 1 1/2 cups salsa
- Pepper
- Salt

Directions:
1. Add chicken into the instant pot. Season chicken with pepper and salt.
2. Pour salsa over chicken.
3. Seal pot with lid and cook on high pressure for 8 minutes.
4. Once done, allow to release pressure naturally for 10 minutes then release remaining pressure using the quick-release method. Open the lid.
5. Shred the chicken using a fork.
6. Stir well and serve.

Nutritional Value (Amount per Serving):
Calories 226; Fat 5 g; Carbohydrates 7 g; Sugar 4 g; Protein 38 g; Cholesterol 109 mg

Chapter 3: Vegetarian
Cheesy Cauliflower Mashed

Preparation Time: 10 minutes; Cooking Time: 30 minutes; Serve: 16

Ingredients:
- 40 oz frozen cauliflower, steam until warm
- 1 cup Asiago cheese, shredded
- 12 oz cream cheese, softened
- 3/4 cup butter
- 1/2 cup heavy cream
- 5 garlic cloves, roasted
- 2 tsp salt

Directions:
1. Add all ingredients except Asiago cheese into the food processor and process until smooth.
2. Spoon blended cauliflower mixture into the baking dish and top with Asiago cheese.
3. Bake at 400 F for 30 minutes.
4. Serve and enjoy.

Nutritional Value (Amount per Serving):
Calories 201; Fat 19 g; Carbohydrates 4.8 g; Sugar 1.8 g; Protein 4.6 g; Cholesterol 56 mg

Simple Pumpkin Casserole

Preparation Time: 10 minutes; Cooking Time: 30 minutes; Serve: 6

Ingredients:
- 2 eggs
- 15 oz pumpkin puree
- 1/2 tsp dried thyme
- 1/2 tsp dried sage
- 1/2 tsp dried rosemary
- 2 tbsp parmesan cheese, grated
- 6 tbsp ricotta cheese
- 1/2 cup heavy cream
- 3 garlic cloves, minced
- 1/4 tsp salt

Directions:
1. Grease 7*11-inch pan and set aside.
2. In a bowl, whisk eggs with cream, pumpkin puree, garlic, and salt.
3. Pour egg mixture into the prepared pan. Sprinkle ricotta cheese, parmesan cheese, thyme, rosemary, and sage over egg mixture.
4. Bake at 350 F for 25-30 minutes.
5. Serve and enjoy.

Nutritional Value (Amount per Serving):
Calories 120; Fat 7.7 g; Carbohydrates 7.8 g; Sugar 2.5 g; Protein 6.3 g; Cholesterol 77 mg

Delicious Cauliflower Rice

Preparation Time: 10 minutes; Cooking Time: 40 minutes; Serve: 8

Ingredients:
- 6 cups grated cauliflower
- 2 tbsp fresh cilantro, chopped
- 10 oz can tomatoes with green chilis
- 1/8 tsp red pepper flakes
- 1/2 tsp salt

Directions:
1. Grease 1 1/2-quart baking dish and set aside.
2. Add can tomatoes into the blender and blend well.

3. Add grated cauliflower, cilantro, tomatoes, red pepper flakes, and salt into the prepared baking dish and stir until well combined.
4. Bake at 350 F for 40 minutes. Stir halfway through.
5. Serve and enjoy.

Nutritional Value (Amount per Serving):
Calories 24; Fat 0.1 g; Carbohydrates 5.3 g; Sugar 1.8 g; Protein 1.7 g; Cholesterol 0 mg

Green Beans with Jicama

Preparation Time: 10 minutes; Cooking Time: 45 minutes; Serve: 6
Ingredients:
- 12 oz green beans, sliced in half
- 1 medium jicama, cubed
- 1 tsp dried thyme
- 1 tsp dried rosemary
- 3 garlic cloves
- 3 tbsp olive oil
- 1/2 tsp salt

Directions:
1. Preheat the oven to 400 F.
2. Add green beans, jicama, thyme, rosemary, garlic, oil, and salt into the mixing bowl and toss well.
3. Spread green beans and jicama mixture on a parchment-lined baking sheet and bake for 45 minutes. Stir vegetables after every 15 minutes.
4. Serve and enjoy.

Nutritional Value (Amount per Serving):
Calories 73; Fat 7.1 g; Carbohydrates 2.9 g; Sugar 0.6 g; Protein 0.4 g; Cholesterol 0 mg

Roasted Garlic Mushrooms

Preparation Time: 10 minutes; Cooking Time: 25 minutes; Serve: 8
Ingredients:
- 1 lb mushrooms
- 1 tsp dried oregano
- 2 tbsp parmesan cheese, grated
- 2 tbsp balsamic vinegar
- 2 tbsp olive oil
- 10 garlic cloves, minced
- 1/2 tsp pepper
- 1 tsp salt

Directions:
1. Preheat the oven to 400 F. Line baking sheet with foil.
2. In a mixing bowl, toss mushrooms with garlic, oil, oregano, pepper, and salt.
3. Spread mushrooms on a baking sheet and bake for 15 minutes.
4. Drizzle vinegar on top of mushrooms and sprinkle with parmesan cheese and bake for 10 minutes more.
5. Serve and enjoy.

Nutritional Value (Amount per Serving):
Calories 61; Fat 4.5 g; Carbohydrates 3.5 g; Sugar 1 g; Protein 3.2 g; Cholesterol 3 mg

Sauteed Mushrooms & Green Beans

Preparation Time: 10 minutes; Cooking Time: 16 minutes; Serve: 6
Ingredients:
- 1 lb green beans, cut into 1-inch pieces
- 1 tsp dried thyme
- 2 tbsp sun-dried tomatoes, chopped
- 6.5 oz can mushroom, drained
- 1/2 cup dry white wine

- 1 1/2 tsp garlic, minced
- 2 tbsp olive oil
- Pepper
- Salt

Directions:
1. Add green beans into the salted boiling water and cook for 4-5 minutes. Drain well and let it cool.
2. Heat olive oil in a large pan over medium-high heat.
3. Add garlic and saute for 1 minute.
4. Add thyme, tomatoes, mushrooms, and wine and stir well. Cook over high heat for 2 minutes.
5. Add green beans and saute for 1 minute.
6. Season with pepper and salt.
7. Serve and enjoy.

Nutritional Value (Amount per Serving):
Calories 90; Fat 4.9 g; Carbohydrates 8 g; Sugar 1.9 g; Protein 2.1g; Cholesterol 8 mg

Spinach Mushroom Cauliflower Rice

Preparation Time: 10 minutes; Cooking Time: 15 minutes; Serve: 4

Ingredients:
- 10 oz cauliflower rice
- 2 cups spinach
- 3 cups mushrooms, sliced
- 2 garlic cloves
- 1/2 cup onion, chopped
- 1 tbsp olive oil
- 1 tbsp soy sauce

Directions:
1. Cook cauliflower rice according to the packet instructions.
2. Heat olive oil in a pan over medium heat. Add onion and saute until onion is softened.
3. Add mushrooms and saute until cooked. Add garlic and saute for a minute.
4. Add soy sauce and cauliflower rice and stir well and cook for 1-2 minutes.
5. Add spinach and cook until spinach is wilted.
6. Serve and enjoy.

Nutritional Value (Amount per Serving):
Calories 95; Fat 5 g; Carbohydrates 9.2 g; Sugar 4.5 g; Protein 5.4 g; Cholesterol 0 mg

Flavors Zucchini in Sauce

Preparation Time: 10 minutes; Cooking Time: 20 minutes; Serve: 4

Ingredients:
- 2 lbs zucchini, cubed
- 1 tbsp paprika
- 3 tbsp olive oil
- Pepper
- Salt

For sauce:
- 2 tbsp fresh basil, chopped
- 2 tbsp fresh dill, chopped
- 1 tbsp tomato paste
- 2 garlic cloves, minced
- 1 cup sour cream
- Salt

Directions:
1. Preheat the oven to 400 F.
2. In a large bowl, toss zucchini with oil, paprika, pepper, and salt.
3. Spread zucchini on a baking tray and bake for 20 minutes.
4. Meanwhile, add all sauce ingredients into a medium pan and stir well and bring to simmer. Turn off the heat.

5. Add zucchini to the sauce and stir everything well.
6. Serve and enjoy.

Nutritional Value (Amount per Serving):
Calories 156; Fat 13.5 g; Carbohydrates 9.3 g; Sugar 2.6 g; Protein 2.5 g; Cholesterol 9 mg

Roasted Asparagus

Preparation Time: 10 minutes; Cooking Time: 15 minutes; Serve: 4

Ingredients:
- 36 asparagus spears, cut the ends
- 1/2 tsp garlic powder
- 1 tbsp olive oil
- Pepper
- Salt

Directions:
1. Preheat the oven to 400 F.
2. Add asparagus into the large bowl. Drizzle with oil.
3. Season with garlic powder, pepper, and salt. Toss well.
4. Arrange asparagus on a parchment-lined baking sheet and cook for 15 minutes.
5. Serve and enjoy.

Nutritional Value (Amount per Serving):
Calories 74; Fat 3.8 g; Carbohydrates 8.7 g; Sugar 4.2 g; Protein 4.8 g; Cholesterol 0 mg

Spinach Cheese Squares

Preparation Time: 10 minutes; Cooking Time: 40 minutes; Serve: 9

Ingredients:
- 3 eggs
- 8 oz cheddar cheese, grated
- 1/2 tsp paprika
- 1/2 cup ricotta cheese
- 16 oz frozen spinach, cooked and drained
- Pepper
- Salt

Directions:
1. Preheat the oven to 350 F. Grease 8*8-inch baking dish and set aside.
2. Add eggs, paprika, ricotta cheese, pepper, and salt into the blender and blend until smooth. Stir in spinach and cheese.
3. Pour egg mixture into the prepared baking dish and bake for 35 minutes.
4. Slice and serve.

Nutritional Value (Amount per Serving):
Calories 154; Fat 11.1 g; Carbohydrates 3.1 g; Sugar 0.5 g; Protein 11.2 g; Cholesterol 85 mg

Healthy Broccoli Casserole

Preparation Time: 10 minutes; Cooking Time: 20 minutes; Serve: 12

Ingredients:
- 2 lbs broccoli florets, steamed
- 8 oz cheddar cheese, shredded
- 4 oz mayonnaise
- 4 oz sour cream
- 8 oz cream cheese, softened
- 1/2 tbsp garlic powder
- 1 tbsp dried parsley
- 1 tbsp dried onion, minced
- 1/2 tsp pepper
- 1/2 tsp salt

Directions:
1. Preheat the oven to 350 F. Grease 9*13-inch baking dish and set aside.

2. Add broccoli, half cheddar cheese, and remaining ingredients into the mixing bowl and mix well.
3. Transfer broccoli mixture into the prepared baking dish and top with remaining cheddar cheese.
4. Bake for 20 minutes.
5. Serve and enjoy.

Nutritional Value (Amount per Serving):
Calories 227; Fat 18.2 g; Carbohydrates 8.8 g; Sugar 2.1 g; Protein 8.7 g; Cholesterol 47 mg

Roasted Brussels Sprouts

Preparation Time: 10 minutes; Cooking Time: 40 minutes; Serve: 8

Ingredients:
- 2 lbs brussels sprouts, trimmed and quartered
- 6 garlic cloves, sliced
- 2 tbsp olive oil
- 1 tsp salt

Directions:
1. Preheat the oven to 400 F.
2. In a bowl, toss brussels sprouts with garlic, oil, and salt.
3. Spread brussels sprouts on a baking sheet and roast in preheated oven for 40 minutes.
4. Serve and enjoy.

Nutritional Value (Amount per Serving):
Calories 43; Fat 3.6 g; Carbohydrates 2.2 g; Sugar 0.5 g; Protein 0.6 g; Cholesterol 0 mg

Crispy Brussels Sprouts

Preparation Time: 10 minutes; Cooking Time: 14 minutes; Serve: 2

Ingredients:
- 1/2 lb Brussels sprouts, trimmed and halved
- 1 tbsp chives, chopped
- 1/4 tsp cayenne
- 1/2 tsp chili powder
- 1/2 tbsp olive oil
- Pepper
- Salt

Directions:
1. Add all ingredients into the large bowl and toss well.
2. Spread Brussels sprouts in air fryer basket and air fry at 370 F for 14 minutes.
3. Serve and enjoy.

Nutritional Value (Amount per Serving):
Calories 82; Fat 4.1 g; Carbohydrates 10.9 g; Sugar 2.6 g; Protein 4 g; Cholesterol 0 mg

Lemon Garlic Broccoli

Preparation Time: 10 minutes; Cooking Time: 8 minutes; Serve: 12

Ingredients:
- 3 lbs broccoli florets
- 1 tsp garlic powder
- 1/4 cup fresh lemon juice
- 1/2 cup olive oil
- 1 tsp salt

Directions:
1. Steam broccoli florets until tender and drain well.
2. Add broccoli into the large mixing bowl.

3. Add olive oil, garlic powder, lemon juice, and salt into the blender and blend until smooth.
4. Pour oil mixture over broccoli and toss well.
5. Serve and enjoy.

Nutritional Value (Amount per Serving):
Calories 113; Fat 8.8 g; Carbohydrates 7.8 g; Sugar 2.1 g; Protein 3.3 g; Cholesterol 0 mg

Broccoli Mushroom Stir Fry

Preparation Time: 10 minutes; Cooking Time: 15 minutes; Serve: 4
Ingredients:
- 2 cups broccoli, cut into florets
- 1/2 cup carrot, shredded
- 1/4 cup vegetable broth
- 2 tsp fresh ginger, grated
- 2 cups mushrooms, sliced
- 1 tbsp sesame seeds, toasted
- 2 tbsp soy sauce
- 2 tbsp rice wine vinegar
- 1/4 cup cashews
- 1 tbsp garlic, minced
- 1/4 cup onion, chopped

Directions:
1. Add broccoli, ginger, mushrooms, garlic, onion, and broth in a saucepan and cook over high heat until broccoli is softened.
2. Add soy sauce, vinegar, cashews, and carrot and stir well and simmer for 2 minutes.
3. Sprinkle with sesame seeds and serve.

Nutritional Value (Amount per Serving):
Calories 97; Fat 4.5 g; Carbohydrates 9.4 g; Sugar 2.7 g; Protein 4.6 g; Cholesterol 0 mg

Cabbage Chaffle

Preparation Time: 10 minutes; Cooking Time: 8 minutes; Serve: 2
Ingredients:
- 1 egg, lightly beaten
- 1/2 bacon slice, chopped
- 1 1/2 tbsp green onion, sliced
- 2 tbsp cabbage, chopped
- 2 tbsp almond flour
- 1/3 cup mozzarella cheese, grated
- Pepper
- Salt

Directions:
1. Heat waffle maker and lightly grease.
2. Add all ingredients in a bowl and stir to combine.
3. Pour half of the batter in the hot waffle maker and cook until golden brown.
4. Serve and enjoy.

Nutritional Value (Amount per Serving):
Calories 233; Fat 19 g; Carbohydrates 7 g; Sugar 1.4 g; Protein 12 g; Cholesterol 90 mg

Broccoli Chaffle

Preparation Time: 10 minutes; Cooking Time: 4 minutes; Serve: 1
Ingredients:
- 1 egg
- 1 tbsp almond flour
- 1/8 tsp onion powder
- 1/8 tsp garlic powder
- 1/4 cup broccoli florets, chopped
- 1/2 cup cheddar cheese, shredded

Directions:
1. Heat waffle maker and lightly grease.

2. Add all ingredients into the mixing bowl and mix until well combined.
3. Pour batter into the hot waffle maker and cook for 4 minutes.
4. Serve and enjoy.

Nutritional Value (Amount per Serving):
Calories 474; Fat 38 g; Carbohydrates 9.5 g; Sugar 1.9 g; Protein 28.4 g; Cholesterol 164 mg

Dill Zucchini Chaffle

Preparation Time: 10 minutes; Cooking Time: 20 minutes; Serve: 4

Ingredients:
- 2 eggs
- 1 cup mozzarella cheese, grated
- 2 cups zucchini, grated & squeeze out excess liquid
- 1 tbsp fresh dill, chopped
- 1 garlic clove, minced
- 1 tbsp onion, minced

Directions:
1. Heat waffle maker and lightly grease.
2. In a bowl, whisk eggs. Add remaining ingredients and stir to combine.
3. Pour 1/4 of batter into the hot waffle maker and cook for 5 minutes.
4. Serve and enjoy.

Nutritional Value (Amount per Serving):
Calories 65; Fat 3.6 g; Carbohydrates 3.2 g; Sugar 1.3 g; Protein 5.7 g; Cholesterol 86 mg

Grilled Cauliflower Wedges

Preparation Time: 10 minutes; Cooking Time: 20 minutes; Serve: 8

Ingredients:
- 1 large cauliflower head, cut into 8 wedges
- 1/2 tsp ground turmeric
- 2 tbsp olive oil
- 1/2 tsp crushed red pepper flakes

Directions:
1. Heat a grill to medium-high heat.
2. Brush cauliflower wedges with oil and sprinkle with turmeric and crushed red pepper flakes.
3. Place cauliflower wedges on a hot grill, covered, and cook over medium-high heat for 8-10 minutes on each side.
4. Serve and enjoy.

Nutritional Value (Amount per Serving):
Calories 57; Fat 3.6 g; Carbohydrates 5.7 g; Sugar 2.5 g; Protein 2.1 g; Cholesterol 0 mg

Zucchini Chaffle

Preparation Time: 10 minutes; Cooking Time: 10 minutes; Serve: 2

Ingredients:
- 1 egg
- 1/2 cup parmesan cheese, shredded
- 1 cup zucchini, grated and squeeze out excess liquid
- 1 tsp dried basil
- 1/4 cup mozzarella cheese, shredded
- Pepper
- Salt

Directions:

1. Heat waffle maker and lightly grease.
2. In a medium bowl, whisk the egg. Add remaining ingredients and stir to combine.
3. Pour half of the batter into the waffle maker and cook for 4-5 minutes.
4. Serve and enjoy.

Nutritional Value (Amount per Serving):
Calories 131; Fat 8.3 g; Carbohydrates 3.1 g; Sugar 1.2 g; Protein 12.5 g; Cholesterol 102 mg

Mac and Cheese

Preparation Time: 10 minutes; Cooking Time: 20 minutes; Serve: 4
Ingredients:
- 1 large cauliflower head, cut into florets
- 1 cup heavy cream
- 1 tsp Dijon mustard
- 2 oz cream cheese
- 1/8 tsp garlic powder
- 1/4 tsp pepper
- 2 cups cheddar cheese, shredded
- 1/2 tsp kosher salt

Directions:
1. Preheat the oven to 375 F.
2. Add water and salt to the pot and bring to boil.
3. Spray a baking dish with cooking spray and set aside.
4. Add cauliflower florets into the boiling water and cook for 5 minutes. Drain well and transfer to a baking dish.
5. Add cream into the saucepan and bring to simmer, whisk in mustard and cream cheese until smooth.
6. Stir in 1 1/2 cup cheese, pepper, garlic, and salt. Whisk until cheese melts for 2 minutes. Season with pepper and salt.
7. Remove pan from heat and pour over cauliflower florets and stir well.
8. Top with remaining cheese and bake for 15 minutes.
9. Serve and enjoy.

Nutritional Value (Amount per Serving):
Calories 435; Fat 35 g; Carbohydrates 13 g; Sugar 5.4 g; Protein 20 g; Cholesterol 116 mg

Roasted Cauliflower

Preparation Time: 10 minutes; Cooking Time: 20 minutes; Serve: 4
Ingredients:
- 4 cups cauliflower florets
- 3 tbsp olive oil
- 1/2 cup cherry tomatoes, halved
- 2 tbsp fresh parsley, chopped
- 2 garlic cloves, sliced
- 1 tbsp capers, drained
- Pepper
- Salt

Directions:
1. Preheat the oven to 450 F.
2. In a bowl, toss together cherry tomatoes, cauliflower, oil, garlic, capers, pepper, and salt and spread on a baking tray.
3. Roast for 20 minutes.
4. Garnish with parsley and serve.

Nutritional Value (Amount per Serving):
Calories 123; Fat 10.7 g; Carbohydrates 6.9 g; Sugar 3 g; Protein 2.4 g; Cholesterol 0 mg

Tasty Brussel Sprouts Skewers

Preparation Time: 10 minutes; Cooking Time: 10 minutes; Serve: 8
Ingredients:
- 24 Brussel sprouts, trimmed and cut into half
- 1/4 tsp garlic powder
- 1/4 tsp black pepper
- 2 tbsp balsamic vinegar
- 1/4 cup olive oil
- 1/2 tsp salt

Directions:
1. Preheat the grill to medium-high heat.
2. Season Brussel sprouts with garlic powder, pepper, and salt and brush with olive oil.
3. Thread Brussel sprouts onto the soaked wooden skewers and places them on a hot grill.
4. Cook for 5 minutes on each side.
5. Transfer skewers to a plate and drizzle with balsamic vinegar.
6. Serve and enjoy.

Nutritional Value (Amount per Serving):
Calories 80; Fat 6.5 g; Carbohydrates 5.3 g; Sugar 1.3 g; Protein 2 g; Cholesterol 0 mg

Italian Sauteed Mushrooms

Preparation Time: 10 minutes; Cooking Time: 10 minute; Serve: 6
Ingredients:
- 1 lb mushrooms, sliced
- 3/4 cup Italian dressing
- 2 tbsp fresh parsley, chopped
- 1 red bell pepper, sliced
- 1/2 onion, diced
- Pepper
- Salt

Directions:
1. Spray pan with cooking spray and heat over medium-high heat.
2. Add mushrooms and salt and sauté for 5-7 minutes. Add red bell pepper, onion, and Italian dressing and bring to boil.
3. Turn heat to medium and cook for 3 minutes. Season with pepper and salt.
4. Garnish with parsley and serve.

Nutritional Value (Amount per Serving):
Calories 113; Fat 8.6 g; Carbohydrates 8 g; Sugar 5.1 g; Protein 2.8 g; Cholesterol 20 mg

Eggplant & Zucchini

Preparation Time: 10 minutes; Cooking Time: 5 hours; Serve: 6
Ingredients:
- 1 lb eggplant, peeled and cut 1-inch cubes
- 1 zucchini, chopped
- 3 fresh tomatoes, diced
- 1/2 onion, diced
- 1 red bell pepper, chopped
- 3 oz feta cheese, crumbled
- 2 tsp dried basil
- 1 tbsp garlic, minced
- 1 tbsp olive oil
- Pepper
- Salt

Directions:
1. Add all ingredients except feta cheese into the slow cooker and stir well.
2. Cover and cook on low for 5 hours.
3. Top with crumbled feta cheese and serve.

Nutritional Value (Amount per Serving):
Calories 71; Fat 3.3 g; Carbohydrates 9.5 g; Sugar 4.9 g; Protein 2.7 g; Cholesterol 3 mg

Cauliflower Soup

Preparation Time: 10 minutes; Cooking Time: 25 minutes; Serve: 8
Ingredients:
- 1 cauliflower head, chopped
- 1 tbsp ginger, grated
- 8 cups vegetable broth
- 1 onion, diced
- 4 carrots, shredded
- 1 tbsp olive oil
- 1 tbsp curry powder
- 1 tsp turmeric powder
- 6 oz unsweetened coconut milk
- 1/4 tsp red pepper flakes
- Pepper
- Salt

Directions:
1. Heat olive oil in a large saucepan over medium heat. Add onion and sauté for 5 minutes.
2. Add cauliflower, red pepper flakes, carrots, and broth and bring to boil. Turn heat to low and simmer until vegetables are softened.
3. Add curry powder, turmeric, and ginger and stir well.
4. Puree the soup using a blender until smooth.
5. Add coconut milk and stir well.
6. Season soup with pepper and salt.
7. Serve and enjoy.

Nutritional Value (Amount per Serving):
Calories 130; Fat 8.4 g; Carbohydrates 8.2 g; Sugar 3.8 g; Protein 6.2 g; Cholesterol 0 mg

Tomato Basil Soup

Preparation Time: 10 minutes; Cooking Time: 20 minutes; Serve: 6
Ingredients:
- 28 oz can tomatoes, diced
- 1/4 tsp Italian seasoning
- 1 tsp garlic, minced
- 1 onion, chopped
- 2 tbsp butter
- 1/4 cup fresh basil leaves
- 1/2 cup heavy cream
- 1 1/2 cups vegetable stock
- 1 tbsp olive oil
- Pepper
- Salt

Directions:
1. Heat butter and oil in a medium saucepan over medium-high heat. Add onion and sauté for 5 minutes.
2. Add garlic and sauté for 30 seconds. Add tomatoes, Italian seasoning, and broth and stir well. Bring to boil over high heat.
3. Turn heat to medium-low and simmer for 8 minutes.
4. Puree the soup using an immersion blender until smooth.
5. Stir in basil and heavy cream.
6. Season soup with pepper and salt.
7. Stir well and serve.

Nutritional Value (Amount per Serving):
Calories 100; Fat 10 g; Carbohydrates 2.6 g; Sugar 1.1 g; Protein 0.6 g; Cholesterol 24 mg

Pesto Zucchini Noodles

Preparation Time: 10 minutes; Cooking Time: 5 minutes; Serve: 2
Ingredients:
- 2 zucchini, spiralized using a slicer
- For pesto:
- 6 tbsp walnuts
- 1 tbsp fresh lemon juice
- 2 cups fresh spinach
- 2 tbsp olive oil

Directions:
1. Add all pesto ingredients into the blender and blend until smooth.
2. Add zucchini noodles into the large bowl.
3. Pour pesto over zucchini noodles and toss well.
4. Season with pepper and salt.
5. Serve and enjoy.

Nutritional Value (Amount per Serving):
Calories 186; Fat 17 g; Carbohydrates 8.2 g; Sugar 3.7 g; Protein 3.9 g; Cholesterol 0 mg

Grilled Zucchini

Preparation Time: 10 minutes; Cooking Time: 10 minutes; Serve: 4
Ingredients:
- 16 oz zucchini, sliced 1/4-inch thick
- 1 tsp dried parsley
- 1 tbsp red wine vinegar
- 1 tbsp olive oil
- 1/2 tsp garlic powder
- 1 tsp dried basil
- Pepper
- Salt

Directions:
1. Heat a grill to medium-high heat.
2. Add zucchini slices and remaining ingredients into the mixing bowl and toss well.
3. Place zucchini slices on a hot grill. Cover and cook for 2-3 minutes.
4. Flip zucchini slices and cook for 2-3 minutes more.
5. Serve and enjoy.

Nutritional Value (Amount per Serving):
Calories 50; Fat 3.7 g; Carbohydrates 4.1 g; Sugar 2.1 g; Protein 1.5 g; Cholesterol 0 mg

Parmesan Asparagus

Preparation Time: 10 minutes; Cooking Time: 12 minutes; Serve: 4
Ingredients:
- 1 lb asparagus, wash, trimmed, and cut the ends
- 1 tbsp dried parsley
- 2 garlic cloves, minced
- 2 tbsp olive oil
- 3 oz parmesan cheese, shaved
- 1 tsp dried oregano
- Pepper
- Salt

Directions:
1. Preheat the oven to 425 F. Spray a baking tray with cooking spray.
2. Arrange asparagus on a baking tray.
3. Drizzle olive oil over asparagus and season with pepper and salt.
4. Spread cheese, oregano, parsley, and garlic over asparagus and bake for 10-12 minutes.

5. Serve and enjoy.

Nutritional Value (Amount per Serving):
Calories 155; Fat 11.8 g; Carbohydrates 6 g; Sugar 2.2 g; Protein 9.5 g; Cholesterol 15 mg

Eggplant Curry

Preparation Time: 10 minutes; Cooking Time: 27 minutes; Serve: 8

Ingredients:
- 2 lbs eggplant, diced
- 1/2 tsp turmeric powder
- 1 tsp apple cider vinegar
- 1 tbsp garlic, minced
- 2 tbsp olive oil
- 1 green chili, sliced
- 1 cup half and half
- 1 tsp mustard seeds
- 1 tsp cumin seeds
- 1 tsp curry powder
- 1 onion, diced
- Pepper
- Salt

Directions:
1. Heat oil in a medium saucepan over medium heat. Add mustard seeds and cumin seeds and sauté for 30 seconds.
2. Add eggplant and sauté for 8-10 minutes. Add garlic, green chili, and onion and sauté for 2-3 minutes.
3. Add turmeric, curry powder, pepper, and salt and cook for 1 minute.
4. Add vinegar and cook for 3-5 minutes.
5. Add half and half and cook for 5-7 minutes.
6. Stir well and serve.

Nutritional Value (Amount per Serving):
Calories 86; Fat 7.2 g; Carbohydrates 4.7 g; Sugar 1.5 g; Protein 1.6 g; Cholesterol 11 mg

Easy Roasted Artichoke Hearts

Preparation Time: 10 minutes; Cooking Time: 25 minutes; Serve: 6

Ingredients:
- 18 oz frozen artichoke hearts, defrosted
- 1 tbsp olive oil
- Pepper
- Salt

Directions:
1. Preheat the oven to 400 F.
2. Arrange artichoke hearts on a baking sheet and drizzle with olive oil. Season with pepper and salt.
3. Roast in preheated oven for 25 minutes.
4. Serve and enjoy.

Nutritional Value (Amount per Serving):
Calories 25; Fat 2.8 g; Carbohydrates 0.3 g; Sugar 0.1 g; Protein 0.1 g; Cholesterol 0 mg

Spinach Broccoli Curry

Preparation Time: 10 minutes; Cooking Time: 30 minutes; Serve: 4

Ingredients:
- 1 cup broccoli florets
- 1 tbsp red curry paste
- 2 tsp soy sauce
- 1/2 cup coconut cream

- 1/4 onion, sliced
- 4 tbsp olive oil
- 1/2 cup spinach
- 1 tsp ginger, minced
- 1 tsp garlic, minced

Directions:
1. Heat 2 tbsp oil to a pan over medium-high heat. Add onion and cook until softened.
2. Add garlic and sauté for minutes. Turn heat to medium-low and add broccoli and stir everything well.
3. Once broccoli is cooked then move vegetables to the other side of the pan.
4. Add curry paste and cook for a minute. Add spinach and cook until wilted.
5. Add coconut cream, remaining oil, ginger, and soy sauce. Stir well and simmer for 5 minutes.
6. Serve and enjoy.

Nutritional Value (Amount per Serving):
Calories 217; Fat 22 g; Carbohydrates 5.5 g; Sugar 1.8 g; Protein 1.8 g; Cholesterol 0 mg

Ratatouille

Preparation Time: 10 minutes; Cooking Time: 4 hours; Serve: 8
Ingredients:
- 1 cup fresh basil, chopped
- 2 summer squash, sliced
- 1 bell pepper, chopped
- 1 eggplant, chopped
- 1 tbsp garlic, minced
- 1 onion, chopped
- 2 tbsp olive oil
- 1/4 tsp red pepper flakes
- 1 tsp dried oregano
- 2 tbsp tomato paste
- 1 cup cherry tomatoes, chopped
- 1/4 tsp pepper
- 1/2 tsp sea salt

Directions:
1. Add all ingredients except basil into the crockpot and stir well.
2. Cover and cook on high for 4 hours.
3. Stir well and serve.

Nutritional Value (Amount per Serving):
Calories 59; Fat 3.8 g; Carbohydrates 6.5 g; Sugar 4 g; Protein 1.3 g; Cholesterol 0 mg

Zucchini Spinach Soup

Preparation Time: 10 minutes; Cooking Time: 25 minutes; Serve: 6
Ingredients:
- 6 medium zucchini, chopped
- 1 cup baby spinach
- 4 cups of water
- 1 cup unsweetened coconut milk
- Pepper
- Salt

Directions:
1. Add zucchini and water in a large pot and cook over medium heat. Bring to boil.
2. Turn heat to low and simmer for 25 minutes.
3. Remove from heat and add coconut milk and spinach.
4. Puree the soup using an immersion blender until smooth. Season with pepper and salt.
5. Serve and enjoy.

Nutritional Value (Amount per Serving):
Calories 60; Fat 3.2 g; Carbohydrates 7 g; Sugar 3.6 g; Protein 2.8 g; Cholesterol 0 mg

Carrot Tomato Soup

Preparation Time: 10 minutes; Cooking Time: 4 hours; Serve: 4
Ingredients:
- 14.5 oz can tomatoes, diced
- 1 tbsp turmeric
- 1 cup unsweetened coconut milk
- 4 medium carrots, peeled and chopped
- 1 tsp ground cumin
- 1 tsp ground coriander
- Pepper
- Salt

Directions:
1. Add all ingredients into the slow cooker and stir well.
2. Cover and cook on low for 4 hours.
3. Puree the soup using an immersion blender until smooth. Season with pepper and salt.
4. Serve and enjoy.

Nutritional Value (Amount per Serving):
Calories 157; Fat 14.7 g; Carbohydrates 7 g; Sugar 3.1 g; Protein 1.8 g; Cholesterol 0 mg

Creamy Pumpkin Soup

Preparation Time: 10 minutes; Cooking Time: 8 hours; Serve: 4
Ingredients:
- 2 cups pumpkin puree
- 4 cups of water
- 1/4 tsp ground nutmeg
- 1 cup unsweetened coconut milk

Directions:
1. Add all ingredients into the crockpot and stir well.
2. Cover and cook on low for 8 hours.
3. Puree the soup using an immersion blender until smooth.
4. Stir well and serve.

Nutritional Value (Amount per Serving):
Calories 164; Fat 14.4 g; Carbohydrates 8.9 g; Sugar 2.9 g; Protein 2.4 g; Cholesterol 0 mg

Stir Fried Eggplant

Preparation Time: 10 minutes; Cooking Time: 25 minutes; Serve: 4
Ingredients:
- 4 cups eggplant, sliced
- 1 green pepper, sliced
- 1 tsp red pepper flakes
- 6 tbsp tamari sauce
- 1 tbsp olive oil
- 2 garlic cloves, minced
- 1 medium onion, chopped
- 1/2 tsp ground ginger

Directions:
1. Add olive into the pan and heat over medium-high heat.
2. Add onion and garlic into the pan and cook for 6-8 minutes.
3. Turn heat to medium and add eggplant and green pepper. Stir well and cook for few minutes.
4. Add red pepper flakes, ginger, and tamari and stir well.
5. Cook eggplant mixture for 12 minutes. Stir well.
6. Serve and enjoy.

Nutritional Value (Amount per Serving):

Calories 74; Fat 3.7 g; Carbohydrates 9.9 g; Sugar 4.9 g; Protein 2.1 g; Cholesterol 0 mg

Cheesy Zucchini Casserole

Preparation Time: 10 minutes; Cooking Time: 25 minutes; Serve: 6
Ingredients:
- 2 eggs
- 4 cup zucchini, grated
- 1 tbsp garlic, minced
- 1/2 cup cheddar cheese, shredded
- 1 cup mozzarella cheese, shredded
- 1/2 cup parmesan cheese, grated
- 1/2 cup onion, diced
- 1/2 tsp salt

Directions:
1. Preheat the oven to 375 F. Spray baking dish with cooking spray and set aside.
2. Add zucchini and salt into the colander and set aside for 10 minutes.
3. After 10 minutes squeeze out all liquid from zucchini.
4. Combine together zucchini, cheddar cheese, mozzarella cheese, 1/2 parmesan cheese, eggs, garlic, and onion and pour into the prepared baking dish.
5. Bake for 25 minutes.
6. Serve and enjoy.

Nutritional Value (Amount per Serving):
Calories 117; Fat 4.6 g; Carbohydrates 4.6 g; Sugar 1.9 g; Protein 9.3 g; Cholesterol 73 mg

Roasted Vegetables

Preparation Time: 10 minutes; Cooking Time: 30 minutes; Serve: 6
Ingredients:
- 1 eggplant, sliced
- 1 onion, sliced
- 1 bell pepper, cut into strips
- 2 zucchini, sliced
- 2 tomatoes, quartered
- 5 fresh basil leaves, sliced
- 2 tsp Italian seasoning
- 2 tbsp olive oil
- Pepper
- Salt

Directions:
1. Preheat the oven to 400 F. Line baking sheet with parchment paper.
2. Add all ingredients except basil leaves into the mixing bowl and toss well.
3. Transfer veggie mixture on a prepared baking sheet and roast for 30 minutes.
4. Garnish with basil leaves and serve.

Nutritional Value (Amount per Serving):
Calories 80; Fat 5.4 g; Carbohydrates 8 g; Sugar 4.6 g; Protein 1.7 g; Cholesterol 1 mg

Creamy Asparagus Soup

Preparation Time: 10 minutes; Cooking Time: 13 minutes; Serve: 4
Ingredients:
- 2 lbs asparagus, trimmed and cut into pieces
- 1 small onion, chopped
- 2 tbsp butter
- 1/2 cup heavy whipping cream
- 2 oz parmesan cheese, shredded
- 4 garlic cloves, minced
- 4 cups vegetable broth
- 1/2 tsp salt

Directions:
1. Add broth into the large microwave-safe bowl and microwave on high for 5 minutes.

2. Melt butter in a large pot over low heat. Add chopped onion, garlic, salt, and asparagus to the pot and saute for 5 minutes.
3. Add broth and bring to boil. Turn heat to low and simmer for 2-3 minutes or until tender.
4. Puree the soup using a blender until smooth.
5. Add cream. Stir well and heat over medium heat.
6. Remove pot from heat. Stir in parmesan cheese.
7. Serve and enjoy.

Nutritional Value (Amount per Serving):
Calories 229; Fat 17 g; Carbohydrates 12 g; Sugar 5.5 g; Protein 7.7 g; Cholesterol 63 mg

Broccoli Soup

Preparation Time: 10 minutes; Cooking Time: 15 minutes; Serve: 8
Ingredients:
- 4 cups broccoli, cut into florets
- 1 tbsp olive oil
- 3 cups cheddar cheese, shredded
- 1 cup heavy cream
- 3 1/2 cups vegetable broth
- 2 garlic cloves, minced
- Pepper
- Salt

Directions:
1. Heat olive oil in a large pot over medium heat. Add garlic and sauté for a minute.
2. Add broth, broccoli, and heavy cream and bring to boil, reduce heat and simmer for 15 minutes.
3. Add shredded cheese and stir constantly until cheese is melted. Season with pepper and salt.
4. Remove from heat and serve.

Nutritional Value (Amount per Serving):
Calories 271; Fat 22.1 g; Carbohydrates 4.6 g; Sugar 1.3 g; Protein 14.3 g; Cholesterol 65 mg

Roasted Herb Zucchini

Preparation Time: 10 minutes; Cooking Time: 15 minutes; Serve: 4
Ingredients:
- 1 lb zucchini, sliced
- 1 garlic clove, minced
- 2 tbsp olive oil
- 1 oz parmesan cheese, grated
- 1 tsp dried mix herbs

Directions:
1. Preheat the oven to 450 F.
2. Add all ingredients except parmesan cheese into the large bowl and toss well.
3. Transfer the zucchini mixture to the baking dish and bake for 10 minutes.
4. Sprinkle parmesan cheese over zucchini.
5. Return to the oven and cook for 5 minutes more.
6. Serve and enjoy.

Nutritional Value (Amount per Serving):
Calories 110; Fat 8.7 g; Carbohydrates 6 g; Sugar 2.1 g; Protein 4 g; Cholesterol 5 mg

Asian Zucchini Noodles

Preparation Time: 10 minutes; Cooking Time: 5 minutes; Serve: 4
Ingredients:

- 2 large zucchini, spiralized zucchini using a slicer
- 1/2 cup red cabbage, sliced

For sauce:
- 1 lime juice
- 1 tbsp water
- 1 tbsp sesame oil
- 2 tbsp olive oil
- 1 carrot, peeled and julienned
- 1 green onion, green part only, chopped
- 1/2 cup almond butter
- 1 tbsp soy sauce
- 1 tsp fresh ginger, grated

Directions:
1. In a small bowl, whisk together all sauce ingredients.
2. Add zucchini, green onion, cabbage, and carrot in a large bowl.
3. Pour sauce over zucchini mixture and toss well.
4. Serve and enjoy.

Nutritional Value (Amount per Serving):
Calories 123; Fat 11.6 g; Carbohydrates 5.2 g; Sugar 2 g; Protein 1.3 g; Cholesterol 0 mg

Healthy Zucchini Garlic Noodles

Preparation Time: 10 minutes; Cooking Time: 5 minutes; Serve: 4
Ingredients:
- 4 small zucchini, ends trimmed and spiralized
- 1/3 cup olive oil
- 2 garlic cloves
- 2 cups fresh basil leaves
- 1/4 cup parmesan cheese, grated
- 2 tsp lemon juice
- Pepper
- Salt

Directions:
1. Add garlic, basil, olive oil, parmesan cheese, and lemon juice into the food processor and pulse until well blended. Season with pepper and salt.
2. In a large bowl, combine together pesto and zucchini noodles.
3. Serve and enjoy.

Nutritional Value (Amount per Serving):
Calories 189; Fat 18.5 g; Carbohydrates 5.1 g; Sugar 2.2 g; Protein 3.9 g; Cholesterol 4 mg

Zucchini Stir Fry

Preparation Time: 10 minutes; Cooking Time: 5 minutes; Serve: 2
Ingredients:
- 2 medium zucchini, chopped
- 1 tbsp olive oil
- 1 tbsp fresh lemon juice
- 1 green onion, green part only, chopped
- Pepper
- Salt

Directions:
1. Heat oil in a pan over medium-high heat.
2. Add zucchini and sauté for 3-5 minutes. Season with pepper and salt.
3. Stir in lemon juice and green onion.
4. Serve and enjoy.

Nutritional Value (Amount per Serving):
Calories 96; Fat 7.4 g; Carbohydrates 7.3 g; Sugar 3.7 g; Protein 2.6 g; Cholesterol 0 mg

Tofu Stir Fry

Preparation Time: 10 minutes; Cooking Time: 5 minutes; Serve: 3
Ingredients:
- 8 oz extra firm tofu, pressed and cut into cubes
- 1 tsp coconut aminos
- 3 tsp nutritional yeast
- 1/4 cup button mushrooms, chopped
- 1/4 cup onion, chopped
- 4 cherry tomatoes, chopped
- 4 cups baby spinach

Directions:
1. Spray pan with cooking spray and heat over medium heat.
2. Add mushrooms and onion and sauté until onions are soft, about 2-3 minutes.
3. Add tofu and stir well and cook for 1-2 minutes.
4. Add liquid aminos and nutritional yeast and stir everything well.
5. Add tomatoes and spinach and cook for 3-4 minutes.
6. Serve and enjoy.

Nutritional Value (Amount per Serving):
Calories 91; Fat 3.6 g; Carbohydrates 8.1 g; Sugar 1.1 g; Protein 9.7 g; Cholesterol 0 mg

Zucchini with Herbs

Preparation Time: 10 minutes; Cooking Time: 45 minutes; Serve: 6
Ingredients:
- 2 1/2 lbs zucchini, cut into quarters
- 6 garlic cloves, crushed
- 10 oz cherry tomatoes cut in half
- 1/2 tsp black pepper
- 1/3 cup parsley, chopped
- 1 tsp dried basil
- 1/2 cup parmesan cheese, shredded
- 3/4 tsp salt

Directions:
1. Preheat the oven to 350 F. Spray baking dish with cooking spray and set aside.
2. Add all ingredients except parsley into the large bowl and stir well to combine.
3. Pour egg mixture into the prepared baking dish.
4. Bake for 35 minutes.
5. Garnish with parsley and serve.

Nutritional Value (Amount per Serving):
Calories 52; Fat 2 g; Carbohydrates 5.7 g; Sugar 2.6 g; Protein 4.3 g; Cholesterol 6 mg

Curried Squash Coconut Soup

Preparation Time: 10 minutes; Cooking Time: 25 minutes; Serve: 4
Ingredients:
- 1 1/2 lbs summer squash, ends trimmed and cut into 1-inch pieces
- 3/4 tsp curry powder
- 1 garlic clove, minced
- 1 onion, chopped
- 1 tbsp olive oil
- 1/2 lime juice
- 1/4 cup coconut milk
- 4 cups vegetable stock
- Pepper
- Salt

Directions:
1. Heat oil in the large pot over medium heat. Add onion to the pot and sauté for 8 minutes.

2. Add curry powder and garlic and sauté for 30 seconds. Add squash and sauté for 2 minutes.
3. Add stock and bring to boil. Turn heat to medium-low and simmer for 15 minutes.
4. Puree the soup using an immersion blender until smooth.
5. Stir in lime juice and coconut milk. Season with pepper and salt.
6. Serve and enjoy.

Nutritional Value (Amount per Serving):
Calories 87; Fat 5 g; Carbohydrates 11 g; Sugar 4.2 g; Protein 1.3 g; Cholesterol 0 mg

Healthy Pumpkin Soup

Preparation Time: 10 minutes; Cooking Time: 45 minutes; Serve: 4

Ingredients:
- 1 cup pumpkin puree
- 1 1/2 cups vegetable broth
- 1/2 cup heavy cream
- 1 bay leaf
- 1/8 tsp nutmeg
- 1/2 tsp ginger, minced
- 2 garlic cloves, minced
- 1/4 onion, chopped
- 4 tbsp butter
- 1/4 tsp coriander
- 1/4 tsp cinnamon
- 1/2 tsp pepper
- 1/2 tsp salt

Directions:
1. Melt butter in a saucepan over medium-low heat.
2. Add ginger, garlic, and onion to the pan and sauté for 2-3 minutes. Add spices and stir well and cook for 2 minutes.
3. Add broth and pumpkin puree and mix well. Bring to boil. Turn heat to low and simmer for 20 minutes.
4. Puree the soup using a blender until smooth then simmer for 20 minutes.
5. Remove pan from heat and add heavy cream and stir well.
6. Serve and enjoy.

Nutritional Value (Amount per Serving):
Calories 196; Fat 17.8 g; Carbohydrates 7.5 g; Sugar 2.7 g; Protein 3.2 g; Cholesterol 0 mg

Chapter 4: Meat Recipes
Easy Ranch Pork Chops

Preparation Time: 10 minutes; Cooking Time: 35 minutes; Serve: 6
Ingredients:
- 6 pork chops, boneless
- 1 oz ranch seasoning
- 2 tbsp olive oil
- 1 tsp dried parsley

Directions:
1. Preheat the oven to 400 F.
2. Line baking sheet with parchment paper and set aside.
3. Mix together oil, dried parsley, and ranch seasoning and rub over pork chops.
4. Place pork chops on a prepared baking sheet and bake for 35 minutes.
5. Serve and enjoy.

Nutritional Value (Amount per Serving):
Calories 311; Fat 24.6 g; Carbohydrates 0 g; Sugar 0 g; Protein 18 g; Cholesterol 69 mg

Flavorful Beef Chili

Preparation Time: 10 minutes; Cooking Time: 7 hours 30 minutes; Serve: 8
Ingredients:
- 2 lbs ground beef
- 1/4 tsp chili powder
- 1 tsp cumin powder
- 4 oz can green chilies
- 6 oz can tomato paste
- 30 oz can tomatoes
- 1 tbsp olive oil
- 1/2 onion, chopped
- 1 tsp pepper
- 1 tsp salt

Directions:
1. Heat olive oil in a pan over medium heat.
2. Add onion and saute until softened. Add ground beef and cook until browned.
3. Transfer meat mixture into the slow cooker. Stir in tomatoes, seasoning, green chilies, and tomato paste.
4. Cover and cook on low for 7 hours.
5. Add 1/4 cup water and stir well.
6. Serve and enjoy.

Nutritional Value (Amount per Serving):
Calories 195; Fat 12.1 g; Carbohydrates 6 g; Sugar 3.1 g; Protein 15.9 g; Cholesterol 52 mg

Mexican Beef

Preparation Time: 10 minutes; Cooking Time: 8 hours; Serve: 6
Ingredients:
- 2 lbs chuck roast
- 2 tsp garlic powder
- 2 tsp onion powder
- 1 tsp chili powder
- 1 tsp ground cumin
- 1 onion, diced
- 1 lime juice
- 15 oz can fire-roasted tomatoes
- 1 cup beef broth
- Pepper
- Salt

Directions:
1. Season chuck roast with pepper and salt. Add chuck roast in the slow cooker along with the remaining ingredients.
2. Cover and cook on low for 8 hours.

3. Shred the meat using a fork.
4. Stir well and serve.

Nutritional Value (Amount per Serving):
Calories 368; Fat 13 g; Carbohydrates 7.7 g; Sugar 3.3 g; Protein 51.9 g; Cholesterol 153 mg

Easy Beef Stroganoff

Preparation Time: 10 minutes; Cooking Time: 6 hours; Serve: 4
Ingredients:
- 1 lb beef stew meat
- 8 oz mushrooms, sliced
- 1 cup beef stock
- 3 tbsp tomato paste
- 1 tsp paprika
- 2 bacon slices, diced
- 2 garlic cloves, crushed
- 1 onion, sliced

Directions:
1. Add all ingredients into the slow cooker and stir well.
2. Cover and cook on low for 6 hours.
3. Stir well and serve.

Nutritional Value (Amount per Serving):
Calories 303; Fat 11.5 g; Carbohydrates 7.7 g; Sugar 3.7 g; Protein 41.4 g; Cholesterol 112 mg

Healthy Beef Stroganoff

Preparation Time: 10 minutes; Cooking Time: 8 hours; Serve: 10
Ingredients:
- 2 1/2 lbs beef stew meat
- 1/2 tsp xanthan gum
- 8 oz cream cheese, softened
- 1 cup sour cream
- 8 oz mushrooms, sliced
- 1 can cream of mushroom soup
- Pepper
- Salt

Directions:
1. Spray slow cooker from inside with cooking spray.
2. Add meat, mushrooms, and cream of mushroom soup into the slow cooker and stir well.
3. Cover and cook on low for 8 hours.
4. About a half-hour before serving add cream cheese and stir until cream cheese completely incorporated.
5. Add sour cream and stir well. Season with pepper and salt.
6. Serve and enjoy.

Nutritional Value (Amount per Serving):
Calories 370; Fat 21.6 g; Carbohydrates 4.5 g; Sugar 0.9 g; Protein 38 g; Cholesterol 136 mg

Keto Butter Beef

Preparation Time: 10 minutes; Cooking Time: 8 hours; Serve: 4
Ingredients:
- 3 lbs beef roast
- 1 cup of water
- 1 stick butter
- 1 jar banana pepper rings, drained and reserved 1/4 cup juice
- 1 tbsp Italian dressing seasoning mix
- 2 tbsp ranch dressing seasoning mix

Directions:
1. Add the meat into the slow cooker.
2. Pour remaining ingredients over meat and stir well.
3. Cover and cook on low for 8 hours.
4. Shred the meat using a fork and serve.

Nutritional Value (Amount per Serving):
Calories 862; Fat 44.1 g; Carbohydrates 6.3 g; Sugar 2.5 g; Protein 103.4 g; Cholesterol 365 mg

Crispy Crusted Pork Chops

Preparation Time: 10 minutes; Cooking Time: 15 minutes; Serve: 2
Ingredients:
- 2 pork chops, bone-in
- 1 tbsp olive oil
- 1 cup pork rinds, crushed
- 1/2 tsp garlic powder
- 1/2 tsp onion powder
- 1/2 tsp paprika
- 1/2 tsp parsley

Directions:
1. Preheat the air fryer to 400 F.
2. In a large bowl, mix together pork rinds, garlic powder, onion powder, parsley, and paprika.
3. Brush pork chops with oil and coat with pork rind mixture and place into the air fryer basket.
4. Cook pork chops for 10 minutes. Turn pork chops and air fry for 5 minutes more.
5. Serve and enjoy.

Nutritional Value (Amount per Serving):
Calories 413; Fat 32.7 g; Carbohydrates 1.3 g; Sugar 0.4 g; Protein 28.5 g; Cholesterol 92 mg

Hearty Taco Soup

Preparation Time: 10 minutes; Cooking Time: 2 hours 10 minutes; Serve: 8
Ingredients:
- 2 lbs ground beef
- 1/4 cup fresh cilantro, chopped
- 4 cups chicken stock
- 2 tbsp taco seasoning
- 16 oz cream cheese
- 20 oz can tomatoes, diced

Directions:
1. Brown ground beef in a pan over medium-high heat.
2. Transfer cooked ground beef to the slow cooker along with remaining ingredients and stir well.
3. Cover and cook on high for 2 hours.
4. Stir and serve.

Nutritional Value (Amount per Serving):
Calories 287; Fat 24.2 g; Carbohydrates 6.5 g; Sugar 2.9 g; Protein 12 g; Cholesterol 85 mg

Beef Fajitas

Preparation Time: 10 minutes; Cooking Time: 8 minutes; Serve: 4
Ingredients:
- 1 lb beef flank steak, sliced
- 1/2 tbsp chili powder
- 3 tbsp olive oil
- 2 bell peppers, sliced

- 1 tsp garlic powder
- 1 tsp paprika
- 1 1/2 tsp cumin
- Pepper
- Salt

Directions:
1. In a mixing bowl, toss sliced steak with remaining ingredients.
2. Add half meat mixture into the air fryer basket and cook at 390 F for 8 minutes. Stir the mixture after 3 minutes.
3. Cook remaining half mixture.
4. Serve and enjoy.

Nutritional Value (Amount per Serving):
Calories 330; Fat 18.1 g; Carbohydrates 6.2 g; Sugar 3.3 g; Protein 35.5 g; Cholesterol 101 mg

Beef & Broccoli

Preparation Time: 10 minutes; Cooking Time: 25 minutes; Serve: 2
Ingredients:
- 1/2 lb beef stew meat, cut into pieces
- 1 tbsp vinegar
- 1 garlic clove, minced
- 1 tbsp olive oil
- 1/2 cup broccoli florets
- 1 onion, sliced
- Pepper
- Salt

Directions:
1. Preheat the oven to 390 F.
2. Add meat and remaining ingredients into the large bowl and toss well and spread on a baking sheet.
3. Bake for 25 minutes.
4. Serve and enjoy.

Nutritional Value (Amount per Serving):
Calories 304; Fat 14.2 g; Carbohydrates 7.3 g; Sugar 2.8 g; Protein 35.8 g; Cholesterol 101 mg

Easy Pulled Pork

Preparation Time: 10 minutes; Cooking Time: 40 minutes; Serve: 12
Ingredients:
- 5 lbs pork shoulder, boneless & cut into chunks
- 2 tbsp garlic powder
- 2 tbsp smoked paprika
- 1 tbsp black pepper
- 1 1/2 tbsp salt

Directions:
1. Add all ingredients into the instant pot and mix well.
2. Cover pot with lid and cook on high pressure for 40 minutes.
3. Once done, allow to release pressure naturally for 10 minutes, then release the remaining pressure manually. Remove lid.
4. Shred the pork using a fork.
5. Serve and enjoy.

Nutritional Value (Amount per Serving):
Calories 561; Fat 40.6 g; Carbohydrates 2 g; Sugar 0.5 g; Protein 44.5 g; Cholesterol 170 mg

Juicy Pork Tenderloin

Preparation Time: 10 minutes; Cooking Time: 4 hours; Serve: 8
Ingredients:
- 3 lbs pork tenderloin
- 2 tbsp olive oil
- 1 lemon juice
- 4 garlic clove, chopped
- Pepper
- Salt

Directions:
1. Add pork into the slow cooker.
2. Add olive oil, lemon juice, garlic, pepper, and salt over pork.
3. Cover and cook on low for 4 hours.
4. Slice and serve.

Nutritional Value (Amount per Serving):
Calories 277; Fat 9.5 g; Carbohydrates 0.6 g; Sugar 0.1 g; Protein 44.7 g; Cholesterol 124 mg

Meatballs

Preparation Time: 10 minutes; Cooking Time: 15 minutes; Serve: 4
Ingredients:
- 1 lb ground pork
- 1 tsp paprika
- 1 tsp garlic powder
- 1 tsp onion powder
- 1/2 tsp ground cumin
- 1/2 tsp coriander
- 1/2 tsp dried thyme
- Pepper
- Salt

Directions:
1. Preheat the oven to 400 F.
2. Add all ingredients into the large bowl and mix until well combined.
3. Make small balls from the meat mixture and place them on a baking sheet and bake for 15 minutes.
4. Serve and enjoy.

Nutritional Value (Amount per Serving):
Calories 170; Fat 4.1 g; Carbohydrates 1.5 g; Sugar 0.4 g; Protein 30 g; Cholesterol 83 mg

Lemon Pepper Pork Chops

Preparation Time: 10 minutes; Cooking Time: 15 minutes; Serve: 4
Ingredients:
- 4 pork chops, boneless
- 1 tsp lemon pepper seasoning
- Salt

Directions:
1. Preheat the air fryer to 400 F.
2. Season pork chops with lemon pepper seasoning, and salt and place in air fryer basket and cook for 15 minutes.
3. Serve and enjoy.

Nutritional Value (Amount per Serving):
Calories 257; Fat 19.9 g; Carbohydrates 0.3 g; Sugar 0 g; Protein 18 g; Cholesterol 69 mg

Meatballs

Preparation Time: 10 minutes; Cooking Time: 15 minutes; Serve: 4

Ingredients:
- 1 lb ground lamb
- 1 tsp onion powder
- 1 tbsp garlic, minced
- 1 tsp ground coriander
- 1 tsp ground cumin
- Pepper
- Salt

Directions:
1. Preheat the oven to 400 F.
2. Add all ingredients into the large bowl and mix until well combined.
3. Make small balls from meat mixture and place on a parchment-lined baking sheet.
4. Bake for 15 minutes.
5. Serve and enjoy.

Nutritional Value (Amount per Serving):
Calories 218; Fat 8.5 g; Carbohydrates 1.4 g; Sugar 0.2 g; Protein 32.1 g; Cholesterol 102 mg

Simple Steak with Mushrooms

Preparation Time: 10 minutes; Cooking Time: 18 minutes; Serve: 4

Ingredients:
- 1 lb steaks, cut into 1-inch cubes
- 2 tbsp olive oil
- 8 oz mushrooms, halved
- 1/2 tsp garlic powder
- 1 tsp Worcestershire sauce
- Pepper
- Salt

Directions:
1. Add steak cubes and remaining ingredients into the bowl and toss well.
2. Transfer meat mixture into the air fryer basket and air fry at 400 F for 18 minutes. Stir halfway through.
3. Serve and enjoy.

Nutritional Value (Amount per Serving):
Calories 300; Fat 12.8 g; Carbohydrates 2.4 g; Sugar 1.3 g; Protein 42.8 g; Cholesterol 102 mg

Meatloaf

Preparation Time: 10 minutes; Cooking Time: 20 minutes; Serve: 4

Ingredients:
- 1 egg, lightly beaten
- 3 tbsp almond flour
- 1 lb ground pork
- 1 onion, chopped
- 1 tbsp thyme, chopped
- 1/4 tsp garlic powder
- Pepper
- Salt

Directions:
1. Preheat the oven to 390 F.
2. Grease loaf pan and set aside.
3. Add all ingredients into the mixing bowl and mix until well combined.
4. Pour meat mixture into the prepared loaf pan and bake for 20 minutes.
5. Serve and enjoy.

Nutritional Value (Amount per Serving):
Calories 311; Fat 15.7 g; Carbohydrates 7.7 g; Sugar 2.1 g; Protein 36 g; Cholesterol 124 mg

Easy & Tasty Steak

Preparation Time: 10 minutes; Cooking Time: 18 minutes; Serve: 2

Ingredients:
- 12 oz steaks
- 1 tsp olive oil
- 1/2 tsp garlic powder
- 1/4 tsp onion powder
- Pepper
- Salt

Directions:
1. Coat steaks with oil and season with garlic powder, onion powder, pepper, and salt.
2. Place steaks into the air fryer basket and air fry at 400 F for 18 minutes. Stir halfway through.
3. Serve and enjoy.

Nutritional Value (Amount per Serving):
Calories 362; Fat 10.9 g; Carbohydrates 0.8 g; Sugar 0.3 g; Protein 61.6 g; Cholesterol 153 mg

Meatballs

Preparation Time: 10 minutes; Cooking Time: 12 minutes; Serve: 6

Ingredients:
- 2 lbs ground beef
- 2 eggs, lightly beaten
- 3 oz parmesan cheese, shredded
- 2 oz pork rind, crushed
- Pepper
- Salt

Directions:
1. Add all ingredients into the bowl and mix until well combined.
2. Make small balls from meat mixture and place into the air fryer basket and air fry at 350 F for 8 minutes.
3. Turn meatballs and cook for 4 minutes more.
4. Serve and enjoy.

Nutritional Value (Amount per Serving):
Calories 401; Fat 17.3 g; Carbohydrates 0.6 g; Sugar 0.1 g; Protein 58.4 g; Cholesterol 213 mg

Cheesy Burger Patties

Preparation Time: 10 minutes; Cooking Time: 15 minutes; Serve: 6

Ingredients:
- 2 lbs ground beef
- 1 cup mozzarella cheese, grated
- 1 tsp onion powder
- 1 tsp garlic powder
- Pepper
- Salt

Directions:
1. Preheat the oven to 400 F.
2. Add all ingredients into the large bowl and mix until well combined.
3. Make patties from meat mixture and place on a parchment-lined baking sheet.
4. Bake for 15 minutes.
5. Serve and enjoy.

Nutritional Value (Amount per Serving):
Calories 297; Fat 10.3 g; Carbohydrates 0.8 g; Sugar 0.3 g; Protein 47.3 g; Cholesterol 138 mg

Burger Patties

Preparation Time: 10 minutes; Cooking Time: 12 minutes; Serve: 4

Ingredients:
- 1 lb ground beef
- 1/2 tsp onion powder
- 1/2 tsp garlic powder
- 2 tsp dried parsley
- 1/8 tsp dried dill
- 1/2 tsp paprika
- 1/2 tsp dried dill
- Pepper
- Salt

Directions:
1. Add all ingredients into the large bowl and mix until well combined.
2. Make four even shape patties from meat mixture and place into the air fryer basket and cook at 350 F for 12 minutes. Turn patties halfway through.
3. Serve and enjoy.

Nutritional Value (Amount per Serving):
Calories 214; Fat 7.1 g; Carbohydrates 0.7 g; Sugar 0.2 g; Protein 34.6 g; Cholesterol 101 mg

Simple Sirloin Steak

Preparation Time: 10 minutes; Cooking Time: 14 minutes; Serve: 2

Ingredients:
- 1 lb sirloin steaks
- 1 tsp olive oil
- Pepper
- Salt

Directions:
1. Brush steak with oil and season with pepper and salt.
2. Place steak into the air fryer basket and air fry at 400 F for 14 minutes. Turn steak halfway through.
3. Serve and enjoy.

Nutritional Value (Amount per Serving):
Calories 441; Fat 16.5 g; Carbohydrates 0 g; Sugar 0 g; Protein 68.8 g; Cholesterol 203 mg

Meatballs

Preparation Time: 10 minutes; Cooking Time: 12 minutes; Serve: 4

Ingredients:
- 1 egg, lightly beaten
- 4 oz ground lamb meat
- 1/2 tbsp lemon zest
- 1 tbsp oregano, chopped
- Pepper
- Salt

Directions:
1. Preheat the oven to 400 F.
2. Line cooking tray with parchment paper and set aside.
3. Add all ingredients into the bowl and mix until just combined.
4. Make small balls from meat mixture and place on a parchment-lined baking sheet.
5. Bake for 12 minutes.
6. Serve and enjoy.

Nutritional Value (Amount per Serving):
Calories 77; Fat 5 g; Carbohydrates 1 g; Sugar 0.2 g; Protein 6.8 g; Cholesterol 61 mg

Beef Stew

Preparation Time: 10 minutes; Cooking Time: 26 minutes; Serve: 8

Ingredients:
- 15 oz beef, cut into pieces
- 3 tbsp olive oil

- 14 oz frozen okra, cut into pieces
- 2 tomatoes, chopped
- 4 cups of water
- 1 small onion, chopped
- 1/4 cup fresh cilantro, chopped
- 1 tbsp garlic, minced
- 4 oz tomato paste

Directions:
1. Heat oil in a saucepan over medium-high heat.
2. Add onion, garlic, and cilantro and sauté for a minute. Add okra and stir well and cook for 10 minutes.
3. Add tomatoes, tomato paste, and water into the pan and stir well.
4. Add meat and stir everything well. Turn heat to low and simmer for 15 minutes.
5. Serve and enjoy.

Nutritional Value (Amount per Serving):
Calories 186; Fat 8.8 g; Carbohydrates 8.8 g; Sugar 3.7 g; Protein 18.2 g; Cholesterol 48 mg

Rosemary Beef Tips

Preparation Time: 10 minutes; Cooking Time: 12 minutes; Serve: 4

Ingredients:
- 1 lb rib-eye steak, cut into 1-inch cubes
- 1 tsp paprika
- 2 tsp onion powder
- 1 tsp garlic powder
- 2 tbsp coconut aminos
- 2 tsp rosemary, crushed
- Pepper
- Salt

Directions:
1. Add meat and remaining ingredients into the bowl and mix well and let it marinate for 5 minutes.
2. Add the meat into the air fryer basket and air fry at 380 F for 12 minutes. Stir halfway through.
3. Serve and enjoy.

Nutritional Value (Amount per Serving):
Calories 355; Fat 24.5 g; Carbohydrates 3.7 g; Sugar 0.7 g; Protein 28.7 g; Cholesterol 95 mg

Montreal Steak Tips

Preparation Time: 10 minutes; Cooking Time: 5 minutes; Serve: 3

Ingredients:
- 1 lb steak, cut into cubes
- 1 tsp olive oil
- 1 tsp Montreal steak seasoning
- Pepper
- Salt

Directions:
1. In a bowl, add steak cubes and remaining ingredients and toss well.
2. Add marinated steak cubes into the air fryer basket and cook at 400 F for 5 minutes.
3. Serve and enjoy.

Nutritional Value (Amount per Serving):
Calories 317; Fat 9.1 g; Carbohydrates 0 g; Sugar 0 g; Protein 54.6 g; Cholesterol 136 mg

Beef Kebabs

Preparation Time: 10 minutes; Cooking Time: 10 minutes; Serve: 4

Ingredients:
- 1 lb beef chuck ribs, cut into 1-inch pieces
- 2 tbsp soy sauce
- 1/3 cup sour cream
- 1/2 onion, cut into 1-inch pieces
- 1 bell pepper, cut into 1-inch pieces

Directions:
1. Add meat, soy sauce, and sour cream into the bowl and mix well. Cover and place in the refrigerator overnight.
2. Thread marinated meat, onion, and bell peppers pieces onto the soaked wooden skewers.
3. Place skewers into the air fryer basket and air fry at 400 F for 10 minutes. Turn halfway through.
4. Serve and enjoy.

Nutritional Value (Amount per Serving):
Calories 371; Fat 30.2 g; Carbohydrates 5 g; Sugar 2.3 g; Protein 20.6 g; Cholesterol 84 mg

Delicious Beef Kebabs

Preparation Time: 10 minutes; Cooking Time: 15 minutes; Serve: 4

Ingredients:
- 1 lb ground beef
- 1/2 cup onion, minced
- 1/4 tsp ground cinnamon
- 1/4 tsp ground cardamom
- 1/2 tsp cayenne
- 1/2 tsp turmeric
- 1 tbsp ginger garlic paste
- 1/4 cup cilantro, chopped
- 1 tsp salt

Directions:
1. Add meat and remaining ingredients into the large bowl and mix until well combined.
2. Make kebabs into sausage shapes and place them into the air fryer basket and air fry at 350 F for 15 minutes. Turn kebabs halfway through.
3. Serve and enjoy.

Nutritional Value (Amount per Serving):
Calories 225; Fat 7.4 g; Carbohydrates 2.6 g; Sugar 0.7 g; Protein 34.9 g; Cholesterol 101 mg

Meatballs

Preparation Time: 10 minutes; Cooking Time: 10 minutes; Serve: 4

Ingredients:
- 1 egg, lightly beaten
- 1 lb ground beef
- 2 tbsp taco seasoning
- 1 tbsp garlic, minced
- 1/2 cup cheddar cheese, shredded
- 1/4 cup cilantro, chopped
- 1/4 cup onion, chopped
- Pepper
- Salt

Directions:
1. Add ground beef and remaining ingredients into the large bowl and mix until well combined.

2. Make small meatballs from meat mixture and place it into the air fryer basket and cook at 400 F for 10 minutes.
3. Serve and enjoy.

Nutritional Value (Amount per Serving):
Calories 299; Fat 13.4 g; Carbohydrates 2.4 g; Sugar 0.5 g; Protein 40.1 g; Cholesterol 159 mg

Easy Steak Fajitas

Preparation Time: 10 minutes; Cooking Time: 4 hours; Serve: 6
Ingredients:
- 2 lbs beef, sliced
- 2 tbsp fajita seasoning
- 20 oz salsa
- 1 onion, sliced
- 2 bell pepper, sliced

Directions:
1. Add salsa into the crockpot.
2. Add meat, bell peppers, onion, and fajita seasoning to the slow cooker. Stir well.
3. Cover and cook on high for 4 hours.
4. Serve and enjoy.

Nutritional Value (Amount per Serving):
Calories 337; Fat 9.7 g; Carbohydrates 12.7 g; Sugar 5.7 g; Protein 47.9 g; Cholesterol 135 mg

Simple Spice Pork Chops

Preparation Time: 10 minutes; Cooking Time: 12 minutes; Serve: 4
Ingredients:
- 8 oz pork chops, boneless
- 1 tsp onion powder
- 1 tsp paprika
- 1 tsp olive oil
- Pepper
- Salt

Directions:
1. Brush pork chops with oil.
2. Mix together remaining ingredients and rub over pork chops.
3. Place pork chops into the air fryer basket and cook at 380 F for 12 minutes. Turn pork chops halfway through.
4. Serve and enjoy.

Nutritional Value (Amount per Serving):
Calories 195; Fat 15.3 g; Carbohydrates 0.8 g; Sugar 0.3 g; Protein 12.9 g; Cholesterol 49 mg

Curried Pork Chops

Preparation Time: 10 minutes; Cooking Time: 6 hours; Serve: 8
Ingredients:
- 2 lbs pork chops
- 1 tbsp dried rosemary
- 1/4 cup olive oil
- 1 tbsp ground cumin
- 1 tbsp fresh chives, chopped
- 1 tbsp curry powder
- 1 tbsp dried thyme
- 1 tbsp fennel seeds
- 1 tsp salt

Directions:
1. In a small bowl, mix cumin, rosemary, 2 tbsp oil, fennel seeds, chives, curry powder, thyme, and salt and rub over pork chops.

2. Place pork chops into the crockpot.
3. Pour remaining olive oil over pork chops.
4. Cover and cook on low for 6 hours.
5. Serve and enjoy.

Nutritional Value (Amount per Serving):
Calories 427; Fat 35 g; Carbohydrates 1.7 g; Sugar 0.1 g; Protein 25.9 g; Cholesterol 98 mg

Salsa Pork Chops

Preparation Time: 10 minutes; Cooking Time: 3 hours 10 minutes; Serve: 8

Ingredients:
- 8 pork chops, bone-in
- 1/2 cup salsa
- 3 tbsp olive oil
- 1 tsp garlic powder
- 1/4 cup fresh lime juice
- 1/2 tsp ground cumin
- Pepper
- Salt

Directions:
1. Heat oil in a pan over medium-high heat.
2. Add pork chops in a pan and cook until browned from both sides.
3. Place pork chops into the crockpot.
4. Pour remaining ingredients over pork chops.
5. Cover and cook on high for 3 hours.
6. Serve and enjoy.

Nutritional Value (Amount per Serving):
Calories 307; Fat 25.2 g; Carbohydrates 1.5 g; Sugar 0.6 g; Protein 18.3 g; Cholesterol 1.5 mg

Lemon Pepper Pork Tenderloin

Preparation Time: 10 minute; Cooking Time: 20 minutes; Serve: 6

Ingredients:
- 2 lbs pork tenderloin
- 1 garlic clove, minced
- 1 tsp fresh parsley, minced
- 1 tsp fresh lemon juice
- 2 tbsp olive oil
- 1/2 tsp kosher salt

Directions:
1. Add all ingredients except pork tenderloin into the zip-lock bag and mix well.
2. Add pork tenderloin zip-lock bag. Seal bag and place in the refrigerator overnight.
3. Preheat a grill to medium-high heat.
4. Place pork tenderloin on hot grill and cook for 15-20 minutes.
5. Slice and serve.

Nutritional Value (Amount per Serving):
Calories 257; Fat 10 g; Carbohydrates 0.2 g; Sugar 0 g; Protein 39.6 g; Cholesterol 110 mg

Grilled Lamb Chops

Preparation Time: 10 minutes; Cooking Time: 8 minutes; Serve: 6

Ingredients:
- 6 lamb chops
- 1/2 tsp Pepper
- 2 tbsp olive oil
- 2 tbsp fresh mint, chopped
- 1/2 tsp kosher salt

Directions:

1. Preheat a grill to high heat.
2. Brush lamb chops with oil and season with pepper and salt.
3. Place lamb chops on grill, cover, and cook for 5 minutes.
4. Flip lamb chops and cook for 3 minutes.
5. Garnish with mint. Serve.

Nutritional Value (Amount per Serving):
Calories 301; Fat 19.7 g; Carbohydrates 5 g; Sugar 0 g; Protein 25 g; Cholesterol 0 mg

Grilled Steak Kababs

Preparation Time: 10 minutes; Cooking Time: 15 minutes; Serve: 4

Ingredients:
- 1 lb beef sirloin, cut into 1-inch pieces
- 2 tsp olive oil
- 1 onion, cut into 1-inch pieces
- 1 green bell pepper, cut into 1-inch pieces
- 1 cup mushrooms
- 1 tbsp fresh parsley, chopped
- 1 tsp garlic, minced
- 3 tbsp butter
- Pepper
- Salt

Directions:
1. Preheat a grill to medium-high heat.
2. Thread the beef, bell pepper, mushrooms, and onion onto the skewers.
3. Brush meat and vegetables with olive oil and season with pepper and salt.
4. Place skewers on hot grill and cooks for 4-5 minutes per side.
5. Melt butter in a pan over medium-low heat.
6. Add garlic and sauté for a minute.
7. Remove pan from heat and stir in parsley, pepper, and salt.
8. Brush butter mixture all over kababs.
9. Serve and enjoy.

Nutritional Value (Amount per Serving):
Calories 301; Fat 19 g; Carbohydrates 5 g; Sugar 0 g; Protein 25 g; Cholesterol 0 mg

Lamb Chops

Preparation Time: 10 minutes; Cooking Time: 10 minutes; Serve: 6

Ingredients:
- 12 lamb chops, trim excess fat
- For rub:
- 1/2 tsp ground coriander
- 1 tbsp chili powder
- 1 tbsp turmeric powder
- 1 tsp kosher salt

Directions:
1. Heat the grill to medium-high heat.
2. In a small bowl, mix together ground coriander, chili powder, turmeric, and salt and rub all over lamb chops.
3. Place lamb chops on hot grill and cook for 3-5 minutes on each side or until cooked.
4. Serve and enjoy.

Nutritional Value (Amount per Serving):
Calories 648; Fat 52 g; Carbohydrates 1.4 g; Sugar 0.1 g; Protein 38 g; Cholesterol 160 mg

Lamb Roast

Preparation Time: 10 minutes; Cooking Time: 8 hours; Serve: 8

Ingredients:
- 4 lbs lamb roast, boneless
- 1/2 tsp thyme
- 1 tsp oregano
- 3 garlic cloves, cut into slivers
- 1/2 tsp marjoram
- 1/4 tsp pepper
- 2 tsp salt

Directions:
1. Using a sharp knife make small cuts all over the meat then insert garlic slivers into the cuts.
2. In a small bowl, mix together marjoram, thyme, oregano, pepper, and salt and rub all over lamb roast.
3. Place lamb roast into the slow cooker.
4. Cover and cook on low for 8 hours.
5. Serve and enjoy.

Nutritional Value (Amount per Serving):
Calories 605; Fat 48.2 g; Carbohydrates 0.7 g; Sugar 0 g; Protein 38.3 g; Cholesterol 161 mg

Flank Steak

Preparation Time: 10 minutes; Cooking Time: 9 hours; Serve: 6

Ingredients:
- 1 1/2 lbs flank steak
- 2 bell pepper, sliced
- 1 1/2 tsp chili powder
- 15 oz salsa
- 1/4 tsp pepper
- 3 garlic cloves, minced
- 1 onion, chopped
- 1/2 tsp salt

Directions:
1. Add all ingredients into the large zip-lock bag and mix well.
2. Place a zip-lock bag into the refrigerator overnight.
3. Add marinated steak into the crockpot.
4. Cover and cook on low for 9 hours.
5. Slice and serve.

Nutritional Value (Amount per Serving):
Calories 264; Fat 9.8 g; Carbohydrates 10.1 g; Sugar 5 g; Protein 33.4 g; Cholesterol 62 mg

Lamb Kebabs

Preparation Time: 10 minutes; Cooking Time: 10 minutes; Serve: 6

Ingredients:
- 1 1/2 lbs Lamb, cut into 2-inch pieces
- 5 tbsp olive oil
- 1 1/2 tbsp fresh parsley, chopped
- 1 1/2 tbsp fresh mint leaves, chopped
- 1 1/2 tbsp fresh rosemary, chopped
- 1/8 tsp crushed red pepper flakes
- 1 lemon zest, grated
- 4 garlic cloves, minced
- 2 tsp fresh oregano, chopped
- 1 1/2 tsp black pepper
- 1 tsp kosher salt

Directions:
1. Add lamb chunks and remaining ingredients into the zip-lock bag and mix well.
2. Seal bag and place in the refrigerator overnight.
3. Preheat the grill to medium-high heat.
4. Thread marinated lamb chunks onto the skewers.

5. Place skewers onto the hot grill and cook for 8-10 minutes, turn skewers twice during cooking.
6. Serve and enjoy.

Nutritional Value (Amount per Serving):
Calories 321; Fat 20.2 g; Carbohydrates 2.1 g; Sugar 0.1 g; Protein 32.2 g; Cholesterol 102 mg

Lamb Patties

Preparation Time: 10 minutes; Cooking Time: 15 minutes; Serve: 4
Ingredients:
- 1 lb ground lamb
- 1 tsp ground cumin
- 1/4 cup fresh parsley, chopped
- 1/4 cup onion, minced
- 1 tbsp garlic, minced
- 1/4 tsp pepper
- 1/4 tsp cayenne pepper
- 1/2 tsp ground allspice
- 1 tsp ground cinnamon
- 1 tsp ground coriander
- 1 tsp kosher salt

Directions:
1. Preheat the oven to 450 F.
2. Add all ingredients into the large bowl and mix until well combined.
3. Make small balls from meat mixture and place on a baking sheet and lightly flatten the meatballs with back on spoon.
4. Bake for 12-15 minutes.
5. Serve and enjoy.

Nutritional Value (Amount per Serving):
Calories 223; Fat 8.5 g; Carbohydrates 2.6 g; Sugar 0.4 g; Protein 32.3 g; Cholesterol 102 mg

Beef Kofta

Preparation Time: 10 minutes; Cooking Time: 10 minutes; Serve: 8
Ingredients:
- 2 lbs ground beef
- 1 onion, minced
- 2 tsp cumin
- 1 cup fresh parsley, chopped
- 4 garlic cloves, minced
- 1/4 tsp pepper
- 1 tsp salt

Directions:
1. Add all ingredients into the mixing bowl and mix until just combined.
2. Shape meat mixture into the kabab shapes and cook in a hot pan for 4-6 minutes on each side.
3. Serve and enjoy.

Nutritional Value (Amount per Serving):
Calories 223; Fat 7.3 g; Carbohydrates 2.5 g; Sugar 0.7 g; Protein 35 g; Cholesterol 101 mg

Herb Beef Patties

Preparation Time: 10 minutes; Cooking Time: 8 minutes; Serve: 5
Ingredients:
- 1 lb ground beef
- 1 egg, lightly beaten
- 3 tbsp almond flour
- 1 small onion, grated
- 2 tbsp fresh parsley, chopped
- 1 tsp dry oregano

- 1 tsp dry mint
- Pepper
- Salt

Directions:
1. Add all ingredients into the bowl and mix until combined.
2. Make small patties from the meat mixture.
3. Heat grill pan over medium-high heat.
4. Place patties in a hot pan and cook for 4-5 minutes on each side.
5. Serve and enjoy.

Nutritional Value (Amount per Serving):
Calories 284; Fat 15 g; Carbohydrates 5.3 g; Sugar 1.3 g; Protein 32.5 g; Cholesterol 114 mg

Tasty Pork Kabobs

Preparation Time: 10 minutes; Cooking Time: 15 minutes; Serve: 2

Ingredients:
- 1 lb pork tenderloin, cut into 1-inch pieces
- 1/2 tsp paprika
- 1/2 tsp oregano
- 1/2 tsp garlic powder
- 1 tbsp Italian seasoning
- 1 onion, cut into 1-inch pieces
- 2 tbsp olive oil
- Pepper
- Salt

Directions:
1. In a bowl, add all ingredients and mix well and place in the refrigerator for overnight.
2. Heat grill over medium-high heat.
3. Thread marinated pork pieces and onion pieces onto the skewers and grill for 15 minutes. Turn skewers after every 3-4 minutes.
4. Serve and enjoy.

Nutritional Value (Amount per Serving):
Calories 493; Fat 24.2 g; Carbohydrates 7 g; Sugar 3.2 g; Protein 60.2 g; Cholesterol 170 mg

Meatballs

Preparation Time: 10 minutes; Cooking Time: 20 minutes; Serve: 4

Ingredients:
- 1 lb ground lamb
- 1 egg, lightly beaten
- 3 tbsp olive oil
- 2 tbsp fresh parsley, chopped
- 1 tbsp garlic, minced
- 1/4 tsp red pepper flakes
- 1 tsp ground cumin
- 2 tsp fresh oregano, chopped
- 1/4 tsp pepper
- 1 tsp kosher salt

Directions:
1. Preheat the oven to 425 F. Line baking sheet with parchment paper.
2. Add all ingredients except oil into the mixing bowl and mix until well combined.
3. Make small meatballs from meat mixture and place them on a prepared baking sheet.
4. Drizzle oil over meatballs and bake for 20 minutes.
5. Serve and enjoy.

Nutritional Value (Amount per Serving):
Calories 325; Fat 20.2 g; Carbohydrates 1.7 g; Sugar 0.2 g; Protein 33.6 g; Cholesterol 124 mg

Classic Pork Cacciatore

Preparation Time: 10 minutes; Cooking Time: 6 hours; Serve: 6
Ingredients:
- 1 1/2 lbs pork chops
- 1 cup beef broth
- 1 garlic clove, minced
- 1 tsp dried oregano
- 2 tbsp olive oil
- 3 tbsp tomato paste
- 14 oz can tomatoes, diced
- 2 cups mushrooms, sliced
- 1 small onion, diced
- 1/4 tsp pepper
- 1/2 tsp salt

Directions:
1. Heat oil in a pan over medium-high heat.
2. Add pork chops in the pan and cook until brown on both sides.
3. Transfer pork chops into the crockpot.
4. Pour remaining ingredients over the pork chops.
5. Cover and cook on low for 6 hours.
6. Serve and enjoy.

Nutritional Value (Amount per Serving):
Calories 441; Fat 33.2 g; Carbohydrates 7.3 g; Sugar 4.3 g; Protein 28.2 g; Cholesterol 98 mg

Meatballs

Preparation Time: 10 minutes; Cooking Time: 4 hours; Serve: 6
Ingredients:
- 1 egg
- 2 tbsp fresh parsley, chopped
- 1 garlic clove, minced
- 1/2 lb ground beef
- 1/2 lb ground pork
- 14 oz can tomatoes, crushed
- 2 tbsp fresh basil, chopped
- 1/4 tsp pepper
- 1/2 tsp salt

Directions:
1. In a bowl, mix together beef, pork, egg, parsley, garlic, pepper, and salt until well combined.
2. Make small balls from the meat mixture.
3. Arrange meatballs into the slow cooker.
4. Pour crushed tomatoes, basil, pepper, and salt over meatballs.
5. Cover and cook on low for 4 hours.
6. Serve and enjoy.

Nutritional Value (Amount per Serving):
Calories 150; Fat 4.4 g; Carbohydrates 3.8 g; Sugar 2.3 g; Protein 23 g; Cholesterol 89 mg

Greek Pork Chops

Preparation Time: 10 minutes; Cooking Time: 6 minutes; Serve: 8
Ingredients:
- 8 pork chops, boneless
- 4 tsp dried oregano
- 2 tbsp Worcestershire sauce
- 3 tbsp fresh lemon juice
- 1/4 cup olive oil
- 1 tsp ground mustard
- 2 tsp garlic powder
- 2 tsp onion powder
- Pepper
- Salt

Directions:
1. Whisk together oil, garlic powder, onion powder, oregano, Worcestershire sauce, lemon juice, mustard, pepper, and salt.
2. Place pork chops in a baking dish then pour marinade over pork chops and coat well. Place in the freezer overnight.
3. Preheat the grill. Arrange marinated pork chops on hot grill and cook for 3 minutes on each side.
4. Serve and enjoy.

Nutritional Value (Amount per Serving):
Calories 324; Fat 26.5 g; Carbohydrates 2.5 g; Sugar 1.3 g; Protein 18.4 g; Cholesterol 69 mg

Italian Pork Roast

Preparation Time: 10 minutes; Cooking Time: 6 hours; Serve: 8

Ingredients:
- 2 lbs lean pork roast, boneless
- 1/2 cup parmesan cheese, grated
- 28 oz can tomatoes, diced
- 1 tsp dried oregano
- 1 tsp dried basil
- 1 tsp garlic powder
- 1 tbsp parsley
- Pepper
- Salt

Directions:
1. Add the meat into the slow cooker.
2. Mix together tomatoes, oregano, basil, garlic powder, parsley, cheese, pepper, and salt and pour over meat.
3. Cover and cook on low for 6 hours.
4. Serve and enjoy.

Nutritional Value (Amount per Serving):
Calories 239; Fat 8.5 g; Carbohydrates 5.7 g; Sugar 3.5 g; Protein 33.9 g; Cholesterol 94 mg

Simple Pork Carnitas

Preparation Time: 10 minutes; Cooking Time: 8 hours 3 minutes; Serve: 8

Ingredients:
- 3 lbs pork roast
- 1 fresh lime juice
- 2 tbsp olive oil
- 2 tbsp fresh cilantro, chopped

Directions:
1. Place pork roast in crockpot.
2. Cover and cook on low for 8 hours.
3. Remove meat from crockpot and shred using the fork.
4. Heat oil in a large pan over medium-high heat.
5. Add shredded meat to the pan and cook for 2-3 minutes.
6. Remove from heat. Add lime juice and stir well.
7. Garnish with cilantro and serve.

Nutritional Value (Amount per Serving):
Calories 384; Fat 19.5 g; Carbohydrates 0.5 g; Sugar 0.1 g; Protein 48.5 g; Cholesterol 146 mg

Meatloaf

Preparation Time: 10 minutes; Cooking Time: 55 minutes; Serve: 6

Ingredients:
- 2 lbs ground beef
- 1/4 cup green onion, chopped
- 1/2 cup sunflower seed flour
- 1/2 cup salsa, low-fodmap
- 2 eggs, lightly beaten
- 2 tbsp olive oil
- 1 tsp oregano
- 1 tsp paprika
- 1 tsp cumin
- 1/4 cup fresh cilantro, chopped
- 1 red bell pepper, diced
- 1/2 tsp salt

Directions:
1. Preheat the oven to 375 F. Grease loaf pan and set aside.
2. Add meat in a bowl.
3. Cook bell pepper in olive oil over medium heat, about 5 minutes.
4. Transfer bell pepper in meat bowl.
5. Add remaining ingredients to the meat mixture and mix until just combined.
6. Transfer meat mixture into the loaf pan and bake for 50-55 minutes.
7. Slice and serve.

Nutritional Value (Amount per Serving):
Calories 377; Fat 15.9 g; Carbohydrates 5.8 g; Sugar 2 g; Protein 51.1 g; Cholesterol 190 mg

Pork Roast

Preparation Time: 10 minutes; Cooking Time: 8 hours; Serve: 6

Ingredients:
- 3 lbs pork shoulder roast, boneless and cut into 4 pieces
- 1 tbsp fresh oregano
- 2/3 cup grapefruit juice
- 1/2 tbsp cumin
- Pepper
- Salt

Directions:
1. Season meat with pepper and salt and place into the crockpot.
2. Add cumin, oregano, and grapefruit juice into the blender and blend until smooth.
3. Pour blended mixture over meat and stir well.
4. Cover and cook on low for 8 hours.
5. Remove meat from crockpot and shred using a fork.
6. Return shredded meat into the crockpot and stir well.
7. Serve and enjoy.

Nutritional Value (Amount per Serving):
Calories 594; Fat 46.4 g; Carbohydrates 2.8 g; Sugar 1.8 g; Protein 38.5 g; Cholesterol 161 mg

Tasty Burger Patties

Preparation Time: 10 minutes; Cooking Time: 10 minutes; Serve: 6

Ingredients:
- 1 lb ground lamb
- 1 lb ground beef
- 1 tbsp dried oregano
- 1 tbsp dried thyme
- 1 tsp cumin
- 1/2 cup green onion, chopped
- 2 tbsp olive oil
- 1 tsp dried rosemary
- 1 tsp pepper
- 1 1/2 tsp salt

Directions:
1. Add all ingredients into the large bowl and mix until well combined.
2. Make six even shape patties from the meat mixture.

3. Grill patties over medium heat for 5 minutes on each side.
4. Serve and enjoy.

Nutritional Value (Amount per Serving):
Calories 330; Fat 15.2 g; Carbohydrates 1.9 g; Sugar 0.2 g; Protein 44.5 g; Cholesterol 136 mg

Cabbage Skillet

Preparation Time: 10 minutes; Cooking Time: 10 minutes; Serve: 4

Ingredients:
- 1 lb ground beef
- 2 cups cabbage, shredded
- 1/2 cup salsa
- 3/4 cup cheddar cheese, shredded
- 2 tsp chili powder
- Pepper
- Salt

Directions:
1. Heat pan over medium heat.
2. Add ground beef in a pan and cook until brown. Drain excess fat.
3. Add cabbage, seasoning, and salsa to the pan and bring to boil.
4. Cover pan and turn heat to medium and cook for 10 minutes.
5. Remove pan from heat and mix in cheddar cheese until melted.
6. Serve and enjoy.

Nutritional Value (Amount per Serving):
Calories 318; Fat 14.4 g; Carbohydrates 5.1 g; Sugar 2.3 g; Protein 40.8 g; Cholesterol 124 mg

Italian Shredded Beef

Preparation Time: 10 minutes; Cooking Time: 20 minutes; Serve: 8

Ingredients:
- 2 lbs beef chuck roast, cut into chunks
- 2 tbsp red wine vinegar
- 14.5 oz can fire-roasted tomatoes
- 1 cup bell pepper, chopped
- 1 cup carrots, chopped
- 1/2 tbsp dried red pepper
- 1 tbsp Italian seasoning
- 1 tbsp garlic, minced
- 1 cup onion, chopped
- 1 tsp salt

Directions:
1. Add all ingredients into the instant pot and stir well.
2. Seal pot and cook on high pressure for 20 minutes.
3. Once done, then release pressure using the quick-release method. Open the lid.
4. Shred the meat using a fork.
5. Serve and enjoy.

Nutritional Value (Amount per Serving):
Calories 446; Fat 32.1 g; Carbohydrates 6.3 g; Sugar 3.1 g; Protein 30.5 g; Cholesterol 118 mg

Meatballs

Preparation Time: 10 minutes; Cooking Time: 20 minutes; Serve: 6

Ingredients:
- 1 egg, lightly beaten
- 2 lbs lean ground beef
- 2 tsp coriander
- 1 tsp garlic, minced
- 1 small onion, grated
- 1 tbsp fresh mint, chopped

- 1/4 cup fresh parsley, minced
- 1/2 tsp allspice
- 1 tsp oregano
- 1 tsp cinnamon
- 2 tsp cumin
- 1 tsp paprika
- 1/4 tsp pepper
- 1/2 tsp salt

Directions:
1. Preheat the oven to 400 F.
2. Add all ingredients into the large bowl and mix until well combined.
3. Make small balls from the meat mixture and place them on the baking sheet.
4. Bake for 15-20 minutes.
5. Serve and enjoy.

Nutritional Value (Amount per Serving):
Calories 291; Fat 15.7 g; Carbohydrates 2.7 g; Sugar 0.7 g; Protein 32.2 g; Cholesterol 128 mg

Rosemary Pork Chops

Preparation Time: 10 minutes; Cooking Time: 35 minutes; Serve: 4

Ingredients:
- 4 pork chops, boneless
- 3 garlic cloves, minced
- 1 tsp dried rosemary, crushed
- 1/4 tsp pepper
- 1/4 tsp sea salt

Directions:
1. Preheat the oven to 425 F. Line baking sheet with parchment paper.
2. Season pork chops with pepper and salt.
3. Combine together garlic and rosemary and rub all over pork chops.
4. Place pork chops on the baking sheet.
5. Roast pork chops for 10 minutes.
6. Turn oven temperature to 350 F and roast for 25 minutes.
7. Serve and enjoy.

Nutritional Value (Amount per Serving):
Calories 261; Fat 19.9 g; Carbohydrates 1 g; Sugar 0 g; Protein 18.1 g; Cholesterol 69 mg

Meatloaf

Preparation Time: 10 minutes; Cooking Time: 40 minutes; Serve: 4

Ingredients:
- 2 eggs
- 1 1/2 lbs ground beef
- 1 1/2 tsp chili powder
- 1 1/2 tsp ground mustard
- 4 oz tomato sauce, sugar-free
- 1 tbsp Worcestershire sauce
- 2 tbsp garlic, minced
- 1/3 tsp ground pepper
- 1/2 cup pork rinds, crushed
- 1/3 cup onion, chopped

Directions:
1. Preheat the oven to 375 F.
2. In a mixing bowl, add all ingredients and mix well until combined.
3. Spray loaf pan with cooking spray. Add beef mixture into the loaf pan.
4. Bake in preheated oven for 45 minutes.
5. Cut into the slices and serve.

Nutritional Value (Amount per Serving):
Calories 406; Fat 14 g; Carbohydrates 9.3 g; Sugar 4.9 g; Protein 56.3 g; Cholesterol 236 mg

Rosemary Dijon Pork Chops

Preparation Time: 10 minutes; Cooking Time: 10 minutes; Serve: 4
Ingredients:
- 4 pork chops, boneless
- 2 tbsp olive oil
- 1/4 cup Dijon mustard
- 2 tbsp fresh rosemary, chopped
- 1/4 cup coconut aminos
- 1/2 tsp salt

Directions:
1. In a bowl, mix together rosemary, coconut aminos, olive oil, Dijon mustard, and salt.
2. Add pork chops to the bowl and coat well.
3. Cover and place in the refrigerator for 1 hour.
4. Heat grill over medium-high heat.
5. Place marinated pork chops onto the hot grill and cook for 5 minutes on each side.
6. Serve and enjoy.

Nutritional Value (Amount per Serving):
Calories 347; Fat 27.8 g; Carbohydrates 4.9 g; Sugar 0.1 g; Protein 18.7 g; Cholesterol 69 mg

Italian Beef Chuck Roast

Preparation Time: 10 minutes; Cooking Time: 45 minutes; Serve: 8
Ingredients:
- 3 1/2 lbs beef chuck roast, cut into cubes
- 1/2 tsp garlic powder
- 1/2 tsp dried thyme
- 5 carrots, peeled and diced
- 2 cups chicken broth
- 1 onion, diced
- 2 tbsp olive oil
- 1 tbsp Italian seasoning
- 1 tsp pepper
- 1 tsp salt

Directions:
1. Season meat with spices and set aside.
2. Add oil into the instant pot and set the pot on sauté mode.
3. Add onion and sauté for 5 minutes.
4. Add remaining ingredients and stir well.
5. Seal pot and cook on high for 40 minutes.
6. Release pressure using the quick-release method. Open the lid.
7. Stir well and serve.

Nutritional Value (Amount per Serving):
Calories 788; Fat 59.6 g; Carbohydrates 5.8 g; Sugar 2.8 g; Protein 53.7 g; Cholesterol 206 mg

Smoked Tenderloin

Preparation Time: 10 minutes; Cooking Time: 35 minutes; Serve: 6
Ingredients:
- 2 pork tenderloin
- For rub:
- 1 tbsp onion powder
- 1 tbsp smoked paprika
- 1 tbsp garlic powder
- 1/2 tbsp salt

Directions:
1. Preheat the oven to 425 F.
2. In a small bowl, combine together all rub ingredients.

3. Coat pork tenderloin with the rub.
4. Heat oven-safe pan over medium-high heat.
5. Spray pan with cooking spray. Sear pork on all sides until lightly golden brown.
6. Place pan into the oven and roast for about 25-30 minutes.
7. Slice and serve.

Nutritional Value (Amount per Serving):
Calories 171; Fat 4.1 g; Carbohydrates 2.6 g; Sugar 0.9 g; Protein 29.6 g; Cholesterol 81 mg

Minced Pork

Preparation Time: 10 minutes; Cooking Time: 20 minutes; Serve: 4
Ingredients:
- 14 oz minced pork
- 1/4 cup green bell pepper, chopped
- 2 tbsp water
- 3/4 cup ketchup, sugar-free
- 1/2 onion, chopped
- 1/2 tbsp olive oil
- Pepper
- Salt

Directions:
1. Heat oil in a pan over medium heat.
2. Add chopped bell pepper and onion in the pan and cook until softened.
3. Add pork, pepper, and salt in a pan and cook until browned.
4. Add water and ketchup and mix well. Bring to boil.
5. Serve and enjoy.

Nutritional Value (Amount per Serving):
Calories 210; Fat 5.3 g; Carbohydrates 10.9 g; Sugar 7 g; Protein 26.2 g; Cholesterol 72 mg

Spicy Pepper Beef

Preparation Time: 10 minutes; Cooking Time: 4 hours 15 minutes; Serve: 6
Ingredients:
- 2 lbs beef chuck, sliced
- 1 cup chicken broth
- 1 small onion, sliced
- 2 cups bell pepper, chopped
- 1 tsp sriracha sauce
- 1/3 cup parsley, chopped
- 2 garlic cloves, minced
- 1 tsp black pepper
- 2 tsp salt

Directions:
1. Place meat on the bottom of the Crockpot and top with onion and bell pepper. Season with garlic, pepper, and salt.
2. Mix broth and sriracha together and pour into the Crockpot.
3. Cover and cook on high for 4 hours.
4. Garnish with parsley and serve.

Nutritional Value (Amount per Serving):
Calories 314; Fat 10.4 g; Carbohydrates 5.1 g; Sugar 2.7 g; Protein 47.4 g; Cholesterol 136 mg

Greek Beef Roast

Preparation Time: 10 minutes; Cooking Time: 8 hours 10 minutes; Serve: 8
Ingredients:
- 2 1/2 lbs beef round roast
- 1/2 cup red wine

- 1/2 cup chicken broth
- 1 small onion, sliced
- 1/2 tsp marjoram
- 1/2 tsp thyme
- 1 tsp basil
- 1/4 tsp black pepper
- 1 tsp kosher salt

Directions:
1. In a small bowl, mix together all spices and rub all over beef roast.
2. Place roast in the slow cooker and top with onion.
3. Pour broth and red wine into the slow cooker.
4. Cover and cook on low for 8 hours.
5. Shred meat using a fork and stir well.
6. Serve and enjoy.

Nutritional Value (Amount per Serving):
Calories 284; Fat 11 g; Carbohydrates 1.4 g; Sugar 0.5 g; Protein 39.3 g; Cholesterol 122 mg

Meatloaf

Preparation Time: 10 minutes; Cooking Time: 40 minutes; Serve: 8
Ingredients:
- 2 eggs
- 2 lbs ground beef
- 1/2 cup marinara sauce, without sugar
- 1 cup cottage cheese
- 1 lb mozzarella cheese, cut into cubes
- 2 tsp Italian seasoning
- 1/4 cup basil pesto
- 1/2 cup parmesan cheese, grated
- 1 tsp salt

Directions:
1. Preheat the oven to 400 F.
2. A grease casserole dish with butter and set aside.
3. Add all ingredients into the large bowl and mix until well combined.
4. Transfer bowl mixture to the prepared dish and bake for 40 minutes.
5. Serve and enjoy.

Nutritional Value (Amount per Serving):
Calories 299; Fat 11.5 g; Carbohydrates 3.8 g; Sugar 1.7 g; Protein 43 g; Cholesterol 124 mg

Beef Ribs

Preparation Time: 10 minutes; Cooking Time: 35 minutes; Serve: 4
Ingredients:
- 2 lbs beef short ribs
- 2 tsp garlic, minced
- 1/4 cup Swerve
- 1/3 cup coconut aminos
- 1/2 cup chicken stock
- 1 tbsp ginger, grated
- 1 tsp five-spice powder

Directions:
1. In a bowl, whisk together stock, ginger, spice powder, garlic, swerve, and coconut aminos.
2. Place ribs into the instant pot. Pour stock mixture over the ribs.
3. Seal pot with lid and cook on high for 35 minutes.
4. Allow releasing pressure naturally then open the lid.
5. Serve and enjoy.

Nutritional Value (Amount per Serving):

Calories 493; Fat 20.6 g; Carbohydrates 5.6 g; Sugar 0.2 g; Protein 65.8 g; Cholesterol 206 mg

Rosemary Lamb Roast

Preparation Time: 10 minutes; Cooking Time: 4 hours; Serve: 6
Ingredients:
- 4 lbs lamb leg
- 1 fresh lemon juice
- 1 tbsp olive oil
- 4 tbsp rosemary
- 4 garlic cloves, sliced
- Pepper
- Salt

Directions:
1. Make deep incisions all over the meat.
2. Push rosemary and garlic into the incisions and drizzle with oil. Season with pepper and salt.
3. Place lamb leg into the slow cooker.
4. Pour lemon juice over the lamb leg.
5. Cook lamb on high for 4 hours.
6. Slice and serve.

Nutritional Value (Amount per Serving):
Calories 576; Fat 22.9 g; Carbohydrates 2.2 g; Sugar 0.2 g; Protein 85.5 g; Cholesterol 263 mg

Steak Bites

Preparation Time: 10 minutes; Cooking Time: 8 hours 10 minutes; Serve: 4
Ingredients:
- 3 lbs round steak, cut into 1-inch cubes
- 1/2 cup chicken broth
- 1/2 tsp black pepper
- 4 tbsp butter, sliced
- 1 tsp garlic powder
- 1 tbsp onion, minced
- 1/2 tsp salt

Directions:
1. Place meat cubes in the slow cooker and pour broth over the meat.
2. Sprinkle with garlic powder, onion, pepper, and salt.
3. Place butter slices on top of the meat.
4. Cover and cook on low for 8 hours.
5. Serve and enjoy.

Nutritional Value (Amount per Serving):
Calories 845; Fat 44.4 g; Carbohydrates 1 g; Sugar 0.4 g; Protein 103.6 g; Cholesterol 320 mg

Apple Cider Pork Chops

Preparation Time: 10 minutes; Cooking Time: 45 minutes; Serve: 8
Ingredients:
- 2 1/2 lbs pork chops
- 1 medium onion, sliced
- 1/2 cup olive oil
- 1 1/4 cup apple cider vinegar

Directions:
1. Heat olive oil in a pan over medium heat.
2. Add pork chops and cook until brown.
3. Once all pork chops are browned then add onion and vinegar and mix well.
4. Cover pan and cook for 45 minutes.

5. Serve and enjoy.

Nutritional Value (Amount per Serving):
Calories 575; Fat 47.8 g; Carbohydrates 1.6 g; Sugar 0.7 g; Protein 32 g; Cholesterol 122 mg

Beef Barbacoa

Preparation Time: 10 minutes; Cooking Time: 8 hours 10 minutes; Serve: 8

Ingredients:
- 3 lbs chuck roast, trimmed and cut into 2" cubes
- 1 tbsp ground cumin
- 3 bay leaves
- 3 tbsp apple cider vinegar
- 1/4 cup lime juice
- 4 oz can green chilies, diced
- 3 chipotles in adobo, chopped
- 3 garlic cloves, minced
- 1/2 tsp ground cloves
- 1 tbsp onion powder
- 1 tbsp dried oregano
- 1/2 cup chicken broth
- Pepper
- Salt

Directions:
1. Add all ingredients into the slow cooker and stir to combine.
2. Cover and cook on low for 8 hours. Discard bay leaves.
3. Shred meat using fork and season with pepper and salt.
4. Serve and enjoy.

Nutritional Value (Amount per Serving):
Calories 389; Fat 14.9 g; Carbohydrates 3.3 g; Sugar 0.4 g; Protein 57.3 g; Cholesterol 174 mg

Lamb Curry

Preparation Time: 10 minutes; Cooking Time: 20 minutes; Serve: 4

Ingredients:
- 1 lb lamb shoulder, cut into cubes
- 1 1/2 cups chicken stock
- 2 tsp dried thyme
- 2 garlic cloves, minced
- 2 tbsp curry powder
- 2 carrot, chopped
- 1 onion, chopped
- 2 tbsp cilantro, chopped
- 1 scallion, chopped
- 1/4 cup water
- 1/2 tsp salt

Directions:
1. Add meat, curry powder, and onion to the pot and cook on sauté mode for 3-4 minutes. Add stock and stir well.
2. Add remaining ingredients to the pot and stir well.
3. Seal pot with lid and cook on high for 20 minutes.
4. Allow releasing pressure naturally then open the lid.
5. Stir well and serve.

Nutritional Value (Amount per Serving):
Calories 253; Fat 9.1 g; Carbohydrates 8.8 g; Sugar 3.2 g; Protein 33.3 g; Cholesterol 102 mg

Beef Mushroom Stew

Preparation Time: 10 minutes; Cooking Time: 1 hour 45 minutes; Serve: 10

Ingredients:
- 3 lbs beef stew meat
- 1/4 tsp thyme

- 1/4 tsp dried basil
- 1 tsp onion powder
- 1 cauliflower head, cut into florets
- 2 celery stalks, chopped
- 8 oz mushrooms, sliced
- 3/4 tsp garlic powder
- 5 cups of water
- 2 cups vegetable juice
- 4 cups beef stock
- 2 garlic cloves, minced
- 1/2 onion, chopped
- 1/4 cup olive oil
- 1 ½ tbsp sea salt

Directions:
1. Heat oil in a large stockpot over high heat.
2. Add garlic and onion to the pot and sauté until softened. Add meat and cook for 10 minutes.
3. Add remaining ingredients and stir well and cook over high heat for 30 minutes.
4. Turn heat to low and simmer until meat and vegetables are tender, about 1 hour.
5. Serve and enjoy.

Nutritional Value (Amount per Serving):
Calories 329; Fat 13.9 g; Carbohydrates 5.6 g; Sugar 3.1 g; Protein 44.1 g; Cholesterol 122 mg

Meatloaf

Preparation Time: 10 minutes; Cooking Time: 30 minutes; Serve: 6
Ingredients:
- 2 eggs
- 3 tbsp olive oil
- 2 lbs ground beef
- 1 1/2 cups water
- 1 tsp garlic salt
- 1/2 tsp sage
- 1 tsp parsley
- 1 tsp oregano
- 1 tsp thyme
- 1 tsp rosemary

Directions:
1. Pour water into the instant pot and place trivet in the pot. Grease loaf pan and set aside.
2. Add all ingredients into the large bowl and mix until well combined.
3. Transfer bowl mixture into the prepared loaf pan and press down gently.
4. Place loaf pan on top of the trivet.
5. Seal pot with lid and cook on high for 30 minutes.
6. Allow releasing pressure naturally. Open the lid.
7. Serve and enjoy.

Nutritional Value (Amount per Serving):
Calories 366; Fat 18 g; Carbohydrates 0.9 g; Sugar 0.2 g; Protein 47.9 g; Cholesterol 190 mg

Chili Chuck Roast

Preparation Time: 10 minutes; Cooking Time: 65 minutes; Serve: 4
Ingredients:
- 2 lbs chuck roast
- 8 oz can green chilies, chopped
- 2 lemon juice
- 1 onion, sliced
- 1 tbsp oregano
- 1 tbsp cumin
- 3 garlic cloves, minced
- 1/2 cup water
- 1/2 tsp pepper

Directions:
1. Add all ingredients into the instant pot and stir well.

2. Seal pot with lid and cook on high for 60 minutes.
3. Release pressure using a quick-release method than open the lid.
4. Remove meat from pot and shred the meat using a fork.
5. Return shredded meat to the pot and cook on sauté mode for 5 minutes.
6. Serve and enjoy.

Nutritional Value (Amount per Serving):
Calories 532; Fat 19.7 g; Carbohydrates 8 g; Sugar 1.8 g; Protein 76.4 g; Cholesterol 229 mg

Tasty Ground Beef

Preparation Time: 10 minutes; Cooking Time: 8 minutes; Serve: 4
Ingredients:
- 1 lb ground beef
- 1/2 tsp stevia drops
- 1 tsp red pepper, crushed
- 1/2 tsp fresh ginger, minced
- 2 garlic cloves, minced
- 1 tbsp olive oil
- 3 tbsp green onion, sliced
- 2 1/2 tbsp soy sauce

Directions:
1. Heat olive oil in a pan over medium heat.
2. Add garlic and meat and cook until meat is brown about 6 minutes.
3. Add red pepper, ginger, soy sauce, and stevia. Mix well. Stir for 2 minutes.
4. Garnish with green onion and serve.

Nutritional Value (Amount per Serving):
Calories 260; Fat 10.7 g; Carbohydrates 4 g; Sugar 1.8 g; Protein 35.5 g; Cholesterol 101 mg

Juicy & Tender Chuck Roast

Preparation Time: 10 minutes; Cooking Time: 80 minutes; Serve: 4
Ingredients:
- 2 lbs chuck roast
- 1 onion, sliced
- 2 cups chicken broth
- 2 tbsp olive oil
- Pepper
- Salt

Directions:
1. Add oil into the instant pot and set the pot on sauté mode. Season meat with pepper and salt.
2. Place meat into the pot and sear from all the sides until browned.
3. Pour broth over the meat. Seal pot with lid and cook on high for 70 minutes.
4. Release pressure using a quick-release method than open the lid.
5. Serve and enjoy.

Nutritional Value (Amount per Serving):
Calories 580; Fat 26.5 g; Carbohydrates 3.1 g; Sugar 1.5 g; Protein 77.6 g; Cholesterol 229 mg

Zucchini Lamb Curry

Preparation Time: 10 minutes; Cooking Time: 25 minutes; Serve: 4
Ingredients:
- 1 lb lamb, cut into cubes
- 1 zucchini, diced
- 1/2 cup coconut milk
- 1 cup tomatoes, diced
- 1 tsp ginger, grated
- 2 tsp garlic, minced
- 1 tbsp olive oil
- 1 1/2 tbsp curry powder

- 1 carrot, sliced
- 1 onion, diced

Directions:
1. In a bowl, mix together meat, coconut milk, garlic, and ginger.
2. Cover bowl and place in the refrigerator overnight.
3. Transfer meat into the instant pot along with the marinade.
4. Add oil, tomatoes, onion, and carrot. Stir well.
5. Seal pot with lid and cook on high for 20 minutes.
6. Allow releasing pressure naturally. Open the lid.
7. Add zucchini and cook on sauté mode for 5 minutes.
8. Serve and enjoy.

Nutritional Value (Amount per Serving):
Calories 314; Fat 14.6 g; Carbohydrates 10.8 g; Sugar 4.7 g; Protein 33.7 g; Cholesterol 102 mg

Easy Pork Soup

Preparation Time: 10 minutes; Cooking Time: 30 minutes; Serve: 2

Ingredients:
- 1/2 lb ground pork
- 1/2 tsp ground ginger
- 1 tbsp soy sauce
- 1 tbsp olive oil
- 2 cup chicken stock
- 1 1/2 cup cabbage, chopped
- 1 cup carrot, peeled and shredded
- Pepper
- 1 small onion, chopped
- Salt

Directions:
1. Add oil into the instant pot and set the pot on sauté mode.
2. Add meat to the pot and sauté for 3-4 minutes.
3. Add remaining ingredients and stir to combine.
4. Seal pot with lid and cook on high for 25 minutes.
5. Release pressure using a quick-release method than open the lid. Season soup with pepper and salt.
6. Serve and enjoy.

Nutritional Value (Amount per Serving):
Calories 288; Fat 11.7 g; Carbohydrates 13.4 g; Sugar 6.7 g; Protein 32.4 g; Cholesterol 83 mg

Herb Pork Chops

Preparation Time: 10 minutes; Cooking Time: 35 minutes; Serve: 4

Ingredients:
- 4 pork chops, boneless
- 1 tsp dried rosemary, crushed
- 1 tbsp fresh rosemary, chopped
- 2 garlic cloves, minced
- 1/4 tsp pepper
- 1/4 tsp salt

Directions:
1. Preheat the oven to 425 F.
2. Spray a baking tray with cooking spray and set aside.
3. Season pork chops with pepper and salt and set aside.
4. In a small bowl, mix together garlic and rosemary and rub over pork chops.
5. Place pork chops on the baking sheet and roast in preheated oven for 10 minutes.
6. Turn heat to 350 F and roast for 25 minutes more.
7. Serve and enjoy.

Nutritional Value (Amount per Serving):

Calories 260; Fat 19.9 g; Carbohydrates 0.8 g; Sugar 0 g; Protein 18.1 g; Cholesterol 69 mg

Beef Chili

Preparation Time: 10 minutes; Cooking Time: 6 hours 10 minutes; Serve: 6

Ingredients:
- 1 lb ground beef
- 1 large onion, chopped
- 1 tsp garlic powder
- 1 tsp paprika
- 2 1/2 tsp chili powder
- 1 tbsp Worcestershire sauce
- 1 tbsp parsley, chopped
- 1 tsp onion powder
- 4 carrots, chopped
- 1 bell pepper, seeded and chopped
- 1/2 tsp salt

Directions:
1. Add meat in pan and brown over high heat.
2. Transfer brown beef into the slow cooker.
3. Add remaining ingredients into the slow cooker and mix well.
4. Cover and cook on high for 6 hours.
5. Stir well and serve.

Nutritional Value (Amount per Serving):

Calories 207; Fat 9.2 g; Carbohydrates 9.8 g; Sugar 4.9 g; Protein 20.9 g; Cholesterol 64 mg

Chapter 5: Fish & Seafood

Simple Cajun Salmon

Preparation Time: 10 minutes; Cooking Time: 8 minutes; Serve: 4

Ingredients:
- 4 salmon fillets
- 1 tsp Cajun seasoning
- 1/4 cup butter, melted

Directions:
1. Preheat the air fryer to 375 F.
2. Brush salmon fillets with butter and season with Cajun seasoning.
3. Place salmon fillets in the air fryer basket and cook for 8 minutes.
4. Serve and enjoy.

Nutritional Value (Amount per Serving):
Calories 337; Fat 22.5 g; Carbohydrates 0 g; Sugar 0 g; Protein 34.7 g; Cholesterol 109 mg

Tasty Crab Cakes

Preparation Time: 10 minutes; Cooking Time: 10 minutes; Serve: 5

Ingredients:
- 2 eggs, lightly beaten
- 18 oz can crab meat, drained
- 1 tsp Old bay seasoning
- 1 1/2 tbsp Dijon mustard
- 2 1/2 tbsp mayonnaise
- 1/4 cup almond flour
- 1 1/2 tsp dried parsley
- 1 tbsp dried celery
- Pepper
- Salt

Directions:
1. Preheat the air fryer to 320 F.
2. Add all ingredients into the mixing bowl and mix until just combined.
3. Make small patties from crab mixture and place into the air fryer basket and cook for 10 minutes.
4. Serve and enjoy.

Nutritional Value (Amount per Serving):
Calories 125; Fat 5.1 g; Carbohydrates 4.2 g; Sugar 2.4 g; Protein 16.4 g; Cholesterol 127 mg

White Fish Fillets

Preparation Time: 10 minutes; Cooking Time: 12 minutes; Serve: 2

Ingredients:
- 12 oz white fish fillets
- 1/2 tsp lemon pepper seasoning
- 1/2 tsp garlic powder
- 1/2 tsp onion powder
- Pepper
- Salt

Directions:
1. Preheat the air fryer to 350 F.
2. Spray fish fillets with cooking spray and season with onion powder, lemon pepper seasoning, garlic powder, pepper, and salt.
3. Place fish fillets into the air fryer basket and cook for 12 minutes.
4. Serve and enjoy.

Nutritional Value (Amount per Serving):
Calories 298; Fat 12.8 g; Carbohydrates 1.3 g; Sugar 0.4 g; Protein 41.9 g; Cholesterol 131 mg

Spicy Air Fryer Shrimp

Preparation Time: 10 minutes; Cooking Time: 6 minutes; Serve: 4
Ingredients:
- 1 lb shrimp
- 1 tsp steak seasoning
- 1/4 tsp red pepper flakes
- 2 garlic cloves, minced
- 2 tsp olive oil
- 1 tbsp parsley, chopped
- 2 tsp fresh lemon juice
- 1 tsp lemon zest, grated
- Pepper
- Salt

Directions:
1. Add shrimp and remaining ingredients into the mixing bowl and toss well.
2. Spread shrimp into the air fryer basket and cook at 400 F for 6 minutes.
3. Serve and enjoy.

Nutritional Value (Amount per Serving):
Calories 159; Fat 4.3 g; Carbohydrates 2.5 g; Sugar 0.1 g; Protein 26 g; Cholesterol 239 mg

Paprika Herb Salmon

Preparation Time: 10 minutes; Cooking Time: 5 minutes; Serve: 2
Ingredients:
- 2 salmon fillets
- 1/4 tsp paprika
- 1 tsp herb de Provence
- 1 tbsp butter, melted
- 2 tbsp olive oil
- Pepper
- Salt

Directions:
1. Preheat the air fryer to 390 F.
2. Brush salmon fillets with oil and sprinkle with paprika, herb de Provence, pepper, and salt.
3. Place salmon fillets in the air fryer basket and cook for 5 minutes.
4. Drizzle melted butter over salmon and serve.

Nutritional Value (Amount per Serving):
Calories 413; Fat 31.1 g; Carbohydrates 0.2 g; Sugar 0 g; Protein 35.4 g; Cholesterol 94 mg

Quick Cajun Shrimp

Preparation Time: 10 minutes; Cooking Time: 10 minutes; Serve: 4
Ingredients:
- 1 lb shrimp, deveined & peeled
- 3/4 tbsp Cajun seasoning
- 2 tbsp olive oil
- Salt

Directions:
1. Add shrimp, Cajun seasoning, and oil into the bowl and toss well.
2. Spread shrimp into the air fryer basket and air fry at 350 F for 10 minutes.
3. Serve and enjoy.

Nutritional Value (Amount per Serving):
Calories 195; Fat 8.9 g; Carbohydrates 1.7 g; Sugar 0 g; Protein 25.9 g; Cholesterol 239 mg

Garlic Tomato Shrimp

Preparation Time: 10 minutes; Cooking Time: 25 minutes; Serve: 4
Ingredients:

- 1 lb shrimp, peeled
- 1 tbsp garlic, sliced
- 2 cups grape tomatoes
- 1 tbsp olive oil
- Pepper
- Salt

Directions:
1. Preheat the oven to 400 F.
2. Spray a baking dish with cooking spray and set aside.
3. Add shrimp, oil, garlic, tomatoes, pepper, and salt into the large bowl and toss well.
4. Transfer shrimp mixture into the baking dish and bake for 25 minutes.
5. Serve and enjoy.

Nutritional Value (Amount per Serving):
Calories 184; Fat 5.6 g; Carbohydrates 5.9 g; Sugar 2.4 g; Protein 26.8 g; Cholesterol 239 mg

Easy Salmon Patties

Preparation Time: 10 minutes; Cooking Time: 7 minutes; Serve: 2
Ingredients:
- 1 egg, lightly beaten
- 8 oz salmon fillet, minced
- 1/4 tsp garlic powder
- Pepper
- Salt

Directions:
1. Add all ingredients into the bowl and mix until just combined.
2. Make small patties from the salmon mixture and place it into the air fryer basket.
3. Air fry at 390 F for 7 minutes.
4. Serve and enjoy.

Nutritional Value (Amount per Serving):
Calories 183; Fat 9.2 g; Carbohydrates 0.5 g; Sugar 0.3 g; Protein 24.8 g; Cholesterol 132 mg

Rosemary Garlic Shrimp

Preparation Time: 10 minutes; Cooking Time: 10 minutes; Serve: 4
Ingredients:
- 1 lb shrimp, peeled and deveined
- 1/2 tbsp fresh rosemary, chopped
- 2 garlic cloves, minced
- 1 tbsp olive oil
- Pepper
- Salt

Directions:
1. Preheat the oven to 400 F.
2. Spray a baking dish with cooking spray and set aside.
3. Add shrimp and remaining ingredients in a large bowl and toss well.
4. Pour shrimp mixture into the baking dish and bake for 10 minutes.
5. Serve and enjoy.

Nutritional Value (Amount per Serving):
Calories 167; Fat 5.5 g; Carbohydrates 2.3 g; Sugar 0 g; Protein 25.9 g; Cholesterol 239 mg

Lemon Pepper Fish Fillets

Preparation Time: 10 minutes; Cooking Time: 10 minutes; Serve: 2
Ingredients:
- 2 tilapia fillets
- 1/2 tsp lemon pepper seasoning
- 1/2 tsp garlic powder
- 1/2 tsp onion powder

- Salt

Directions:
1. Preheat the air fryer to 350 F.
2. Spray fish fillets with cooking spray. Season with onion powder, lemon pepper seasoning, and salt.
3. Place fish fillets into the air fryer basket and cook for 10 minutes.
4. Serve and enjoy.

Nutritional Value (Amount per Serving):
Calories 99; Fat 1.1 g; Carbohydrates 1.3 g; Sugar 0.4 g; Protein 21.3 g; Cholesterol 55 mg

Slow Cook Shrimp Scampi

Preparation Time: 10 minutes; Cooking Time: 1 hour 30 minutes; Serve: 4
Ingredients:
- 1 lb raw shrimp, peeled and deveined
- 1 tbsp fresh lemon juice
- 2 tbsp fresh parsley, chopped
- 1 tbsp garlic, minced
- 2 tbsp butter
- 2 tbsp olive oil
- 1/2 cup white cooking wine
- 1/4 cup chicken broth
- Pepper
- Salt

Directions:
1. Add broth, lemon juice, parsley, garlic, butter, olive oil, wine, pepper, and salt into the slow cooker.
2. Add shrimp and stir well.
3. Cover and cook on high for 1 hour 30 minutes.
4. Serve and enjoy.

Nutritional Value (Amount per Serving):
Calories 255; Fat 14.8 g; Carbohydrates 3.1 g; Sugar 0.2 g; Protein 26.4 g; Cholesterol 254 mg

Delicious Crab Cakes

Preparation Time: 10 minutes; Cooking Time: 10 minutes; Serve: 4
Ingredients:
- 8 oz crab meat
- 2 tbsp mayonnaise
- 2 green onion, chopped
- 1/4 cup bell pepper, chopped
- 1 tsp old bay seasoning
- 1 tbsp Dijon mustard
- 2 tbsp almond flour
- Pepper
- Salt

Directions:
1. Preheat the air fryer to 370 F.
2. Add all ingredients into the mixing bowl and mix until just combined.
3. Make four equal shapes of patties from mixture and place into the air fryer basket and cook for 10 minutes.
4. Serve and enjoy.

Nutritional Value (Amount per Serving):
Calories 167; Fat 10.7 g; Carbohydrates 7.1 g; Sugar 1.6 g; Protein 10.6 g; Cholesterol 32 mg

Tuna Chaffle

Preparation Time: 10 minutes; Cooking Time: 8 minutes; Serve: 2

Ingredients:
- 1 egg, lightly beaten
- 1 can tuna, drained
- 1 dill pickle, sliced
- 1 tbsp mayonnaise
- 1/3 cup cheddar cheese, shredded

Directions:
1. Heat waffle maker and lightly grease.
2. Add all ingredients in a bowl and whisk until well combined.
3. Pour half batter in the hot waffle maker and cook for 4 minutes.
4. Serve and enjoy.

Nutritional Value (Amount per Serving):
Calories 305; Fat 18.1 g; Carbohydrates 2.9 g; Sugar 1.1 g; Protein 31.3 g; Cholesterol 131 mg

Tasty Shrimp Fajitas

Preparation Time: 10 minutes; Cooking Time: 22 minutes; Serve: 12

Ingredients:
- 1 lb shrimp
- 1 green bell pepper, diced
- 1 red bell pepper, diced
- 2 tbsp taco seasoning
- 1/2 cup onion, diced
- 1 tbsp olive oil

Directions:
1. Add shrimp and remaining ingredients into the bowl and toss well.
2. Transfer shrimp mixture into the air fryer basket and cook at 390 F for 22 minutes. Stir halfway through.
3. Serve and enjoy.

Nutritional Value (Amount per Serving):
Calories 62; Fat 1.8 g; Carbohydrates 2.1 g; Sugar 0.7 g; Protein 8.8 g; Cholesterol 80 mg

Cajun Scallops

Preparation Time: 10 minutes; Cooking Time: 6 minutes; Serve: 1

Ingredients:
- 4 scallops, rinsed and pat dry
- 1/2 tsp Cajun seasoning
- Pepper
- Salt

Directions:
1. Line air fryer basket with parchment paper.
2. Spray scallops with cooking spray and season with Cajun seasoning, pepper, and salt.
3. Place scallops into the air fryer basket and cook at 400 F for 6 minutes. Turn scallops halfway through.
4. Serve and enjoy.

Nutritional Value (Amount per Serving):
Calories 106; Fat 0.9 g; Carbohydrates 2.9 g; Sugar 0 g; Protein 20.2 g; Cholesterol 40 mg

Flavorful Blackened Shrimp

Preparation Time: 10 minutes; Cooking Time: 6 minutes; Serve: 4

Ingredients:

- 1 lb shrimp, peeled and deveined
- 1 tsp garlic powder
- 1 tsp onion powder
- 2 tbsp olive oil
- 2 tsp paprika
- 1/4 tsp cayenne
- 1 tsp dried oregano
- Pepper
- Salt

Directions:
1. Preheat the air fryer to 400 F.
2. In a large bowl, toss shrimp with remaining ingredients.
3. Transfer shrimp into the air fryer basket and cook for 6 minutes.
4. Serve and enjoy.

Nutritional Value (Amount per Serving):
Calories 204; Fat 9.1 g; Carbohydrates 3.6 g; Sugar 0.5 g; Protein 26.2 g; Cholesterol 239 mg

Blackened Mahi-Mahi Fish Fillets

Preparation Time: 10 minutes; Cooking Time: 12 minutes; Serve: 4
Ingredients:
- 4 Mahi Mahi fillets
- 1/2 tsp cayenne
- 1 tsp oregano
- 1 tsp garlic powder
- 1 tsp cumin
- 1 tsp onion powder
- 1 tsp paprika
- 3 tbsp olive oil
- 1/2 tsp pepper
- 1/2 tsp salt

Directions:
1. Preheat the oven to 450 F. Line baking sheet with foil and set aside.
2. Place fish fillets on the baking sheet and drizzle with oil.
3. In a small bowl, mix together cumin, onion powder, paprika, cayenne, oregano, garlic powder, pepper, and salt.
4. Rub fish fillets with a spice mixture and bake in preheated oven for 10-12 minutes.
5. Serve and enjoy.

Nutritional Value (Amount per Serving):
Calories 189; Fat 11.7 g; Carbohydrates 2.1 g; Sugar 0.5 g; Protein 19.4 g; Cholesterol 86 mg

Tuna Patties

Preparation Time: 10 minutes; Cooking Time: 6 minutes; Serve: 4
Ingredients:
- 1 egg, lightly beaten
- 1/4 cup almond flour
- 8 oz can tuna, drained
- 1 tbsp mustard
- Pepper
- Salt

Directions:
1. Preheat the air fryer to 400 F.
2. Add all ingredients into the large bowl and mix until just combined.
3. Make four equal shapes of patties from mixture and place into the air fryer basket and cook for 6 minutes. Turn patties halfway through.
4. Serve and enjoy.

Nutritional Value (Amount per Serving):
Calories 105; Fat 3.2 g; Carbohydrates 1.5 g; Sugar 0.3 g; Protein 16.9 g; Cholesterol 58 mg

Baked Basa Fillets

Preparation Time: 10 minutes; Cooking Time: 12 minutes; Serve: 4

Ingredients:
- 4 basa fish fillets
- 2 tbsp fresh parsley, chopped
- 1/4 cup green onion, sliced
- 1/2 tsp garlic powder
- 1/4 tsp lemon pepper seasoning
- 4 tbsp fresh lemon juice
- 8 tsp olive oil
- Pepper
- Salt

Directions:
1. Preheat the oven to 425.
2. Place fish fillets in a baking dish.
3. Pour oil and lemon juice over fish fillets. Sprinkle remaining ingredients.
4. Bake for 10-12 minutes.
5. Serve and enjoy.

Nutritional Value (Amount per Serving):
Calories 308; Fat 21.4 g; Carbohydrates 5.4 g; Sugar 3.4 g; Protein 24.1 g; Cholesterol 0 mg

Parmesan Garlic Shrimp

Preparation Time: 10 minutes; Cooking Time: 10 minutes; Serve: 3

Ingredients:
- 1 lb shrimp, peeled and deveined
- 1/4 cup parmesan cheese, grated
- 3 garlic cloves, minced
- 1 tbsp olive oil
- 1/4 tsp oregano
- 1/2 tsp pepper
- 1/2 tsp onion powder
- 1/2 tsp basil

Directions:
1. Preheat the air fryer to 350 F.
2. Add all ingredients into the large bowl and toss well.
3. Line air fryer basket with parchment paper.
4. Add shrimp into the air fryer basket and cook for 10 minutes.
5. Serve and enjoy.

Nutritional Value (Amount per Serving):
Calories 254; Fat 9.1 g; Carbohydrates 4.2 g; Sugar 0.2 g; Protein 37.4 g; Cholesterol 324 mg

Cajun Salmon

Preparation Time: 10 minutes; Cooking Time: 12 minutes; Serve: 4

Ingredients:
- 1 lb salmon fillets
- 1 tsp paprika
- 2 tsp onion powder
- 2 tsp garlic powder
- 2 tsp Cajun seasonings
- 3 tbsp olive oil
- 1/4 cup parsley, minced
- 1 lemon juice
- 1/8 tsp cayenne pepper
- Pepper
- Salt

Directions:
1. Preheat the oven to 475 F.
2. In a small bowl, mix together Cajun seasoning, pepper, garlic powder, onion powder, paprika, cayenne pepper, and salt.

3. Brush fish fillets with oil and rub with spice mixture.
4. Place fish fillets in a baking dish.
5. Pour lemon juice over fish fillets.
6. Bake for 10-12 minutes.
7. Garnish with parsley and serve.

Nutritional Value (Amount per Serving):
Calories 252; Fat 17.6 g; Carbohydrates 2.6 g; Sugar 0.9 g; Protein 22.6 g; Cholesterol 50 mg

Baked Tilapia Fish Fillets

Preparation Time: 10 minutes; Cooking Time: 15 minutes; Serve: 4
Ingredients:
- 1 lb tilapia fillets
- 2 tbsp olive oil
- 2 tbsp dried parsley
- 2 tbsp garlic, minced
- Pepper
- Salt

Directions:
1. Preheat the oven to 400 F. Spray a baking dish with cooking spray and set aside.
2. Place fish fillets baking dish. Drizzle with oil and season with pepper and salt.
3. Sprinkle garlic and parsley over fish fillets and bake for 15 minutes.
4. Serve and enjoy.

Nutritional Value (Amount per Serving):
Calories 160; Fat 8.1 g; Carbohydrates 1.5 g; Sugar 0.1 g; Protein 21.4 g; Cholesterol 55 mg

Baked Halibut

Preparation Time: 10 minutes; Cooking Time: 12 minutes; Serve: 4
Ingredients:
- 1 lb halibut fillets
- 1/4 cup olive oil
- 1/4 tsp garlic powder
- 1/2 tsp paprika
- Pepper
- Salt

Directions:
1. Preheat the oven to 425 F.
2. Place fish fillets in a baking dish.
3. In a small bowl, mix together oil, garlic powder, paprika, pepper, and salt.
4. Brush fish fillets with oil mixture and bake in preheated oven for 10-12 minutes.
5. Serve and enjoy.

Nutritional Value (Amount per Serving):
Calories 270; Fat 15.3 g; Carbohydrates 0.3 g; Sugar 0.1 g; Protein 30.8 g; Cholesterol 53 mg

Grilled Lemon Scallops

Preparation Time: 10 minutes; Cooking Time: 6 minutes; Serve: 4
Ingredients:
- 1 lb jumbo Sea scallops
- 1/2 tsp black pepper
- 1 tsp salt

For dressing:
- 1 tbsp fresh parsley, minced
- 2 tbsp olive oil
- 1/2 tsp black pepper
- 1 fresh lemon juice
- 1/2 tsp red pepper flakes
- 1/2 tsp kosher salt

Directions:
1. Preheat a grill to medium-high heat.
2. In a small bowl, mix together all dressing ingredients and set aside.
3. Season scallops with pepper and salt.
4. Place scallops on a hot grill, covered, and cook for 4 minutes.
5. Flip scallops and cook for 2 minutes more.
6. Transfer scallops to a plate.
7. Pour dressing over scallops.
8. Serve and enjoy.

Nutritional Value (Amount per Serving):
Calories 110; Fat 8.3 g; Carbohydrates 1.5 g; Sugar 0 g; Protein 8.6 g; Cholesterol 40 mg

Baked Swordfish Fillets

Preparation Time: 10 minutes; Cooking Time: 20 minutes; Serve: 2

Ingredients:
- 12 oz swordfish fillets
- 1 garlic clove, minced
- 2 tsp fresh parsley, chopped
- 3 tbsp olive oil
- 1/2 tsp lemon zest, grated
- 1/2 tsp ginger, grated
- 1/8 tsp crushed red pepper

Directions:
1. Preheat the oven to 400 F.
2. In a small bowl, mix together 2 tablespoon oil, lemon zest, red pepper, ginger, garlic, and parsley.
3. Season fish fillets with salt.
4. Heat remaining olive oil in a pan over medium-high heat.
5. Place fish fillets in the pan and cook until lightly browned, about 2-3 minutes.
6. Transfer fish fillets in a baking dish and cook for 8-10 minutes.
7. Pour oil mixture over fish fillets and serve.

Nutritional Value (Amount per Serving):
Calories 449; Fat 29.8 g; Carbohydrates 1.1 g; Sugar 0.1 g; Protein 43.4 g; Cholesterol 85 mg

Lemon Cod

Preparation Time: 10 minutes; Cooking Time: 10 minutes; Serve: 2

Ingredients:
- 1 lb cod fillets, rinsed and pat dry
- 1/8 tsp cayenne pepper
- 1 tbsp fresh lemon juice
- 1 tbsp fresh parsley, chopped
- 1 1/2 tbsp olive oil
- 1/4 tsp salt

Directions:
1. Preheat the oven to 400 F.
2. Place fish fillets in a baking tray.
3. Drizzle with oil and lemon juice and season with cayenne pepper and salt.
4. Bake for 10-12 minutes.
5. Garnish with parsley and serve.

Nutritional Value (Amount per Serving):
Calories 275; Fat 12.6 g; Carbohydrates 0.3 g; Sugar 0.2 g; Protein 40.6 g; Cholesterol 111 mg

Lemon Butter Tilapia

Preparation Time: 10 minutes; Cooking Time: 12 minutes; Serve: 6

Ingredients:
- 1 lb tilapia fillets, cut into 2-inch pieces
- 4 garlic cloves, minced
- 1/4 cup fresh lemon juice
- 3 tbsp fresh parsley, chopped
- 2 tsp dried oregano
- 5 tbsp butter
- Pepper
- Salt

Directions:
1. Melt butter in a pan over medium heat.
2. Add lemon juice and stir well.
3. Add fish pieces into the pan and sprinkle with parsley, oregano, garlic, pepper, and salt and cook for 6 minutes.
4. Flip fish pieces and cook for 6 minutes more.
5. Serve and enjoy.

Nutritional Value (Amount per Serving):
Calories 155; Fat 10.4 g; Carbohydrates 1.3 g; Sugar 0.3 g; Protein 14.5 g; Cholesterol 62 mg

Cajun Catfish Fillets

Preparation Time: 10 minutes; Cooking Time: 15 minutes; Serve: 4

Ingredients:
- 1 lb catfish fillets, cut 1/2-inch thick
- 2 tsp onion powder
- 1 tbsp dried oregano, crushed
- 1/2 tsp ground cumin
- 3/4 tsp chili powder
- 1 tsp crushed red pepper
- Pepper
- Salt

Directions:
1. Preheat the oven to 350 F.
2. In a small bowl, mix together cumin, chili powder, crushed red pepper, onion powder, oregano, pepper, and salt.
3. Rub fish fillets with the spice mixture and place in a baking dish.
4. Bake for 15 minutes.
5. Serve and enjoy.

Nutritional Value (Amount per Serving):
Calories 165; Fat 9 g; Carbohydrates 2.4 g; Sugar 0.6 g; Protein 18 g; Cholesterol 53 mg

Grilled Salmon

Preparation Time: 10 minutes; Cooking Time: 12 minutes; Serve: 4

Ingredients:
- 4 salmon fillets
- 2 tbsp olive oil
- 2 tsp black pepper
- 2 tsp kosher salt

Directions:
1. Heat a grill to high heat.
2. Brush salmon fillets with oil and season with pepper and salt.
3. Place salmon fillets skin side down on the hot grill and cook for 6-8 minutes.
4. Flip salmon fillets, covered, and cook for 2-4 minutes more.

5. Serve and enjoy.

Nutritional Value (Amount per Serving):
Calories 298; Fat 18 g; Carbohydrates 0.7 g; Sugar 0 g; Protein 34.6 g; Cholesterol 78 mg

Lemon Herb Salmon

Preparation Time: 10 minutes; Cooking Time: 10 minutes; Serve: 4

Ingredients:
- 24 oz salmon, cut into 4 pieces
- 2 tbsp lemon juice
- 2 tbsp olive oil
- 1 tsp oregano
- 1 garlic clove, grated
- 1 tbsp yogurt
- 1 tsp lemon zest
- 1/4 tsp pepper
- 1/4 tsp salt

Directions:
1. Preheat the oven to 400 F.
2. Add all ingredients except salmon in a baking dish and mix well.
3. Add salmon and coat well and let it sit for 30 minutes.
4. Bake salmon for 10 minutes.
5. Serve and enjoy.

Nutritional Value (Amount per Serving):
Calories 292; Fat 17.7 g; Carbohydrates 1.1 g; Sugar 0.5 g; Protein 33.4 g; Cholesterol 75 mg

Grilled Mahi Mahi Fish Fillets

Preparation Time: 10 minutes; Cooking Time: 10 minutes; Serve: 3

Ingredients:
- 3 Mahi Mahi fillets
- 1/2 tsp onion powder
- 1/2 tsp garlic powder
- 1 tsp paprika
- 2 tbsp fresh lemon juice
- 1 tsp cumin
- 1 tsp dried oregano
- 1/8 tsp cayenne pepper
- 3 tbsp olive oil
- 1/4 tsp pepper
- 1/2 tsp salt

Directions:
1. Preheat grill to medium-high heat.
2. In a small bowl, mix together spices.
3. Brush fish fillets with oil. Sprinkle with the spice mixture.
4. Grill fish for 4-5 minutes per side.
5. Drizzle with lemon juice and serve.

Nutritional Value (Amount per Serving):
Calories 221; Fat 15.3 g; Carbohydrates 2.1 g; Sugar 0.6 g; Protein 19.4 g; Cholesterol 86 mg

Spicy Grilled Shrimp

Preparation Time: 10 minutes; Cooking Time: 4 minutes; Serve: 6

Ingredients:
- 2 lbs shrimp, peeled and deveined
- 2 tbsp garlic, minced
- 2 tbsp hot sauce
- 4 tbsp fresh parsley, chopped
- 3 tbsp fresh lemon juice
- 1 tbsp chili paste
- 1 tbsp ketchup, sugar-free
- 4 tbsp sesame oil

- 1/3 cup olive oil
- 1 tsp black pepper
- 1 tsp salt

Directions:
1. In a bowl, whisk together olive oil, lemon juice, chili paste, ketchup, garlic, hot sauce, parsley, sesame oil, pepper, and salt.
2. Add shrimp into the zip-lock bag then pour marinade over shrimp.
3. Seal bag, shake well, and place in the freezer for 2 hours.
4. Preheat a grill to high heat.
5. Thread marinated shrimp onto the soaked wooden skewers.
6. Place shrimp skewers on a hot grill and cook for 2 minutes per side.
7. Serve and enjoy.

Nutritional Value (Amount per Serving):
Calories 375; Fat 23 g; Carbohydrates 5 g; Sugar 1.5 g; Protein 35 g; Cholesterol 319 mg

Grilled Cajun Shrimp

Preparation Time: 10 minutes; Cooking Time: 6 minutes; Serve: 4

Ingredients:
- 1 lb shrimp, shelled and deveined
- 2 garlic cloves, chopped
- 2 tbsp butter
- 1 tbsp fresh lemon juice
- 1 tbsp Cajun seasoning

Directions:
1. Melt butter in a pan over medium heat.
2. Add garlic and sauté for a minute. Remove pan from heat.
3. Season shrimp with Cajun seasoning and thread onto the skewers.
4. Heat a grill to medium-high heat.
5. Place skewers on hot grill and cooks for 2-3 minutes per side.
6. Brush shrimp with melted butter mixture and lemon juice.
7. Serve and enjoy.

Nutritional Value (Amount per Serving):
Calories 189; Fat 7.7 g; Carbohydrates 2.3 g; Sugar 0.1 g; Protein 26.1 g; Cholesterol 254 mg

Lemon Garlic Grilled Halibut

Preparation Time: 10 minutes; Cooking Time: 14 minutes; Serve: 4

Ingredients:
- 4 halibut steaks
- 1/2 tsp fresh thyme
- 1/3 cup olive oil
- 1/2 tsp black pepper
- 1/2 tsp Rosemary, chopped
- 2 tbsp fresh lemon juice
- 4 garlic cloves, minced
- 1 tsp sea salt

Directions:
1. In a small bowl, mix together oil, thyme, rosemary, lemon juice, and garlic and set aside.
2. Place halibut steaks into the baking dish.
3. Pour oil mixture on top of halibut steaks and coat well. Cover and place in the refrigerator for 30 minutes.
4. Preheat a grill to medium-high heat.
5. Remove halibut steaks from refrigerator and season with pepper and salt.
6. Place halibut steaks on hot grill and cook for 5-7 minutes.

7. Turn steaks and cook for 5-7 minutes more.
8. Serve and enjoy.

Nutritional Value (Amount per Serving):
Calories 184; Fat 17 g; Carbohydrates 1.5 g; Sugar 0.2 g; Protein 6.1 g; Cholesterol 11 mg

Spicy Tuna Cakes

Preparation Time: 10 minutes; Cooking Time: 10 minutes; Serve: 4

Ingredients:
- 14 oz can tuna, drained
- 1 jalapeno pepper, diced
- 1/4 cup almond flour
- 1/4 cup yogurt
- 1/2 cup fresh cilantro, minced
- 2 tbsp olive oil
- 1/2 tsp ground cumin
- 1/2 tsp garlic powder
- 1/2 lemon juice
- 1 egg, lightly beaten
- Pepper
- Salt

Directions:
1. Add all ingredients except oil into the large bowl and mix until just combined.
2. Heat oil in a pan over medium heat.
3. Make small patties from tuna mixture and place on a hot pan and cook for 5 minutes. Turn patties and cook for 5 minutes more.
4. Serve and enjoy.

Nutritional Value (Amount per Serving):
Calories 217; Fat 10.1 g; Carbohydrates 2.3 g; Sugar 1.6 g; Protein 28.2 g; Cholesterol 72 mg

Greek Tilapia

Preparation Time: 10 minutes; Cooking Time: 17 minutes; Serve: 2

Ingredients:
- 1/2 lb tilapia fillets, remove bones
- 1/3 cup fresh parsley, chopped
- 1 tsp olive oil
- 2 oz feta cheese, crumbled
- 2/3 cup tomatoes, chopped
- 1 1/2 tbsp garlic, minced
- Pepper
- Salt

Directions:
1. Preheat the oven to 400 F.
2. In a medium bowl, mix together tomatoes, garlic, feta, parsley, and olive oil.
3. Spray tilapia fillets with cooking spray and season with pepper and salt.
4. Place tilapia fillets on baking tray and top and with tomato mixture.
5. Bake for 15-17 minutes.
6. Serve and enjoy.

Nutritional Value (Amount per Serving):
Calories 212; Fat 9.6 g; Carbohydrates 6.2 g; Sugar 2.9 g; Protein 26.4 g; Cholesterol 80 mg

Parmesan Cod Fillets

Preparation Time: 10 minutes; Cooking Time: 20 minutes; Serve: 4

Ingredients:
- 1 lb cod, cut into 4 pieces
- 1 tbsp fresh lemon juice
- 1 tsp garlic, minced
- 3/4 cup parmesan cheese, grated
- 4 tbsp butter
- 1 tbsp dried parsley

- 1 tsp dried oregano

Directions:
1. Preheat the oven to 400 F.
2. Add garlic and butter in microwave-safe bowl and microwave until butter is melted. Add lemon juice and stir well.
3. Mix together parmesan cheese, parsley, and oregano in a shallow dish.
4. Dip codpieces into the butter mixture then coat with cheese mixture and place on a parchment-lined baking sheet.
5. Bake for 20 minutes.
6. Serve and enjoy.

Nutritional Value (Amount per Serving):
Calories 285; Fat 16.6 g; Carbohydrates 1.3 g; Sugar 0.1 g; Protein 32.2 g; Cholesterol 106 mg

Greek Baked Salmon

Preparation Time: 10 minutes; Cooking Time: 20 minutes; Serve: 5

Ingredients:
- 1 3/4 lbs salmon fillet
- 1/3 cup artichoke hearts
- 1/4 cup sun-dried tomatoes, drained
- 1/4 cup olives, pitted and chopped
- 1/3 cup basil pesto
- 1 tbsp fresh dill, chopped
- 1/4 cup capers
- 1 tsp paprika
- 1/4 tsp salt

Directions:
1. Preheat the oven to 400 F. Line baking tray with parchment paper.
2. Arrange salmon fillet on a prepared baking tray and sprinkle with paprika and salt.
3. Add remaining ingredients on top of salmon.
4. Bake for 20 minutes.
5. Serve and enjoy.

Nutritional Value (Amount per Serving):
Calories 228; Fat 10.7 g; Carbohydrates 2.6 g; Sugar 0.4 g; Protein 31.6 g; Cholesterol 70 mg

Rosemary Basil Salmon

Preparation Time: 10 minutes; Cooking Time: 15 minutes; Serve: 4

Ingredients:
- 1 lbs salmon, cut into 4 pieces
- 1 tbsp olive oil
- 1/2 tbsp dried rosemary
- 1/4 tsp dried basil
- 1 tbsp dried chives
- Pepper
- Salt

Directions:
1. Place salmon pieces skin side down into the air fryer basket.
2. In a small bowl, mix together olive oil, basil, chives, and rosemary.
3. Brush salmon with oil mixture and air fry at 400 F for 15 minutes.
4. Serve and enjoy.

Nutritional Value (Amount per Serving):
Calories 182; Fat 10.6 g; Carbohydrates 0.3 g; Sugar 0 g; Protein 22 g; Cholesterol 50 mg

Healthy Fish Stew

Preparation Time: 10 minutes; Cooking Time: 35 minutes; Serve: 3

Ingredients:
- 4 cod fillets
- 1 cup of water
- 1 1/2 cups onion, sliced
- 1/8 tsp cayenne
- 1/2 tsp paprika
- 1/4 cup olive oil
- 1/4 tsp pepper
- 1 tsp salt

Directions:
1. Add oil, cayenne, paprika, onion, water, pepper, and salt into the pan and bring to boil over medium-high heat.
2. Turn heat to low and simmer for 10-15 minutes.
3. Add fish fillets and cook for 10-15 minutes or until fish is cooked.
4. Serve and enjoy.

Nutritional Value (Amount per Serving):
Calories 289; Fat 18.3 g; Carbohydrates 5.7 g; Sugar 2.5 g; Protein 27.4 g; Cholesterol 73 mg

Lemon Garlic Baked Shrimp

Preparation Time: 10 minutes; Cooking Time: 13 minutes; Serve: 4

Ingredients:
- 1 1/4 lbs shrimp, peeled and deveined
- 1 tbsp garlic, minced
- 1/4 cup butter
- 2 tbsp fresh parsley, minced
- 1/8 tsp red pepper flakes
- 2 tbsp fresh lemon juice
- Pepper
- Salt

Directions:
1. Preheat the oven to 350 F.
2. Add shrimp in baking dish.
3. Melt butter in a pan over low heat.
4. Add garlic and sauté for 30 seconds.
5. Remove melted butter from heat. Add lemon juice and stir well.
6. Pour butter mixture over shrimp and season shrimp with red pepper flakes, pepper, and salt.
7. Bake for 10-13 minutes.
8. Garnish with parsley and serve.

Nutritional Value (Amount per Serving):
Calories 276; Fat 14 g; Carbohydrates 3.2 g; Sugar 0.2 g; Protein 32.7 g; Cholesterol 329 mg

Garlic Herb Red Snapper Fillet

Preparation Time: 10 minutes; Cooking Time: 15 minutes; Serve: 2

Ingredients:
- 1 lb red snapper fillet
- 1 garlic clove, crushed
- 2 tbsp olive oil
- 3/4 cup white wine
- 2 fresh rosemary sprigs
- 1/4 tsp herb de Provence
- Pepper
- Salt

Directions:
1. Preheat the oven to 400 F. Line baking tray with foil.

2. Season fish fillet with pepper and salt and place on a baking tray.
3. Drizzle oil over fish. Place rosemary, garlic, and herb de Provence on top of fish.
4. Roast in preheated oven for 10 minutes.
5. Slowly pour wine over fish fillet and roast for 5 minutes more.
6. Serve and enjoy.

Nutritional Value (Amount per Serving):
Calories 493; Fat 18.3 g; Carbohydrates 3.7 g; Sugar 0.7 g; Protein 60.3 g; Cholesterol 107 mg

Lemon Paprika Shrimp

Preparation Time: 10 minutes; Cooking Time: 6 minutes; Serve: 4

Ingredients:
- 1 lb shrimp, peeled and deveined
- 1 tsp Spanish paprika
- 1/4 tsp chili flakes
- 1 tbsp garlic, chopped
- 1/3 cup olive oil
- 2 tbsp fresh parsley, chopped
- 2 tbsp fresh lemon juice
- 1 1/2 tbsp dry sherry
- 1/8 tsp pepper
- 1/4 tsp kosher salt

Directions:
1. Heat oil in a pan over medium-high heat.
2. Add chili flakes and garlic and sauté for 1 minute.
3. Add shrimp and season with paprika, pepper, and salt and sauté for 2 minutes or until shrimp turns to pink in color.
4. Add lemon juice and sherry and cook for 2-3 minutes.
5. Garnish with parsley and serve.

Nutritional Value (Amount per Serving):
Calories 311; Fat 19.1 g; Carbohydrates 3.9 g; Sugar 0.2 g; Protein 26.3 g; Cholesterol 239 mg

Nutritious Crab Stew

Preparation Time: 10 minutes; Cooking Time: 13 minutes; Serve: 2

Ingredients:
- 1/2 lb lump crab meat
- 1/2 lb shrimp, shelled and chopped
- 1 celery stalk, chopped
- 1/2 tsp garlic, chopped
- 1/4 onion, chopped
- 2 tbsp heavy cream
- 1 tbsp olive oil
- 2 cups fish stock
- Pepper
- Salt

Directions:
1. Add oil into the instant pot and set the pot on saute mode. Add onion and saute for 3 minutes.
2. Add garlic and saute for 30 seconds. Add remaining ingredients except for heavy cream and stir well.
3. Seal pot and cook on high for 10 minutes.
4. Once done, release pressure using quick release. Remove lid.
5. Stir in heavy cream and serve.

Nutritional Value (Amount per Serving):
Calories 376; Fat 25.5 g; Carbohydrates 5.8 g; Sugar 0.7 g; Protein 48.1 g; Cholesterol 326 mg

Crab Cake Waffles

Preparation Time: 10 minutes; Cooking Time: 6 minutes; Serve: 4
Ingredients:
- 2 eggs, lightly beaten
- 12 oz can wild-caught crab, drained
- 1 tsp olive oil
- 2 tbsp fresh parsley, chopped
- 2 tbsp fresh chives, chopped
- 1/2 cup almond flour
- 1 tbsp paleo mayonnaise
- 1 tbsp lemon juice

Directions:
1. In a bowl, mix together eggs with almond flour, mayo, lemon juice, oil, parsley, chives, and crab until well combined.
2. Heat waffle maker.
3. Divide waffle mixture into the four even patties.
4. Place two patties on the hot waffle maker. Cover and cook for 3 minutes.
5. Serve and enjoy.

Nutritional Value (Amount per Serving):
Calories 186; Fat 8.7 g; Carbohydrates 1.2 g; Sugar 0.4 g; Protein 23.7 g; Cholesterol 178 mg

Baked White Fish Fillets

Preparation Time: 10 minutes; Cooking Time: 30 minutes; Serve: 1
Ingredients:
- 8 oz frozen white fish fillet
- 1/2 tsp Italian seasoning
- 1 1/2 tbsp butter, melted
- 1 tbsp lemon juice
- 1 tbsp fresh parsley, chopped
- 1 tbsp roasted red bell pepper, diced

Directions:
1. Preheat the oven to 400 F. Line baking tray with foil and place fish fillet on a baking tray.
2. Drizzle butter and lemon juice over fish.
3. Sprinkle with Italian seasoning.
4. Top with roasted bell pepper and parsley and bake for 30 minutes.
5. Serve and enjoy.

Nutritional Value (Amount per Serving):
Calories 355; Fat 18.8 g; Carbohydrates 1.3 g; Sugar 0.8 g; Protein 46.8 g; Cholesterol 47 mg

Feta Mint Tuna Patties

Preparation Time: 10 minutes; Cooking Time: 10 minutes; Serve: 6
Ingredients:
- 14 oz can tuna
- 2 tbsp green onions, minced
- 3 tbsp flax meal
- 1/2 cup feta cheese, crumbled
- 1 egg, lightly beaten
- 2 garlic clove, minced
- 3 tbsp olive oil
- 1/2 tsp lemon zest
- 1 tsp dried oregano
- 2 tbsp fresh mint, chopped
- 1 tbsp lemon juice
- Pepper
- Salt

Directions:
1. Add all ingredients except olive oil into the large bowl and mix until just combined.

2. Heat oil in a pan over medium heat.
3. Make small patties from tuna mixture and place it on a hot pan.
4. Cook tuna patties for 5-6 minutes. Turn patties and cook for 3 minutes more.
5. Serve and enjoy.

Nutritional Value (Amount per Serving):
Calories 199; Fat 12.2 g; Carbohydrates 2.3 g; Sugar 0.7 g; Protein 20.5 g; Cholesterol 58 mg

Broiled Tilapia

Preparation Time: 10 minutes; Cooking Time: 5 minutes; Serve: 6
Ingredients:
- 24 oz tilapia fish fillets
- 1/4 tsp cinnamon
- 1/2 tsp paprika
- 1 tsp dry mustard powder
- 1 tbsp olive oil
- 2 lemons, sliced
- 1/8 tsp cayenne pepper
- 1/2 tsp basil
- 1/2 tsp salt

Directions:
1. Line broiler pan with parchment paper and set aside.
2. In a small bowl, mix together all dry spices. Place fish fillets on pan and brush with oil.
3. Sprinkle spice mixture over fish fillets then arrange lemon slices on top of fish fillets.
4. Broil fish fillets for 4-5 minutes.
5. Serve and enjoy.

Nutritional Value (Amount per Serving):
Calories 129; Fat 3.6 g; Carbohydrates 2.2 g; Sugar 0.5 g; Protein 22.4 g; Cholesterol 100 mg

Asian Coconut Shrimp

Preparation Time: 10 minutes; Cooking Time: 10 minutes; Serve: 4
Ingredients:
- 1 lb shrimp, deveined
- 1/2 tsp turmeric
- 1 tbsp garlic, minced
- 1 tbsp ginger, minced
- 1/2 cup unsweetened coconut milk
- 1 tsp garam masala
- 1/2 tsp cayenne pepper
- 1 tsp salt

Directions:
1. Add all ingredients into the saucepan and stir well.
2. Cook shrimp over medium heat until done.
3. Stir well and serve over cauliflower rice.

Nutritional Value (Amount per Serving):
Calories 213; Fat 9.2 g; Carbohydrates 5.3 g; Sugar 1.1 g; Protein 26.8 g; Cholesterol 239 mg

Flavorful Sauteed Shrimp

Preparation Time: 10 minutes; Cooking Time: 5 minutes; Serve: 4
Ingredients:
- 1 lb shrimp
- 1/4 tsp pepper
- 1 tsp Italian seasoning
- 4 tbsp butter
- 1 lemon juice
- 1/2 tsp paprika

- 1/2 tsp salt

Directions:
1. In a bowl, add shrimp, paprika, Italian seasoning, pepper, and salt. Toss well.
2. Melt butter in a pan over medium heat.
3. Add shrimp to the pan and cook for 2-3 minutes on each side.
4. Drizzle lemon juice over shrimp.
5. Serve and enjoy.

Nutritional Value (Amount per Serving):
Calories 244; Fat 13.9 g; Carbohydrates 2.3 g; Sugar 0.4 g; Protein 26.1 g; Cholesterol 270 mg

Delicious Salmon Waffles

Preparation Time: 10 minutes; Cooking Time: 9 minutes; Serve: 5

Ingredients:
- 2 eggs, lightly beaten
- 12 oz can salmon, drained
- 1 tsp olive oil
- 2 tbsp green onion, chopped
- 2 tbsp fresh dill, chopped
- 1/2 cup almond flour
- 1 tbsp paleo mayonnaise
- 1 tbsp fresh lemon juice
- 1/2 tsp salt

Directions:
1. In a bowl, mix together salmon, almond flour, mayo, lemon juice, oil, green onion, dill, eggs, and salt until well combined.
2. Heat waffle maker.
3. Make five even shape patties from the salmon mixture.
4. Place two patties on the hot waffle maker. Cover and cook for 3 minutes.
5. Serve and enjoy.

Nutritional Value (Amount per Serving):
Calories 166; Fat 10.3 g; Carbohydrates 1.7 g; Sugar 0.4 g; Protein 16.6 g; Cholesterol 104 mg

Shrimp Olive Stir Fry

Preparation Time: 10 minutes; Cooking Time: 10 minutes; Serve: 2

Ingredients:
- 1/2 lb shrimp, peeled and deveined
- 1 tbsp garlic, minced
- 1/3 cup olives
- 1 cup mushrooms, sliced
- 2 tbsp olive oil
- 1 cup tomatoes, diced
- 1 small onion, chopped
- Pepper
- Salt

Directions:
1. Heat oil in a pan over high heat.
2. Add onion, mushrooms, and garlic and sauté until onion soften.
3. Add shrimp and tomatoes and stir until shrimp is cooked. Add olives and stir well.
4. Remove pan from heat and set aside for 5 minutes. Season with pepper and salt.
5. Serve and enjoy.

Nutritional Value (Amount per Serving):
Calories 350; Fat 18.8 g; Carbohydrates 10.7 g; Sugar 4.5 g; Protein 38.8 g; Cholesterol 281 mg

Salmon with Baby Carrots

Preparation Time: 10 minutes; Cooking Time: 20 minutes; Serve: 4
Ingredients:
- 2 cups baby carrots
- 1 lb salmon, cut into four pieces
- 2 tbsp olive oil
- Salt

Directions:
1. Preheat the oven to 425 F.
2. Place salmon pieces on the center of the baking sheet.
3. In a bowl, toss together baby carrots and olive oil.
4. Arrange carrot around the salmon and bake for 20 minutes.
5. Season salmon and carrots with salt.
6. Serve and enjoy.

Nutritional Value (Amount per Serving):
Calories 225; Fat 14.1 g; Carbohydrates 3.5 g; Sugar 2 g; Protein 22.3 g; Cholesterol 50 mg

Tomato Lemon Cod Fillets

Preparation Time: 10 minutes; Cooking Time: 5 minutes; Serve: 6
Ingredients:
- 1 1/2 lb cod fillets
- 28 oz can tomatoes, diced
- 3 tbsp olive oil
- 1 tsp oregano
- 1 lemon juice
- 1/2 tsp pepper
- 1 tsp salt

Directions:
1. Add olive oil into the instant pot and set the pot on sauté mode.
2. Add tomatoes, lemon juice, oregano, pepper, and salt and stir for 2 minutes. Add fish fillets and stir well.
3. Seal pot with lid and cook on high for 3 minutes.
4. Once done, release pressure using the quick-release method. Open the lid.
5. Serve and enjoy.

Nutritional Value (Amount per Serving):
Calories 182; Fat 8.1 g; Carbohydrates 7.2 g; Sugar 4.7 g; Protein 21.6 g; Cholesterol 56 mg

Shrimp Soup

Preparation Time: 10 minutes; Cooking Time: 15 minutes; Serve: 8
Ingredients:
- 24 oz shrimp, cooked
- 2 cups mushrooms, sliced
- 8 oz cheddar cheese, shredded
- 1/2 cup butter
- 1 cup heavy whipping cream
- 32 oz fish stock
- Pepper
- Salt

Directions:
1. Add stock and mushrooms to a large pot. Bring to boil over high heat.
2. Turn heat to medium, add cheese, whipping cream, and butter and stir until cheese is melted.
3. Reduce heat and add shrimp. Stir well and cook for 2 minutes more.
4. Serve and enjoy.

Nutritional Value (Amount per Serving):

Calories 377; Fat 28.2 g; Carbohydrates 3 g; Sugar 0.8 g; Protein 27.7 g; Cholesterol 260 mg

Delicious Fish Stew

Preparation Time: 10 minutes; Cooking Time: 15 minutes; Serve: 6

Ingredients:
- 2 lbs white fish fillets
- 1/4 cup green onion, chopped
- 2 red bell peppers, chopped
- 2 tbsp olive oil
- 1/4 tsp red pepper flakes
- 2 cups of water
- 14 oz unsweetened coconut milk
- 14 oz can roasted tomatoes, diced
- 1 tsp salt

Directions:
1. Heat oil in a saucepan over medium heat.
2. Add green onion and bell peppers and cook for 5 minutes.
3. Add fish, water, coconut milk, and tomatoes and cook for 10 minutes.
4. Add red pepper flakes and serve.

Nutritional Value (Amount per Serving):
Calories 510; Fat 44.5 g; Carbohydrates 10.1 g; Sugar 6.1 g; Protein 16.6 g; Cholesterol 0 mg

Pesto Fish Fillets

Preparation Time: 10 minutes; Cooking Time: 10 minutes; Serve: 4

Ingredients:
- 4 tilapia fillets
- 1/4 cup basil pesto
- 1 cup tomatoes, chopped
- 1/2 cup parmesan cheese, grated
- Pepper
- Salt

Directions:
1. Preheat the broiler. Line baking sheet with foil and spray with cooking spray.
2. Arrange fish fillets on a baking sheet and top with parmesan cheese and broil for 10 minutes.
3. Top fish fillets with tomatoes and pesto. Season with pepper and salt.
4. Serve and enjoy.

Nutritional Value (Amount per Serving):
Calories 74; Fat 3 g; Carbohydrates 2.3 g; Sugar 1.2 g; Protein 10 g; Cholesterol 34 mg

Sauteed Lemon Garlic Scallops

Preparation Time: 10 minutes; Cooking Time: 5 minutes; Serve: 2

Ingredients:
- 1 lb frozen bay scallops, thawed, rinsed & pat dry
- 1 tsp garlic, minced
- 2 tbsp olive oil
- 1 tsp parsley, chopped
- 1 tsp lemon juice
- Pepper
- Salt

Directions:
1. Heat oil in a pan over medium heat. Add garlic and sauté for 30 seconds.
2. Add scallops, lemon juice, pepper, and salt, and sauté until scallops turn opaque.
3. Garnish with parsley and serve.

Nutritional Value (Amount per Serving):
Calories 263; Fat 16 g; Carbohydrates 2.6 g; Sugar 0.1 g; Protein 30.1 g; Cholesterol 70 mg

Spicy Garlic Shrimp

Preparation Time: 10 minutes; Cooking Time: 10 minutes; Serve: 2
Ingredients:
- 1 lb shrimp, cooked
- 2 garlic cloves, minced
- 1/2 bell pepper, chopped
- 3 tbsp olive oil
- 1 tsp cumin powder
- 1 tsp chili powder

Directions:
1. Heat oil in a large pan over medium heat.
2. Add shrimp, garlic, bell pepper, cumin powder, and chili powder and sauté until bell pepper is cooked.
3. Serve and enjoy.

Nutritional Value (Amount per Serving):
Calories 417; Fat 25.4 g; Carbohydrates 7.9 g; Sugar 1.6 g; Protein 52.5 g; Cholesterol 478 mg

Lemon Garlic Prawns

Preparation Time: 10 minutes; Cooking Time: 3 minutes; Serve: 2
Ingredients:
- 1/2 lb prawns
- 1 tbsp olive oil
- 1 tbsp garlic, minced
- 1/2 cup fish stock
- 1 tbsp fresh lemon juice
- 1 tbsp lemon zest, grated
- Pepper
- Salt

Directions:
1. Add all ingredients into the instant pot and stir well.
2. Seal pot and cook on high for 3 minutes.
3. Once done, release pressure using quick release. Remove lid.
4. Drain prawns and serve.

Nutritional Value (Amount per Serving):
Calories 215; Fat 9.5 g; Carbohydrates 3.9 g; Sugar 0.4 g; Protein 27.6 g; Cholesterol 239 mg

Chapter 6: Salad Recipes
Southern Chicken Salad
Preparation Time: 10 minutes; Cooking Time: 5 minutes; Serve: 4
Ingredients:
- 3 cups chicken, cooked and shredded
- 1 cup cheddar cheese, shredded
- 8 oz can green chiles, drained and diced
- 1/4 tsp ground cayenne
- 1 tbsp fresh lemon juice
- 2 tbsp sour cream
- 1/2 cup mayonnaise
- 1 garlic clove, minced
- 1 celery rib, diced
- 2 scallions, sliced
- Pepper
- Salt

Directions:
1. In a large mixing bowl, stir together mayonnaise, cayenne, lemon juice, sour cream, and garlic.
2. Add remaining ingredients and mix well.
3. Season salad with pepper and salt.
4. Serve and enjoy.

Nutritional Value (Amount per Serving):
Calories 321; Fat 28 g; Carbohydrates 4 g; Sugar 2.8 g; Protein 33.1 g; Cholesterol 90 mg

Easy Avocado Egg Salad
Preparation Time: 10 minutes; Cooking Time: 5 minutes; Serve: 2
Ingredients:
- 3 hard-boiled eggs, peel and chopped
- 1 tbsp chives, minced
- 1 tbsp fresh lime juice
- 2 tbsp mayonnaise
- 1 avocado, pitted and diced
- Pepper
- Salt

Directions:
1. Add all ingredients into the bowl and mix well.
2. Season salad with pepper and salt.
3. Serve and enjoy.

Nutritional Value (Amount per Serving):
Calories 340; Fat 51.6 g; Carbohydrates 5.2 g; Sugar 2 g; Protein 9.8 g; Cholesterol 246 mg

Keto Italian Salad
Preparation Time: 10 minutes; Cooking Time: 5 minutes; Serve: 8
Ingredients:
For salad:
- 2 romaine hearts, chopped
- 1 tbsp dried basil
- 1 onion, sliced
- 1 cup mild pepper rings
- 1 red bell pepper, sliced into strips
- 1 cucumber, sliced
- 1 package mini pepperoni
- 1 cup parmesan cheese, shredded
- 8 oz mini mozzarella balls
- 1/2 lb provolone, chopped
- 1/2 lb salami, chopped
- 1 tbsp ground black pepper

For dressing:
- 1 tbsp Italian seasoning
- 1/2 tsp garlic powder

- 1/3 cup red wine vinegar
- 1/2 cup olive oil
- 1 tsp salt

Directions:
1. In a small bowl, whisk together all dressing ingredients and set aside.
2. Add all salad ingredients into the large mixing bowl and mix well. Cover and place in the refrigerator for 4 hours.
3. Pour dressing over salad and toss well.
4. Serve and enjoy.

Nutritional Value (Amount per Serving):
Calories 568; Fat 45 g; Carbohydrates 8 g; Sugar 3 g; Protein 28 g; Cholesterol 87 mg

Nutritious Chicken Avocado Salad

Preparation Time: 10 minutes; Cooking Time: 5 minutes; Serve: 6

Ingredients:
- 2 avocados, pitted and diced
- 2 chicken breasts, cooked and chopped
- 2 tbsp fresh parsley, chopped
- 1/2 onion, chopped
- 5 bacon slices, cooked and chopped
- 2 hard-boiled eggs, peeled and chopped
- 2 cups mixed greens
- 2 tbsp fresh lemon juice
- 2 tbsp olive oil
- Pepper
- Salt

Directions:
1. Add avocados, chicken, parsley, onion, bacon, eggs, and mixed greens in a mixing bowl and mix well.
2. For the dressing: In a small bowl, whisk together lemon juice, olive oil, pepper, and salt and pour over salad.
3. Toss well and serve.

Nutritional Value (Amount per Serving):
Calories 255; Fat 17.2 g; Carbohydrates 2.2 g; Sugar 0.6 g; Protein 22.2 g; Cholesterol 115 mg

Delicious Tuna Salad

Preparation Time: 10 minutes; Cooking Time: 5 minutes; Serve: 4

Ingredients:
- 10 oz can tuna, drain well
- 1 tbsp Dijon mustard
- 1/2 cup mayonnaise
- 1/4 tsp black pepper
- 1/2 tbsp fresh dill, chopped
- 2 green onions, chopped
- 1 celery stalk, chopped
- 1 tbsp fresh lemon juice
- 1/2 tsp sea salt

Directions:
1. Add all ingredients into the large mixing bowl and mix until just combined.
2. Stir well and serve immediately.

Nutritional Value (Amount per Serving):
Calories 196; Fat 22.1 g; Carbohydrates 1.9 g; Sugar 0.9 g; Protein 18.9 g; Cholesterol 21 mg

Cucumber Feta Cheese Salad

Preparation Time: 10 minutes; Cooking Time: 5 minutes; Serve: 6

Ingredients:

- 2 cucumbers, chopped
- 1/2 cup feta cheese, crumbled
- 1 tbsp fresh lemon juice
- 1/4 cup olive oil
- 1/4 cup olives, pitted
- 1/4 cup jar pepperoncini peppers
- 1/2 cup onion, chopped
- 1 cup tomatoes, chopped
- Pepper
- Salt

Directions:
1. In a small bowl, mix together lemon juice, olive oil, pepper, and salt.
2. Add cucumber, cheese, olives, pepperoncini peppers, onion, and tomatoes in a mixing bowl and mix well.
3. Pour dressing over salad and toss well.
4. Serve and enjoy.

Nutritional Value (Amount per Serving):
Calories 136; Fat 11.9 g; Carbohydrates 6.8 g; Sugar 3.5 g; Protein 2.9 g; Cholesterol 11 mg

Flavorful Deviled Egg Salad

Preparation Time: 10 minutes; Cooking Time: 5 minutes; Serve: 8
Ingredients:
- 12 hard-boiled eggs, peel and chopped
- 1/4 tsp paprika
- 2 tbsp chives, sliced
- 1 tbsp Dijon mustard
- 1/4 cup onion, diced
- 3/4 cup mayonnaise
- 6 bacon slices, crumbled
- 1/4 tsp pepper
- 1/4 tsp salt

Directions:
1. Add all ingredients into the mixing bowl and mix until just combined.
2. Place salad bowl in the refrigerator until ready to serve.

Nutritional Value (Amount per Serving):
Calories 261; Fat 20 g; Carbohydrates 6.5 g; Sugar 2.1 g; Protein 14 g; Cholesterol 267 mg

Cauliflower Egg Salad

Preparation Time: 10 minutes; Cooking Time: 5 minutes; Serve: 8
Ingredients:
- 10 hard-boiled egg, peeled, remove yolks and chop the white part
- 1 tbsp paprika
- 2 celery stalks, chopped
- 1 cup mayonnaise
- 1/4 cup dill pickle relish
- 1/4 cup mustard
- 5 green onions, chopped
- 10 oz frozen cauliflower florets, cooked
- Pepper
- Salt

Directions:
1. In a medium bowl, add yolks and mash with a fork. Add mayonnaise, mustard, pepper, and salt and mix well. Set aside.
2. In a mixing bowl, mix cauliflower florets, celery, green onions, and egg whites. Add egg yolk mixture and mix well.
3. Sprinkle with paprika and serve.

Nutritional Value (Amount per Serving):
Calories 182; Fat 17.7 g; Carbohydrates 8.1 g; Sugar 4.5 g; Protein 9.5 g; Cholesterol 205 mg

Healthy Mediterranean Salad

Preparation Time: 10 minutes; Cooking Time: 10 minutes; Serve: 6

Ingredients:

For salad:
- 2 cups cucumber, chopped
- 1/2 cup feta cheese, crumbled
- 1/3 cup onion, sliced
- 1 cup artichoke hearts, chopped
- 2 cups grape tomatoes halved

For dressing:
- 1 garlic clove
- 1 tbsp apple cider vinegar
- 2 tbsp sun-dried tomatoes, packed in oil
- 6 tbsp olive oil
- 1/8 tsp black pepper
- 1/4 tsp sea salt

Directions:
1. Add all salad ingredients into the large bowl and mix well.
2. Add all dressing ingredients into the blender and blend until smooth.
3. Pour dressing over salad and toss well.
4. Serve and enjoy.

Nutritional Value (Amount per Serving):
Calories 279; Fat 15.8 g; Carbohydrates 7.8 g; Sugar 2.8 g; Protein 25.6 g; Cholesterol 81 mg

Quick & Easy Greek Salad

Preparation Time: 10 minutes; Cooking Time: 5 minutes; Serve: 4

Ingredients:
- 1 cucumber, chopped
- 1/2 onion, sliced
- 1 green bell pepper, diced
- 1 red bell pepper, diced
- 1 tsp dried oregano
- 1 tbsp red wine vinegar
- 4 tbsp olive oil
- 1/2 cup olives, pitted
- 4 oz feta cheese, diced
- Pepper
- Salt

Directions:
1. Add all ingredients into the bowl and mix well.
2. Season salad with pepper and salt.
3. Serve and enjoy.

Nutritional Value (Amount per Serving):
Calories 225; Fat 20 g; Carbohydrates 6 g; Sugar 5 g; Protein 5 g; Cholesterol 24 mg

Tuna Avocado Salad

Preparation Time: 10 minutes; Cooking Time: 5 minutes; Serve: 6

Ingredients:
- 15 oz can tuna, drained and flaked
- 2 tbsp olive oil
- 2 tbsp fresh lemon juice
- 1/4 cup fresh cilantro, chopped
- 1 small onion, sliced
- 2 avocados, peeled, pitted, and diced
- 1 cucumber, sliced
- Pepper
- Salt

Directions:
1. In a large bowl, mix together cucumber, cilantro, tuna, onion, and avocado.

2. In a small bowl, whisk together olive oil, lemon juice, pepper, and salt and pour over salad.
3. Toss well and serve.

Nutritional Value (Amount per Serving):
Calories 145; Fat 1.1 g; Carbohydrates 3.6 g; Sugar 1.5 g; Protein 18.8 g; Cholesterol 21 mg

Delicious Asian Chicken Salad

Preparation Time: 10 minutes; Cooking Time: 5 minutes; Serve: 8

Ingredients:
For salad:
- 4 cups coleslaw mix
- 2 green onions, sliced
- 1/4 cup almonds, sliced
- 1 cup chicken breasts, cooked and shredded
- 1/2 bell pepper, sliced
- 1 cup red cabbage, shredded

For dressing:
- 1 tsp fresh ginger, grated
- 1 tsp garlic, minced
- 1/2 tbsp sesame oil
- 2 tbsp olive oil
- 2 tbsp rice vinegar
- 1/4 cup coconut aminos

Directions:
1. Add all salad ingredients into the large bowl and mix well.
2. In a small bowl, whisk together all dressing ingredients and pour over salad.
3. Toss well and serve.

Nutritional Value (Amount per Serving):
Calories 118; Fat 7.2 g; Carbohydrates 6.3 g; Sugar 2.4 g; Protein 6.5 g; Cholesterol 16 mg

Shrimp Avocado Salad

Preparation Time: 10 minutes; Cooking Time: 10 minutes; Serve: 6

Ingredients:
- 1 lb shrimp
- 3 bacon slices, cooked and chopped
- 1/4 cup blue cheese, crumbled
- 1 tbsp fresh lemon juice
- 1/2 cup tomatoes, chopped
- 2 1/2 avocados, chopped
- 2 garlic cloves, crushed
- 1 tbsp olive oil
- Pepper
- Salt

Directions:
1. Heat olive oil in a pan over medium heat. Add garlic and saute for a minute.
2. Add shrimp and cook for 5-7 minutes or until shrimp turns to pink in color. Season shrimp with pepper and salt.
3. Remove pan from heat and set aside to cool.
4. Add shrimp and remaining ingredients into the mixing bowl and toss well.
5. Serve and enjoy.

Nutritional Value (Amount per Serving):
Calories 357; Fat 25.6 g; Carbohydrates 9.6 g; Sugar 0.9 g; Protein 23.7 g; Cholesterol 174 mg

Quick Pepperoni Avocado Salad

Preparation Time: 5 minutes; Cooking Time: 5 minutes; Serve: 1

Ingredients:
- 1 oz mozzarella pearls
- 15 pepperoni slices
- 1/2 avocado, cubed
- 1 tbsp fresh lemon juice
- Pepper
- Salt

Directions:
1. Add all ingredients into the medium bowl and toss well.
2. Serve and enjoy.

Nutritional Value (Amount per Serving):
Calories 687; Fat 61.1 g; Carbohydrates 9 g; Sugar 0.8 g; Protein 25.8 g; Cholesterol 112 mg

Flavorful Asian Cucumber Salad

Preparation Time: 10 minutes; Cooking Time: 5 minutes; Serve: 6

Ingredients:
For salad:
- 2 cucumbers, sliced
- 1/4 cup onion, sliced
- 1 carrot, grated

For dressing:
- 1/2 tsp fish sauce
- 1/2 tsp apple cider vinegar
- 1 tsp sesame oil
- 2 tbsp coconut aminos
- 1 garlic clove, minced
- 1 tsp fresh ginger, grated

Directions:
1. Add all salad ingredients into the bowl and mix well.
2. In a small bowl, whisk together all dressing ingredients and pour over salad.
3. Toss well and serve.

Nutritional Value (Amount per Serving):
Calories 35; Fat 0.9 g; Carbohydrates 6.5 g; Sugar 2.4 g; Protein 0.9 g; Cholesterol 0 mg

Tasty Buffalo Chicken Salad

Preparation Time: 10 minutes; Cooking Time: 5 minutes; Serve: 5

Ingredients:
- 3 chicken breasts, boneless, skinless, cooked & shredded
- 1/2 cup sour cream
- 2 tbsp sriracha sauce
- 6 tbsp buffalo sauce
- 4 oz Monterrey jack cheese, diced
- 1/2 cup green onions, diced
- 1/2 cup celery, diced
- Pepper
- Salt

Directions:
1. Add all ingredients into the bowl and mix well.
2. Season salad with pepper and salt.
3. Serve and enjoy.

Nutritional Value (Amount per Serving):
Calories 328; Fat 20.2 g; Carbohydrates 4.4 g; Sugar 0.8 g; Protein 30.1 g; Cholesterol 92 mg

Bacon Broccoli Salad

Preparation Time: 10 minutes; Cooking Time: 5 minutes; Serve: 10

Ingredients:
- 8 cups broccoli florets, chopped

- 1/2 lb bacon, cooked and crumbled
- 2 tbsp apple cider vinegar
- 4 oz cheddar cheese, cubed
- 1/2 cup pumpkin seeds
- 1/4 cup onion, diced
- 3/4 cup mayonnaise
- Pepper
- Salt

Directions:
1. Add all ingredients into the bowl and mix well.
2. Season salad with pepper and salt.
3. Cover salad bowl and place in the refrigerator for 3 hours.
4. Serve and enjoy.

Nutritional Value (Amount per Serving):
Calories 305; Fat 31.3 g; Carbohydrates 7.3 g; Sugar 1.9 g; Protein 15.3 g; Cholesterol 37 mg

Flavors Salmon Salad

Preparation Time: 10 minutes; Cooking Time: 15 minutes; Serve: 4
Ingredients:
- 1 lb salmon fillets
- 1 cup mayonnaise
- 1 onion, chopped
- 4 hard-boiled eggs, peel and diced
- Pepper
- Salt

Directions:
1. Preheat the oven to 425 F. Line baking sheet with parchment paper and set aside.
2. Season salmon fillets with pepper and salt and place on a prepared baking sheet.
3. Bake salmon in preheated oven for 15 minutes. Once done then remove from oven and let it cool completely.
4. Chop salmon into small pieces.
5. Add salmon and remaining ingredients into the large bowl and mix well.
6. Serve and enjoy.

Nutritional Value (Amount per Serving):
Calories 330; Fat 32.7 g; Carbohydrates 3.6 g; Sugar 2 g; Protein 28.2 g; Cholesterol 214 mg

Chipotle Chicken Salad

Preparation Time: 10 minutes; Cooking Time: 5 minutes; Serve: 4
Ingredients:
- 2 cups chicken breast, cooked and diced
- 1 lime juice
- 1/2 tsp apple cider vinegar
- 2 tbsp cilantro, chopped
- 1/3 cup roasted red peppers, diced
- 1 tsp chipotle powder
- 1/2 tsp garlic powder
- 1/2 tsp paprika
- 1 tbsp onion, diced
- 1/4 cup celery, chopped
- 1/2 cup mayonnaise
- 1 1/2 tsp salt

Directions:
1. Add all ingredients into the mixing bowl and mix until just combined.
2. Serve and enjoy.

Nutritional Value (Amount per Serving):
Calories 182; Fat 11.1 g; Carbohydrates 9.7 g; Sugar 3.1 g; Protein 11.2 g; Cholesterol 40 mg

Turkey Salad

Preparation Time: 10 minutes; Cooking Time: 5 minutes; Serve: 1
Ingredients:
- 8 oz turkey meat, cooked and chopped
- 3 tbsp mayonnaise
- 1/4 onion, chopped
- 1 celery stalk, chopped
- 1 bacon slice, cooked and chopped
- Pepper
- Salt

Directions:
1. Add all ingredients into the bowl and mix well.
2. Season salad with pepper and salt.
3. Serve and enjoy.

Nutritional Value (Amount per Serving):
Calories 685; Fat 55.9 g; Carbohydrates 4.5 g; Sugar 2.3 g; Protein 74.6 g; Cholesterol 193 mg

Cauliflower Broccoli Salad

Preparation Time: 10 minutes; Cooking Time: 10 minutes; Serve: 12
Ingredients:
- 3 cups cauliflower florets
- 3 cups broccoli florets
- 1/2 cup pecan pieces
- 8 oz bacon, cooked and crumbled
- 1/2 cup cheddar cheese, shredded
- 1/2 onion, chopped
- 2 tbsp apple cider vinegar
- 1 tbsp Swerve
- 1 cup mayonnaise

Directions:
1. In a large mixing bowl, whisk together mayonnaise, apple cider vinegar, and mayonnaise.
2. Add remaining ingredients to the bowl and mix well.
3. Serve and enjoy.

Nutritional Value (Amount per Serving):
Calories 264; Fat 21.1 g; Carbohydrates 9.5 g; Sugar 2.7 g; Protein 10.3 g; Cholesterol 31 mg

Caprese Chicken Salad

Preparation Time: 10 minutes; Cooking Time: 5 minutes; Serve: 6
Ingredients:
- 3 cups chicken breast, cooked and chopped
- 1 tsp garlic powder
- 1/3 cup fresh basil, chopped
- 1/2 cup mayonnaise
- 1/2 cup onion, chopped
- 1 cup mozzarella, cut into 1/2-inch cubes
- 1 1/2 cups cherry tomatoes, halved
- Pepper
- Salt

Directions:
1. Add all ingredients into the mixing bowl and mix well.
2. Season salad with pepper and salt.
3. Serve and enjoy.

Nutritional Value (Amount per Serving):
Calories 161; Fat 8.7 g; Carbohydrates 7.9 g; Sugar 3 g; Protein 12.7 g; Cholesterol 7.9 mg

Classic Chicken Salad

Preparation Time: 10 minutes; Cooking Time: 5 minutes; Serve: 4
Ingredients:
- 2 cups chicken breast, cooked and chopped
- 1 tsp fresh lemon juice
- 1/4 cup almonds, sliced
- 1/2 cup mayonnaise
- 3 tbsp celery, chopped
- 3 tbsp onion, chopped
- Pepper
- Salt

Directions:
1. Add all ingredients into the bowl and mix well.
2. Season salad with pepper and salt.
3. Serve and enjoy.

Nutritional Value (Amount per Serving):
Calories 218; Fat 9.3 g; Carbohydrates 5.3 g; Sugar 2.2 g; Protein 28.1 g; Cholesterol 32 mg

Lobster Salad

Preparation Time: 10 minutes; Cooking Time: 5 minutes; Serve: 4
Ingredients:
- 2 cups cooked lobster meat, chopped
- 1 tsp tarragon, chopped
- 1/2 cup mayonnaise
- 1 1/2 cups cauliflower florets, cooked
- Pepper
- Salt

Directions:
1. Add all ingredients into the bowl and mix well.
2. Season salad with pepper and salt.
3. Serve salad over lettuce leaves.

Nutritional Value (Amount per Serving):
Calories 189; Fat 10.5 g; Carbohydrates 9.1 g; Sugar 2.8 g; Protein 14.8 g; Cholesterol 113 mg

Healthy Shrimp Salad

Preparation Time: 10 minutes; Cooking Time: 10 minutes; Serve: 2
Ingredients:
For salad:
- 1 lb shrimp, peeled and deveined
- 2 tbsp fresh dill, chopped
- 1 celery stalk, chopped
- 1/4 onion, chopped
- 1 tbsp olive oil
- Pepper
- Salt

For dressing:
- 1 tsp Dijon mustard
- 1 lemon juice
- 1/2 cup mayonnaise

Directions:
1. Preheat the oven to 400 F.
2. Add shrimp, oil, pepper, and salt in a bowl and toss well.
3. Spread shrimp on a baking sheet and bake in preheated oven for 5-6 minutes.
4. In a large mixing bowl, whisk together mayonnaise, lemon juice, and Dijon mustard. Add shrimp, onion, celery, and dill and mix well.

5. Season salad with pepper and salt.
  6. Serve and enjoy.

Nutritional Value (Amount per Serving):
Calories 596; Fat 60.2 g; Carbohydrates 8.8 g; Sugar 2.4 g; Protein 53.7 g; Cholesterol 478 mg

Easy Loaded Cauliflower Salad

Preparation Time: 10 minutes; Cooking Time: 5 minutes; Serve: 6
Ingredients:
- 1 large cauliflower head, cut into florets
- 1/4 cup fresh chives, chopped
- 1 1/2 cups cheddar cheese, shredded
- 1/2 tsp garlic powder
- 1 tbsp lemon juice
- 1/4 cup mayonnaise
- 1/2 cup sour cream
- 6 bacon slices, cooked and chopped
- Pepper
- Salt

Directions:
1. Add cauliflower florets into the boiling water and cook until tender, about 5 minutes. Drain well and let it cool completely.
2. In a mixing bowl, stir together sour cream, garlic powder, lemon juice, and mayonnaise.
3. Add cauliflower florets, bacon, cheese, and chives and mix well.
4. Season salad with pepper and salt.
5. Serve and enjoy.

Nutritional Value (Amount per Serving):
Calories 324; Fat 29.6 g; Carbohydrates 7.1 g; Sugar 2.8 g; Protein 16.9 g; Cholesterol 59 mg

Healthy Greek Salad

Preparation Time: 10 minutes; Cooking Time: 5 minutes; Serve: 4
Ingredients:
For salad:
- 1 avocado, diced
- 1/2 cup olives, pitted
- 7 oz feta cheese, cubed
- 1/2 onion, sliced

For dressing:
- 2 tsp dried oregano
- 1 tsp garlic, minced
- 2 tbsp red wine vinegar
- 1 bell pepper, sliced
- 4 tomatoes, cut into wedges
- 1 large cucumber, sliced

- 1/4 cup olive oil
- 1/4 tsp salt

Directions:
1. Add all salad ingredients into the bowl and mix well.
2. In a small bowl, whisk together all dressing ingredients and pour over salad.
3. Toss well and serve.

Nutritional Value (Amount per Serving):
Calories 414; Fat 35.3 g; Carbohydrates 19.2 g; Sugar 8.9 g; Protein 10.3 g; Cholesterol 44 mg

Healthy Greek Cucumber Salad

Preparation Time: 10 minutes; Cooking Time: 5 minutes; Serve: 6

Ingredients:
- 3 cucumbers, peel and chopped
- 1 tsp dried oregano
- 2 tbsp balsamic vinegar
- 2 tbsp olive oil
- 1/2 onion, chopped
- 1 container feta cheese, crumbled
- 1 can black olives
- 2 cups grape tomatoes, cut into half

Directions:
1. Add all ingredients into the mixing bowl and mix well.
2. Serve and enjoy.

Nutritional Value (Amount per Serving):
Calories 86; Fat 6 g; Carbohydrates 8 g; Sugar 4 g; Protein 2 g; Cholesterol 4 mg

Spinach Egg Bacon Salad

Preparation Time: 10 minutes; Cooking Time: 5 minutes; Serve: 6

Ingredients:
- 4 hard-boiled eggs, peel and chopped
- 4 bacon slices, cooked and crumbled
- 12 cups spinach
- 3 tbsp olive oil
- 1 tbsp Dijon
- 2 tbsp red wine vinegar
- 1 garlic clove, minced
- Pepper
- Salt

Directions:
1. Add spinach, egg, and bacon in a large mixing bowl and mix well.
2. In a small bowl, stir together oil, Dijon, vinegar, and garlic and pour over salad.
3. Season salad with pepper and salt.
4. Serve and enjoy.

Nutritional Value (Amount per Serving):
Calories 189; Fat 15.4 g; Carbohydrates 2.8 g; Sugar 0.5 g; Protein 10.1 g; Cholesterol 2.8 mg

Easy Bacon Ranch Chicken Salad

Preparation Time: 10 minutes; Cooking Time: 5 minutes; Serve: 2

Ingredients:
- 10 oz chicken, cooked and cubed
- 1/4 cup bacon, cooked and crumbled
- 1/4 cup cheddar cheese, shredded
- 1/8 tsp garlic powder
- 1/8 tsp onion powder
- 1/2 tsp parsley
- 1/2 tsp dill
- 1/4 cup sour cream
- 1/4 cup mayonnaise
- Pepper
- Salt

Directions:
1. In a bowl, whisk together mayonnaise, spices, and sour cream.
2. Add remaining ingredients and mix well.
3. Serve and enjoy.

Nutritional Value (Amount per Serving):
Calories 462; Fat 25.8 g; Carbohydrates 8.9 g; Sugar 2.1 g; Protein 46.8 g; Cholesterol 147 mg

Dill Cucumber Salad

Preparation Time: 10 minutes; Cooking Time: 5 minutes; Serve: 4
Ingredients:
- 2 large cucumbers, sliced
- 1 garlic clove, grated
- 2 tbsp fresh dill, chopped
- 1 lemon juice
- 1/4 cup yogurt
- 1/4 cup onion, sliced
- Pepper
- Salt

Directions:
1. Add all ingredients into the bowl and mix well.
2. Season salad with pepper and salt.
3. Serve and enjoy.

Nutritional Value (Amount per Serving):
Calories 26; Fat 0.4 g; Carbohydrates 4.1 g; Sugar 2.1 g; Protein 1.6 g; Cholesterol 1 mg

Nutritious Tuna Salad

Preparation Time: 10 minutes; Cooking Time: 5 minutes; Serve: 1
Ingredients:
- 1 can tuna, drained
- 1/4 lemon zest
- 1 1/2 tsp Dijon mustard
- 2 tbsp feta cheese, crumbled
- 2 cups spinach
- 2 tbsp olive oil

Directions:
1. Add tuna, feta cheese, and spinach into the bowl and mix well.
2. In a small bowl, stir together olive oil, Dijon mustard, and lemon zest and pour over salad.
3. Toss well and serve.

Nutritional Value (Amount per Serving):
Calories 644; Fat 46.9 g; Carbohydrates 4.7 g; Sugar 1.4 g; Protein 52.1 g; Cholesterol 72 mg

Feta Avocado Cucumber Salad

Preparation Time: 10 minutes; Cooking Time: 5 minutes; Serve: 3
Ingredients:
- 1 large cucumber, chopped
- 1 tbsp fresh dill, chopped
- 1/3 cup feta cheese, crumbled
- 1 lemon juice
- 3 avocados, chopped
- Pepper
- Salt

Directions:
1. Add all ingredients into the mixing bowl and mix well.
2. Season salad with pepper and salt.
3. Serve and enjoy.

Nutritional Value (Amount per Serving):
Calories 121; Fat 8.8 g; Carbohydrates 8.2 g; Sugar 2.7 g; Protein 4.4 g; Cholesterol 15 mg

Egg Bacon Salad

Preparation Time: 10 minutes; Cooking Time: 5 minutes; Serve: 6
Ingredients:

- 8 hard-boiled eggs, peel and cut into 8 pieces
- 2 tbsp fresh chives, chopped
- 1/2 cup grape tomatoes, halved
- 1/2 cup blue cheese, crumbled
- 1 avocado, sliced
- 8 bacon slices, cooked and crumbled
- 2 tbsp red wine vinegar
- 3 tbsp yogurt
- 3 tbsp mayonnaise
- Pepper
- Salt

Directions:
1. In a large bowl, mix together eggs, grape tomatoes, cheese, avocado, and bacon.
2. In a small bowl, stir together mayonnaise, vinegar, yogurt, and chives and pour over salad. Toss well.
3. Season salad with pepper and salt.
4. Serve and enjoy.

Nutritional Value (Amount per Serving):
Calories 367; Fat 28.8 g; Carbohydrates 6.9 g; Sugar 2.1 g; Protein 20.5 g; Cholesterol 257 mg

Delicious Antipasto Salad

Preparation Time: 10 minutes; Cooking Time: 10 minutes; Serve: 6
Ingredients:
For salad:
- 1/2 cup olives, sliced
- 1 cup pepperoncini, chopped
- 1 cup cherry tomatoes, halved
- 1 cup artichoke hearts, quartered
- 8 oz mozzarella balls, halved
- 1/2 lb salami
- 2 large romaine hearts, chopped

For dressing:
- 1/2 cup olive oil
- 1/4 tsp red pepper flakes
- 1/2 tsp oregano
- 1 tsp Dijon mustard
- 1/4 cup red wine vinegar
- Pepper
- Salt

Directions:
1. Add all salad ingredients into the large bowl and mix well.
2. In a small bowl, whisk together dressing ingredients and pour over salad.
3. Season salad with pepper and salt.
4. Serve and enjoy.

Nutritional Value (Amount per Serving):
Calories 384; Fat 34.6 g; Carbohydrates 5.3 g; Sugar 1.7 g; Protein 15 g; Cholesterol 54 mg

Cauliflower Shrimp Salad

Preparation Time: 10 minutes; Cooking Time: 10 minutes; Serve: 8
Ingredients:
For salad:
- 5 cups cauliflower florets, cooked
- 1 tbsp fresh dill, chopped
- 1/2 cup can olives, sliced
- 1/3 cup celery, diced
- 1 lb shrimp, cooked

For dressing:
- 1/2 cup mayonnaise
- 1 tsp apple cider vinegar
- 2 tbsp lemon juice
- 1/4 tsp celery seed

- Pepper
- Salt

Directions:
1. Add all salad ingredients into the bowl and mix well.
2. In a small bowl, whisk together all dressing ingredients and pour over salad.
3. Toss well and serve.

Nutritional Value (Amount per Serving):
Calories 153; Fat 6.5 g; Carbohydrates 9.2 g; Sugar 2.6 g; Protein 14.5 g; Cholesterol 123 mg

Cucumber Cabbage Salad

Preparation Time: 10 minutes; Cooking Time: 5 minutes; Serve: 8

Ingredients:
- 1/2 cabbage head, shredded
- 3 tbsp olive oil
- 1/2 lemon juice
- 2 tbsp green onion, chopped
- 2 tbsp fresh dill, chopped
- 2 cucumbers, sliced
- Pepper
- Salt

Directions:
1. Add all ingredients into the bowl and mix well.
2. Season salad with pepper and salt.
3. Serve and enjoy.

Nutritional Value (Amount per Serving):
Calories 71; Fat 5.4 g; Carbohydrates 5.9 g; Sugar 2.8 g; Protein 1.3 g; Cholesterol 0 mg

Zucchini Noodle Salad

Preparation Time: 10 minutes; Cooking Time: 5 minutes; Serve: 8

Ingredients:
For salad:
- 4 zucchini, spiralized
- 1 oz fresh basil, chopped
- 8 oz mozzarella pearls
- 4 oz cherry tomatoes, cut in half

For dressing:
- 1/4 cup olive oil
- 1/4 tsp garlic powder
- 1 tbsp fresh lemon juice
- 3 tbsp red wine vinegar
- Pepper
- Salt

Directions:
1. Add all salad ingredients into the bowl and mix well.
2. In a small bowl, whisk together all dressing ingredients and pour over salad.
3. Toss well and serve.

Nutritional Value (Amount per Serving):
Calories 75; Fat 6.6 g; Carbohydrates 4.1 g; Sugar 2.2 g; Protein 1.5 g; Cholesterol 0 mg

BLT Salad

Preparation Time: 10 minutes; Cooking Time: 5 minutes; Serve: 4

Ingredients:
For salad:
- 1 avocado, peeled, pitted, and sliced
- 1 cup radish sprouts
- 1 green onion, sliced
- 8 bacon slices, cooked and crumbled

- 2 cups cherry tomatoes, halved
- 1 head romaine lettuce, chopped

For dressing:
- 1/4 tsp garlic powder
- 1 tbsp white wine vinegar
- 1 tbsp almond milk
- 1/2 cup mayonnaise
- Pepper
- Salt

Directions:
1. Add all salad ingredients into the bowl and mix well.
2. In a small bowl, whisk together all dressing ingredients and pour over salad.
3. Toss well and serve.

Nutritional Value (Amount per Serving):
Calories 385; Fat 42.9 g; Carbohydrates 9.6 g; Sugar 4.6 g; Protein 16.3 g; Cholesterol 42 mg

Avocado Salmon Salad

Preparation Time: 10 minutes; Cooking Time: 5 minutes; Serve: 2

Ingredients:
- 7 oz smoked salmon
- 1 tbsp fresh lemon juice
- 2 tbsp olive oil
- 2 tbsp cilantro, chopped
- 2 tbsp sunflower seeds
- 1 tsp sesame seeds
- 1 avocado, diced
- 6 oz arugula leaves
- Pepper
- Salt

Directions:
1. Add salmon, cilantro, sunflower seeds, avocado, and arugula leaves into the mixing bowl and toss well.
2. In a small bowl, stir together lemon juice, olive oil, and sesame seeds and pour over salad.
3. Season salad with pepper and salt.
4. Serve and enjoy.

Nutritional Value (Amount per Serving):
Calories 312; Fat 23.7 g; Carbohydrates 5.8 g; Sugar 2 g; Protein 21.8 g; Cholesterol 23 mg

Chapter 7: Snack & Appetizers
Broccoli Nuggets
Preparation Time: 10 minutes; Cooking Time: 20 minutes; Serve: 4
Ingredients:
- 2 cups broccoli florets, cook until soft
- 1/4 cup almond flour
- 1 cup cheddar cheese, shredded
- 2 egg whites
- Pinch of salt

Directions:
1. Preheat the oven to 350 F. Line baking sheet with parchment paper.
2. In a mixing bowl, add broccoli and break broccoli into the small pieces using a masher.
3. Add remaining ingredients and mix until well combined.
4. Drop 20 scoops of broccoli mixture onto the prepared baking sheet and press into a nugget shape.
5. Bake in preheated oven for 20 minutes.
6. Serve and enjoy.

Nutritional Value (Amount per Serving):
Calories 148; Fat 10.4 g; Carbohydrates 3.9 g; Sugar 1.1 g; Protein 10.5 g; Cholesterol 30 mg

Spicy Jalapeno Poppers
Preparation Time: 10 minutes; Cooking Time: 10 minutes; Serve: 20
Ingredients:
- 10 jalapenos, cut in half and remove seeds and ribs
- 4 oz cream cheese, softened
- 4 oz cheddar cheese, shredded
- 4 bacon slices, cook and crumbled

Directions:
1. Preheat the oven to 350 F.
2. In a bowl, mix together cream cheese, cheddar cheese, and bacon.
3. Stuff cheese mixture into each jalapeno half.
4. Arrange jalapeno halves on a baking sheet and bake in preheated oven for 10 minutes.
5. Serve and enjoy.

Nutritional Value (Amount per Serving):
Calories 65; Fat 5.5 g; Carbohydrates 0.7 g; Sugar 0.3 g; Protein 3.3 g; Cholesterol 16 mg

Bacon Cheese Dip
Preparation Time: 5 minutes; Cooking Time: 5 minutes; Serve: 8
Ingredients:
- 2 tbsp bacon, crumbled
- 3 wedges Swiss cheese
- 3 tbsp unsweetened almond milk
- 1/2 cup cottage cheese
- 1/4 tsp salt

Directions:
1. Add all ingredients into the food processor and process until smooth.
2. Serve with fresh vegetables.

Nutritional Value (Amount per Serving):

Calories 201; Fat 14.2 g; Carbohydrates 2.9 g; Sugar 0.6 g; Protein 15.2 g; Cholesterol 45 mg

Roasted Mix Nuts

Preparation Time: 5 minutes; Cooking Time: 20 minutes; Serve: 20
Ingredients:
- 5 cups mixed nuts
- 1 tsp dill
- 1 tsp chives
- 1 tsp fresh parsley
- 1 tsp paprika
- 1 tsp onion powder
- 1 tsp garlic powder
- 1/4 cup olive oil
- 1 tsp salt

Directions:
1. Preheat the oven to 325 F.
2. Add mixed nuts and remaining ingredients into the mixing bowl and mix well.
3. Spread nuts on a parchment-lined baking sheet and bake for 20 minutes. Stir after every 5 minutes.
4. Serve and enjoy.

Nutritional Value (Amount per Serving):
Calories 244; Fat 22.8 g; Carbohydrates 8.3 g; Sugar 1.7 g; Protein 5.7 g; Cholesterol 0 mg

Delicious Avocado Deviled Eggs

Preparation Time: 10 minutes; Cooking Time: 10 minutes; Serve: 12
Ingredients:
- 6 hard-boiled eggs, peeled
- 1 tsp fresh cilantro, chopped
- 1/4 fresh lime juice
- 2 tbsp onion, diced
- 2 tbsp mayonnaise
- 1 avocado, diced
- Pepper
- Salt

Directions:
1. Cut eggs in half lengthwise. Add egg yolks to the mixing bowl and place egg whites onto a serving plate.
2. Add avocado into mixing bowl and mash with egg yolk. Add cilantro, lime juice, onion, mayonnaise, pepper, and salt and mix well.
3. Spoon avocado mixture evenly into the egg white halves.
4. Serve and enjoy.

Nutritional Value (Amount per Serving):
Calories 76; Fat 6.3 g; Carbohydrates 2.5 g; Sugar 0.5 g; Protein 3.1 g; Cholesterol 82 mg

Roasted Pepper Dip

Preparation Time: 5 minutes; Cooking Time: 5 minutes; Serve: 12
Ingredients:
- 12 oz jar roasted red peppers, drained
- 1 tsp xanthan gum
- 1 tbsp tomato paste
- 5 oz coconut cream
- 2/3 cup mayonnaise
- 10 garlic cloves
- 1/2 tsp salt

Directions:
1. Add all ingredients into the food processor and process until red peppers are chopped.

2. Serve and enjoy.

Nutritional Value (Amount per Serving):
Calories 118; Fat 15.5 g; Carbohydrates 6.3 g; Sugar 3.5 g; Protein 0.7 g; Cholesterol 0 mg

Macadamia Hummus

Preparation Time: 10 minutes; Cooking Time: 5 minutes; Serve: 20

Ingredients:
- 1 lb macadamia nuts
- 6 tbsp olive oil
- 1/4 cup hot water
- 1 1/2 tbsp fresh rosemary, chopped
- 1/4 cup fresh lemon juice
- 3 garlic cloves

Directions:
1. Add all ingredients into the food processor and process until smooth.
2. Serve and enjoy.

Nutritional Value (Amount per Serving):
Calories 201; Fat 21.4 g; Carbohydrates 3.5 g; Sugar 1.1 g; Protein 1.9 g; Cholesterol 0 mg

Flavors Chive Dip

Preparation Time: 5 minutes; Cooking Time: 5 minutes; Serve: 10

Ingredients:
- 1 cup chives
- 1/2 cup unsweetened almond milk
- 1 cup mayonnaise
- 1 cup yogurt
- 1 tsp salt

Directions:
1. Add all ingredients into the blender and blend until smooth.
2. Serve and enjoy.

Nutritional Value (Amount per Serving):
Calories 113; Fat 8.4 g; Carbohydrates 7.7 g; Sugar 3.3 g; Protein 1.8 g; Cholesterol 8 mg

Chicken Nuggets

Preparation Time: 5 minutes; Cooking Time: 25 minutes; Serve: 4

Ingredients:
- 1 1/2 lbs chicken breast, boneless & cut into chunks
- 1/4 cup parmesan cheese, shredded
- 1/4 cup mayonnaise
- 1/2 tsp garlic powder
- 1/4 tsp salt

Directions:
1. In a bowl, mix together mayonnaise, cheese, garlic powder, and salt.
2. Add chicken and mix until well coated. Arrange coated chicken in air fryer basket and air fry at 400 F for 25 minutes.
3. Serve and enjoy.

Nutritional Value (Amount per Serving):
Calories 272; Fat 10.5 g; Carbohydrates 4 g; Sugar 1 g; Protein 38.3 g; Cholesterol 117 mg

Turkey Meatballs

Preparation Time: 5 minutes; Cooking Time: 18 minutes; Serve: 6

Ingredients:
- 2 eggs, lightly beaten
- 1 lb ground turkey
- 1 tbsp basil, chopped
- 1/3 cup coconut flour
- 2 cups zucchini, grated
- 1 tsp dried oregano
- 1 tsp cumin
- 1 tbsp dried onion flakes
- 1 tbsp garlic, minced
- 1 tbsp nutritional yeast
- Pepper
- Salt

Directions:
1. Preheat the oven to 400 F.
2. Add all ingredients into the mixing bowl and mix until well combined.
3. Make small balls from meat mixture and place on a parchment-lined baking sheet.
4. Bake for 18 minutes.
5. Serve and enjoy.

Nutritional Value (Amount per Serving):
Calories 191; Fat 10.2 g; Carbohydrates 4.1 g; Sugar 1.2 g; Protein 24.1 g; Cholesterol 132 mg

Cilantro Lime Dip

Preparation Time: 5 minutes; Cooking Time: 5 minutes; Serve: 4

Ingredients:
- 1/2 cup sour cream
- 1/2 cup mayonnaise
- 1 tbsp cilantro lime pesto
- 2 oz olive oil
- 1 lime zest
- 1 oz lime juice
- 2 garlic cloves
- 1 cup fresh cilantro
- 1/4 tsp salt

Directions:
1. Add all ingredients into the food processor and process until smooth.
2. Serve and enjoy.

Nutritional Value (Amount per Serving):
Calories 274; Fat 39.9 g; Carbohydrates 4.7 g; Sugar 1.3 g; Protein 1.5 g; Cholesterol 5 mg

Meatballs

Preparation Time: 10 minutes; Cooking Time: 25 minutes; Serve: 4

Ingredients:
- 1 lb ground chicken
- 1 poblano chili pepper, minced
- 1/2 cup cilantro, chopped
- 1 jalapeno pepper, minced
- 1 habanero pepper, minced
- Salt

Directions:
1. Preheat the air fryer to 400 F.
2. Add all ingredients into the large bowl and mix until well combined.
3. Make small balls from meat mixture and place it into the air fryer basket and cook for 25 minutes.
4. Serve and enjoy.

Nutritional Value (Amount per Serving):
Calories 261; Fat 9 g; Carbohydrates 7 g; Sugar 2 g; Protein 36.1 g; Cholesterol 107 mg

Mediterranean Dip

Preparation Time: 5 minutes; Cooking Time: 5 minutes; Serve: 16

Ingredients:
- 16 oz cream cheese
- 2 tbsp fresh basil
- 1/2 cup sun-dried tomatoes
- 1 cup marinated artichoke hearts
- 1 cup kalamata olives
- 1 cup black olives

Directions:
1. Add cream cheese into the food processor and process until smooth.
2. Add olives, sun-dried tomatoes, basil, and artichokes and process until coarsely chopped.
3. Serve and enjoy.

Nutritional Value (Amount per Serving):
Calories 125; Fat 12.1 g; Carbohydrates 2.2 g; Sugar 0.3 g; Protein 2.4 g; Cholesterol 31 mg

Spicy Walnuts

Preparation Time: 5 minutes; Cooking Time: 5 minutes; Serve: 6

Ingredients:
- 2 cups walnuts
- 1/4 tsp chili powder
- 1 tsp olive oil
- Pepper
- Salt

Directions:
1. Add walnuts, chili powder, oil, pepper, and salt into the bowl and toss well.
2. Add walnuts into the air fryer basket and cook at 320 F for 5 minutes.
3. Serve and enjoy.

Nutritional Value (Amount per Serving):
Calories 265; Fat 25.4 g; Carbohydrates 4.2 g; Sugar 0.5 g; Protein 10 g; Cholesterol 0 mg

Herb Mushrooms

Preparation Time: 5 minutes; Cooking Time: 14 minutes; Serve: 4

Ingredients:
- 1 lb mushroom caps
- 1/2 tsp ground coriander
- 1 tsp rosemary, chopped
- 1 tbsp basil, minced
- 1 garlic clove, minced
- 1/2 tbsp vinegar
- Pepper
- Salt

Directions:
1. Add all ingredients into the bowl and toss well.
2. Add mushroom mixture into the air fryer basket and cook at 350 F for 14 minutes. Shake basket halfway through.
3. Serve and enjoy.

Nutritional Value (Amount per Serving):
Calories 27; Fat 0.4 g; Carbohydrates 4.2 g; Sugar 2 g; Protein 3.6 g; Cholesterol 0 mg

Spicy Brussels Sprouts

Preparation Time: 5 minutes; Cooking Time: 35 minutes; Serve: 6

Ingredients:
- 2 cups Brussels sprouts, halved
- 1/4 tsp cayenne pepper
- 1/4 tsp garlic powder
- 1/4 cup olive oil
- 1/4 tsp salt

Directions:

1. Preheat the oven to 400 F.
2. Add all ingredients into the large bowl and toss well.
3. Transfer Brussels sprouts on a baking sheet and roast for 30-35 minutes. Stir halfway through.
4. Serve and enjoy.

Nutritional Value (Amount per Serving):
Calories 85; Fat 8.5 g; Carbohydrates 2.8 g; Sugar 0.7 g; Protein 1 g; Cholesterol 0 mg

Air Fryer Tofu

Preparation Time: 5 minutes; Cooking Time: 15 minutes; Serve: 4
Ingredients:
- 16 oz extra firm tofu, cut into bite-sized pieces
- 1 tbsp olive oil
- 2 tbsp soy sauce
- 1 garlic clove, minced

Directions:
1. Add tofu, garlic, oil, and soy sauce in a bowl and toss well. Marinate tofu for 15 minutes.
2. Arrange tofu pieces in the air fryer basket and air fry at 370 F for 15 minutes.
3. Serve and enjoy.

Nutritional Value (Amount per Serving):
Calories 115; Fat 8.2 g; Carbohydrates 2.8 g; Sugar 0.8 g; Protein 98 g; Cholesterol 0 mg

Cauliflower Bites

Preparation Time: 5 minutes; Cooking Time: 15 minutes; Serve: 4
Ingredients:
- 1 lb cauliflower florets
- 1 1/2 tsp garlic powder
- 1 tbsp olive oil
- 1 tsp sesame seeds
- 1 tsp ground coriander
- 1/2 tsp dried rosemary
- Pepper
- Salt

Directions:
1. Add cauliflower florets and remaining ingredients into the bowl and toss well and spread on the baking sheet.
2. Bake at 400 F for 15 minutes.
3. Serve and enjoy.

Nutritional Value (Amount per Serving):
Calories 67; Fat 4 g; Carbohydrates 7.1 g; Sugar 3 g; Protein 2.6 g; Cholesterol 0 mg

Crab Dip

Preparation Time: 5 minutes; Cooking Time: 7 minutes; Serve: 4
Ingredients:
- 1 cup crabmeat
- 1/2 cup green onion, sliced
- 2 cups cheese, grated
- 1/4 cup mayonnaise
- 2 tbsp parsley, chopped
- 2 tbsp fresh lemon juice
- 2 tbsp hot sauce
- 1/4 tsp pepper
- 1/2 tsp salt

Directions:
1. In a 6-inch dish, mix together crabmeat, hot sauce, cheese, mayo, pepper, and salt.
2. Place dish in the air fryer basket and cook at 400 F for 7 minutes.

3. Remove dish from air fryer.
4. Drizzle dip with lemon juice.
5. Garnish with parsley and serve.

Nutritional Value (Amount per Serving):
Calories 313; Fat 23.9 g; Carbohydrates 8.8 g; Sugar 3.1 g; Protein 16.2 g; Cholesterol 67 mg

Meatballs

Preparation Time: 10 minutes; Cooking Time: 25 minutes; Serve: 4
Ingredients:
- 1 egg, lightly beaten
- 1 lb ground chicken
- 1/4 cup shallots, chopped
- 2 garlic cloves, minced
- 1/2 cup parmesan cheese, grated
- 1/2 cup almond flour
- 2 tbsp cilantro, chopped
- 1 tbsp olive oil
- 1/2 tsp red pepper flakes
- Pepper
- Salt

Directions:
1. Preheat the oven to 400 F.
2. Add all ingredients into the large bowl and mix until well combined.
3. Make small balls from meat mixture and place them on parchment-lined baking sheet.
4. Bake for meatballs for 15 minutes.
5. Turn meatballs and bake for 10 minutes more.
6. Serve and enjoy.

Nutritional Value (Amount per Serving):
Calories 365; Fat 16.5 g; Carbohydrates 12.6 g; Sugar 1 g; Protein 40.4 g; Cholesterol 151 mg

Broccoli Fritters

Preparation Time: 5 minutes; Cooking Time: 30 minutes; Serve: 4
Ingredients:
- 2 eggs, lightly beaten
- 2 garlic cloves, minced
- 3 cups broccoli florets, steam & chopped
- 2 cups cheddar cheese, shredded
- 1/4 cup almond flour
- Pepper
- Salt

Directions:
1. Preheat the oven to 375 F.
2. Add all ingredients into the large bowl and mix until well combined.
3. Make patties from broccoli mixture and place on a parchment-lined baking sheet and bake for 15 minutes.
4. Turn patties and bake for 15 minutes more.
5. Serve and enjoy.

Nutritional Value (Amount per Serving):
Calories 295; Fat 22 g; Carbohydrates 6.3 g; Sugar 1.7 g; Protein 19.2 g; Cholesterol 141 mg

Vegan Queso

Preparation Time: 5 minutes; Cooking Time: 5 minutes; Serve: 12
Ingredients:

- 1 cup cashews
- 4.5 oz can green chilies, diced
- 3/4 cup unsweetened almond milk
- 1/4 tsp red pepper flakes
- 2 tbsp nutritional yeast
- Salt

Directions:
1. Add all ingredients into the blender and blend until smooth.
2. Serve and enjoy.

Nutritional Value (Amount per Serving):
Calories 76; Fat 5.6 g; Carbohydrates 5.1 g; Sugar 0.6 g; Protein 2.7 g; Cholesterol 68 mg

Kale Spread

Preparation Time: 5 minutes; Cooking Time: 10 minutes; Serve: 10

Ingredients:
- 6 cups kale, chopped
- 1/2 cup hemp hearts
- 1/2 cup extra-virgin olive oil
- 1 tbsp olive oil
- 1 1/4 tsp sea salt
- 1/2 cup green onions
- 3 tbsp apple cider vinegar

Directions:
1. Heat 1 tablespoon of olive oil in a pan over low heat. Add kale and sauté for 5-7 minutes.
2. Transfer kale into a food processor along with remaining ingredients and process until smooth.
3. Serve and enjoy.

Nutritional Value (Amount per Serving):
Calories 116; Fat 10.6 g; Carbohydrates 4.8 g; Sugar 0.2 g; Protein 1.7 g; Cholesterol 0 mg

Spicy Cucumber Salsa

Preparation Time: 10 minutes; Cooking Time: 5 minutes; Serve: 18

Ingredients:
- 2 1/2 cups cucumbers, chopped
- 1 garlic clove, minced
- 1/2 onion, chopped
- 4 jalapeno peppers, chopped
- 2 tomatoes, chopped
- 2 tsp fresh cilantro, chopped
- 2 tsp fresh parsley, chopped
- 2 tbsp fresh lime juice
- 1/2 tsp salt

Directions:
1. Add all ingredients into the bowl and mix well.
2. Serve and enjoy.

Nutritional Value (Amount per Serving):
Calories 9; Fat 0.1 g; Carbohydrates 2.1 g; Sugar 0.9 g; Protein 0.3 g; Cholesterol 0 mg

Guacamole

Preparation Time: 5 minutes; Cooking Time: 5 minutes; Serve: 8

Ingredients:
- 3 medium avocados
- 1 tbsp fresh cilantro, chopped
- 1 tbsp jalapeno pepper, minced
- 3 tbsp fresh lime juice
- 1 tsp garlic, minced
- 1/4 cup onion, diced
- 1/2 cup tomato, diced
- 1/2 tsp sea salt

Directions:

1. Scoop out flesh from avocados and place them into the bowl.
2. Mash avocado flesh until smooth. Add remaining ingredients and mix well.
3. Serve and enjoy.

Nutritional Value (Amount per Serving):
Calories 31; Fat 1.9 g; Carbohydrates 3.5 g; Sugar 0.8 g; Protein 0.6 g; Cholesterol 0 mg

Rosemary Parmesan Tomatoes

Preparation Time: 10 minutes; Cooking Time: 20 minutes; Serve: 6

Ingredients:
- 9 tomatoes, halved
- 1 tbsp dried rosemary
- 2 tbsp olive oil
- 1 cup parmesan cheese, grated
- 1/2 tsp ground black pepper
- 1/4 tsp onion powder
- 5 garlic cloves, minced
- 1 tsp kosher salt

Directions:
1. Heat a grill to medium-low heat.
2. Place tomatoes halves, cut side down, onto the grill and cook for 5-7 minutes.
3. Heat olive oil in a pan over medium heat.
4. Add garlic, rosemary, black pepper, onion powder, and salt and cook for 3-5 minutes. Remove from heat and set aside.
5. Flip each tomato half and brush with olive oil garlic mixture and top with grated parmesan cheese. Close grill and cook for 7-10 minutes more until cheese is melted.
6. Remove tomatoes from the grill and serve hot.

Nutritional Value (Amount per Serving):
Calories 180; Fat 11 g; Carbohydrates 8 g; Sugar 5 g; Protein 10 g; Cholesterol 20 mg

Zucchini Fritters

Preparation Time: 5 minutes; Cooking Time: 8 minutes; Serve: 4

Ingredients:
- 2 medium zucchini, grated and squeezed
- 1/4 cup coconut flour
- 3 cups cauliflower rice
- 1 tbsp olive oil
- 1/2 tsp sea salt

Directions:
1. Add all ingredients except oil into the bowl and mix until well combined.
2. Heat oil in a pan over medium heat.
3. Make small patties from mixture and place on the hot pan and cook for 3-4 minutes on each side.
4. Serve and enjoy.

Nutritional Value (Amount per Serving):
Calories 91; Fat 5.2 g; Carbohydrates 8.8 g; Sugar 4.8 g; Protein 4.3 g; Cholesterol 0 mg

Cauliflower Hummus

Preparation Time: 5 minutes; Cooking Time: 35 minutes; Serve: 8

Ingredients:
- 1 cauliflower head, cut into florets
- 3 tbsp olive oil
- 1/2 tsp ground cumin
- 1 tsp garlic, chopped
- 2 tbsp fresh lemon juice
- 1/3 cup tahini
- Pepper
- Salt

Directions:
1. Preheat the oven to 400 F. Line baking sheet with parchment paper and set aside.
2. Spread cauliflower onto the baking sheet and roast for 30-35 minutes. Stir halfway through.
3. Transfer roasted cauliflower into the food processor along with remaining ingredients and process until smooth.
4. Serve and enjoy.

Nutritional Value (Amount per Serving):
Calories 115; Fat 10.7 g; Carbohydrates 4.2 g; Sugar 0.9 g; Protein 2.4 g; Cholesterol 0 mg

Healthy Carrot Fries

Preparation Time: 5 minutes; Cooking Time: 25 minutes; Serve: 4

Ingredients:
- 4 medium carrots, peel and cut into fries shape
- 1 1/2 tbsp olive oil
- 1 tsp cumin powder
- 1/2 tbsp paprika
- 1/2 tsp salt

Directions:
1. Preheat the oven to 450 F.
2. Add carrots, cumin powder, paprika, oil, and salt into the bowl and toss well.
3. Transfer carrot fries on a baking sheet and bake for 10 minutes.
4. Turn carrot fries and bake for 15 minutes more.
5. Serve and enjoy.

Nutritional Value (Amount per Serving):
Calories 75; Fat 5.5 g; Carbohydrates 6.7 g; Sugar 0.5 g; Protein 3.1 g; Cholesterol 0 mg

Chicken Jalapeno Poppers

Preparation Time: 10 minutes; Cooking Time: 20 minutes; Serve: 12

Ingredients:
- 1/2 cup chicken, cooked and shredded
- 4 oz cream cheese
- 1/4 tsp dried oregano
- 1/4 tsp dried basil
- 6 jalapenos, halved and seed removed
- 1/4 cup green onion, sliced
- 1/4 cup Monterey jack cheese, shredded
- 1/4 tsp garlic powder
- 1/4 tsp salt

Directions:
1. Preheat the air fryer to 370 F. Spray air fryer basket with cooking spray.
2. Mix all ingredients in a bowl except jalapenos.
3. Spoon 1 tablespoon mixture into each jalapeno half and place it into the air fryer basket and cook for 20 minutes.
4. Serve and enjoy.

Nutritional Value (Amount per Serving):
Calories 54; Fat 4.2 g; Carbohydrates 0.9 g; Sugar 0.3 g; Protein 3.1 g; Cholesterol 17 mg

Jalapeno Poppers

Preparation Time: 10 minutes; Cooking Time: 13 minutes; Serve: 5

Ingredients:
- 5 jalapeno peppers, slice in half and deseeded
- 1/4 tsp chili powder
- 1/2 tsp garlic, minced
- 2 tbsp salsa
- 4 oz goat cheese, crumbled
- Pepper
- Salt

Directions:
1. In a small bowl, mix together cheese, salsa, chili powder, garlic, pepper, and salt.
2. Spoon cheese mixture into each jalapeno halves and place in air fryer basket and air fry at 350 F for 13 minutes.
3. Serve and enjoy.

Nutritional Value (Amount per Serving):
Calories 111; Fat 8.3 g; Carbohydrates 2.1 g; Sugar 1.2 g; Protein 7.3 g; Cholesterol 24 mg

Cajun Broccoli Fritters

Preparation Time: 10 minutes; Cooking Time: 10 minutes; Serve: 4

Ingredients:
- 2 eggs, lightly beaten
- 8 oz broccoli florets, chopped
- 1 tbsp olive oil
- 1 cup cheddar cheese, shredded
- 1/2 tsp Cajun seasoning
- 2 tbsp almond flour

Directions:
1. Add all ingredients except oil in a large bowl and mix until well combined.
2. Heat oil in a pan over medium heat. Make patties from mixture and place on a hot pan.
3. Cook patties until lightly browned, about 2-3 minutes on each side.
4. Serve and enjoy.

Nutritional Value (Amount per Serving):
Calories 275; Fat 22.2 g; Carbohydrates 7.3 g; Sugar 1.8 g; Protein 14.4 g; Cholesterol 112 mg

Toasted Pecans

Preparation Time: 5 minutes; Cooking Time: 45 minutes; Serve: 16

Ingredients:
- 4 cups raw pecans
- 1/2 cup butter, melted
- 2 tsp kosher salt

Directions:
1. Preheat the oven to 275 F.
2. Toss pecans with melted butter and spread on a parchment-lined baking sheet.
3. Toast pecans for 45 minutes. Stir after every 15 minutes.
4. Season with salt and serve.

Nutritional Value (Amount per Serving):
Calories 251; Fat 24 g; Carbohydrates 4 g; Sugar 1 g; Protein 2 g; Cholesterol 15 mg

Ranch Dip

Preparation Time: 5 minutes; Cooking Time: 5 minutes; Serve: 8

Ingredients:
- 1 1/2 tbsp ranch seasoning
- 1 cup mayonnaise
- 1/2 cup sour cream

Directions:

1. Add all ingredients in a bowl and mix until well combined.
2. Place in refrigerator for 15 minutes.
3. Serve with fresh vegetables.

Nutritional Value (Amount per Serving):
Calories 151; Fat 12.8 g; Carbohydrates 7.6 g; Sugar 1.9 g; Protein 0.7 g; Cholesterol 14 mg

Tasty Cauliflower Hummus

Preparation Time: 10 minutes; Cooking Time: 15 minutes; Serve: 6
Ingredients:
- 3 cups cauliflower florets
- 1 1/2 tbsp tahini paste
- 2 garlic cloves, crushed
- 3 tbsp fresh lemon juice
- 2 tbsp avocado oil
- 2 tbsp water
- 3 tbsp olive oil
- 1/2 tsp salt

Directions:
1. In a microwave-safe dish mix together cauliflower florets, garlic cloves, avocado oil, water, and salt, and microwave for 15 minutes.
2. Transfer cauliflower mixture into the blender and blend until smooth.
3. Add remaining ingredients and blend until smooth.
4. Serve and enjoy.

Nutritional Value (Amount per Serving):
Calories 104; Fat 9.7 g; Carbohydrates 4.2 g; Sugar 1.4 g; Protein 1.8 g; Cholesterol 0 mg

Feta Jalapeno Poppers

Preparation Time: 10 minutes; Cooking Time: 20 minutes; Serve: 24
Ingredients:
- 12 jalapeno peppers, cut in half and remove seeds
- 1/4 tsp garlic powder
- 1/2 tsp onion powder
- 1/4 cup cilantro, chopped
- 4 oz cheddar cheese, shredded
- 4 oz cream cheese
- 2 oz feta cheese

Directions:
1. Preheat the oven to 425 F.
2. Add all ingredients except jalapeno peppers into the bowl and mix well to combine.
3. Stuff cheese mixture into each jalapeno half and place it on a baking sheet.
4. Bake for 20 minutes.
5. Serve and enjoy.

Nutritional Value (Amount per Serving):
Calories 45; Fat 3.8 g; Carbohydrates 0.9 g; Sugar 0.4 g; Protein 2 g; Cholesterol 12 mg

Tasty Spicy Almonds

Preparation Time: 10 minutes; Cooking Time: 20 minutes; Serve: 6
Ingredients:
- 1 1/2 cups raw almonds
- 1/2 tsp garlic powder
- 1/2 tsp cumin
- 1 1/2 tsp chili powder
- 2 tsp Worcestershire sauce
- 1/2 tsp ground cayenne
- 1/4 tsp onion powder
- 1/4 tsp dried basil
- 2 tbsp butter, melted
- 1/2 tsp sea salt

Directions:

1. Preheat the oven to 350 F.
2. In a large bowl, whisk melted butter, cayenne, onion powder, basil, garlic powder, cumin, chili powder, and Worcestershire sauce.
3. Add almonds and toss to coat. Spread almonds on a parchment-lined baking sheet.
4. Bake for 18-20 minutes. Stir 2-3 times.
5. Season with salt and serve.

Nutritional Value (Amount per Serving):
Calories 177; Fat 15 g; Carbohydrates 6 g; Sugar 1.5 g; Protein 5.2 g; Cholesterol 10 mg

Cauliflower Skewers

Preparation Time: 10 minutes; Cooking Time: 14 minutes; Serve: 6

Ingredients:
- 1 large cauliflower head, cut into florets
- 1/4 cup olive oil
- 1/2 tsp garlic powder
- 1/2 tsp ground ginger
- 1 onion, cut into wedges
- 1 yellow bell pepper, cut into squares
- 1 fresh lemon juice
- 3 tsp curry powder
- 1/2 tsp salt

Directions:
1. In a large bowl, whisk together oil, lemon juice, garlic, ginger, curry powder, and salt.
2. Add cauliflower florets and toss until well coated.
3. Heat the grill to medium heat.
4. Thread cauliflower florets, onion, and bell pepper onto the skewers.
5. Place skewers onto the hot grill and cooks for 6-7 minutes on each side.
6. Serve and enjoy.

Nutritional Value (Amount per Serving):
Calories 125; Fat 8.8 g; Carbohydrates 11 g; Sugar 5 g; Protein 3.4 g; Cholesterol 0 mg

Cheese Bacon Jalapeno Poppers

Preparation Time: 10 minutes; Cooking Time: 8 minutes; Serve: 10

Ingredients:
- 10 jalapeno peppers, cut in half and remove seeds
- 1/8 tsp onion powder
- 5 bacon strips, cut in half
- 1/3 cup cream cheese, softened
- 1/4 tsp garlic powder

Directions:
1. Preheat the air fryer to 370 F.
2. In a small bowl, mix together cream cheese, garlic powder, and onion powder.
3. Stuff cream cheese into each jalapeno half.
4. Wrap each jalapeno half with half bacon strip and place in air fryer basket and cook for 6-8 minutes.
5. Serve and enjoy.

Nutritional Value (Amount per Serving):
Calories 83; Fat 4.4 g; Carbohydrates 6.3 g; Sugar 1.5 g; Protein 4.8 g; Cholesterol 9 mg

Parmesan Spinach Dip

Preparation Time: 10 minutes; Cooking Time: 40 minutes; Serve: 8

Ingredients:
- 1 cup frozen spinach, thawed and squeeze out all liquid
- 1/3 cup water chestnuts, drained and chopped
- 1 cup mayonnaise
- 1 cup parmesan cheese, grated
- 8 oz cream cheese, softened
- 1/4 tsp garlic powder
- 1/2 cup onion, minced
- 1/2 tsp pepper

Directions:
1. Spray air fryer baking dish with cooking spray.
2. Add all ingredients into the bowl and mix until well combined.
3. Transfer bowl mixture into the prepared dish and place dish in the air fryer basket.
4. Cook at 300 F for 40 minutes.
5. Serve and enjoy.

Nutritional Value (Amount per Serving):
Calories 260; Fat 22.4 g; Carbohydrates 9.6 g; Sugar 2.3 g; Protein 6.7 g; Cholesterol 48 mg

Italian Roasted Pepper Dip

Preparation Time: 10 minutes; Cooking Time: 12 minutes; Serve: 8

Ingredients:
- 8 oz cream cheese, softened
- 1/2 cup roasted red peppers
- 1/3 cup basil pesto
- 1/4 cup parmesan cheese, grated
- 1 cup mozzarella cheese, shredded

Directions:
1. Add parmesan cheese and cream cheese into the food processor and process until smooth.
2. Transfer cheese mixture into the air fryer pan and spread evenly. Pour basil pesto on top of the cheese.
3. Sprinkle roasted pepper on top of basil pesto.
4. Sprinkle mozzarella cheese on top of the pepper layer and place dish in air fryer basket and cook at 250 F for 12 minutes.
5. Serve and enjoy.

Nutritional Value (Amount per Serving):
Calories 122; Fat 11.2 g; Carbohydrates 1.7 g; Sugar 0.6 g; Protein 4.3 g; Cholesterol 35 mg

Yummy Chicken Dip

Preparation Time: 10 minutes; Cooking Time: 25 minutes; Serve: 6

Ingredients:
- 2 cups chicken, cooked and shredded
- 1/2 cup sour cream
- 8 oz cream cheese, softened
- 4 tbsp hot sauce
- 1/4 tsp garlic powder

Directions:
1. Preheat the oven to 350 F.
2. Add all ingredients in a large bowl and mix until well combined.
3. Transfer mixture in a baking dish and bake for 25 minutes.
4. Serve dip with vegetables.

Nutritional Value (Amount per Serving):
Calories 245; Fat 18.7 g; Carbohydrates 2.1 g; Sugar 0.3 g; Protein 17.1 g; Cholesterol 86 mg

Spicy Guacamole

Preparation Time: 10 minutes; Cooking Time: 5 minutes; Serve: 8
Ingredients:
- 2 avocados, halved and pitted
- 2 tbsp fresh cilantro, chopped
- 4 tbsp jalapeno, chopped
- 1 tbsp fresh lime juice
- 1/4 small onion, chopped
- 1/2 tsp sea salt

Directions:
1. Add cilantro, onion, pepper, and salt in a food processor and process into a smooth paste.
2. Scoop out the avocado flesh into a bowl and mash with a fork. Add cilantro paste and lime juice and stir to combine.
3. Serve and enjoy.

Nutritional Value (Amount per Serving):
Calories 106; Fat 9.8 g; Carbohydrates 5.2 g; Sugar 0.5 g; Protein 1 g; Cholesterol 0 mg

Garlic Zucchini Dip

Preparation Time: 5 minutes; Cooking Time: 5 minutes; Serve: 6
Ingredients:
- 1 zucchini, diced
- 2 garlic cloves
- 1/2 cup sunflower seeds
- 1/2 cup olive oil
- 2 tbsp salt

Directions:
1. Add all ingredients into the blender and blend until smooth.
2. Serve and enjoy.

Nutritional Value (Amount per Serving):
Calories 173; Fat 18.8 g; Carbohydrates 2.2 g; Sugar 0.7 g; Protein 1.3 g; Cholesterol 0 mg

Chapter 8: Desserts

Lemon Melon Pops

Preparation Time: 5 minutes; Cooking Time: 5 minutes; Serve: 4
Ingredients:
- 3 cups melon, chopped
- 1 tsp fresh lemon juice

Directions:
1. Add lemon juice and melon into the blender and blend until smooth.
2. Pour blended mixture into the Popsicle molds and place in the freezer for 4 hours or until set.
3. Serve and enjoy.

Nutritional Value (Amount per Serving):
Calories 40; Fat 0.2 g; Carbohydrates 9.6 g; Sugar 9.2 g; Protein 1 g; Cholesterol 0 mg

Lemon Cheesecake Mousse

Preparation Time: 5 minutes; Cooking Time: 5 minutes; Serve: 8
Ingredients:
- 2/3 cup lemon curd
- 1 cup heavy cream
- 8 oz cream cheese
- 1/3 cup Swerve

Directions:
1. Add heavy cream in a large bowl and beat until soft peaks form.
2. In a separate bowl, beat cream cheese until smooth. Add swerve and lemon curd and beat until combined.
3. Pour cream cheese mixture into the heavy cream and mix until combined.
4. Place mousse in the refrigerator for 15 minutes before serving.

Nutritional Value (Amount per Serving):
Calories 231; Fat 23.4 g; Carbohydrates 6.6 g; Sugar 5.4 g; Protein 3.8 g; Cholesterol 118 mg

Delicious Brownie Bites

Preparation Time: 5 minutes; Cooking Time: 5 minutes; Serve: 13
Ingredients:
- 1 cup pecans, chopped
- 1/4 cup unsweetened chocolate chips
- 1/2 tsp vanilla
- 1/4 cup Lakanto monkfruit sweetener
- 1/2 cup almond butter
- 1/4 cup unsweetened cocoa powder
- 1/8 tsp pink salt

Directions:
1. Add all ingredients except chocolate chips into the food processor and process until well combined.
2. Transfer batter into the mixing bowl. Add chocolate chips and mix well.
3. Make 13 even shape balls from mixture and place on parchment lined baking sheet.
4. Place baking sheet in freezer for 20 minutes.
5. Serve and enjoy.

Nutritional Value (Amount per Serving):
Calories 111; Fat 9.9 g; Carbohydrates 4.6 g; Sugar 1.3 g; Protein 2.1 g; Cholesterol 0 mg

Chocolate Chaffle

Preparation Time: 10 minutes; Cooking Time: 8 minutes; Serve: 2
Ingredients:
- 1 egg
- 1 tsp vanilla
- 1 1/2 tbsp erythritol
- 2 tsp unsweetened cocoa powder
- 1 tbsp coconut flour
- 2 oz cream cheese, softened
- 1 tsp butter, melted
- 1 tsp cinnamon
- 1/2 tsp baking soda

Directions:
1. Heat waffle maker and lightly grease.
2. In a bowl, whisk egg with vanilla and cream cheese.
3. Add remaining ingredients and stir until just combined.
4. Pour 1/2 of the batter into the hot waffle maker and cook for 4 minutes.
5. Serve and enjoy.

Nutritional Value (Amount per Serving):
Calories 175; Fat 14.8 g; Carbohydrates 5.1 g; Sugar 0.8 g; Protein 5.8 g; Cholesterol 118 mg

Blueberry Muffins

Preparation Time: 10 minutes; Cooking Time: 30 minutes; Serve: 12
Ingredients:
- 3 eggs
- 1/2 cup fresh blueberries
- 2 tsp baking powder, gluten-free
- 1/4 cup Swerve
- 2 1/2 cups almond flour
- 5.5 oz plain yogurt
- 1/2 tsp vanilla
- Pinch of salt

Directions:
1. Preheat the oven to 325 F. Spray a muffin tray with cooking spray and set aside.
2. In a bowl, whisk together yogurt, vanilla, eggs, and salt until smooth.
3. Add almond flour, baking powder, and swerve and blend again until smooth.
4. Add blueberries and stir well. Pour batter into the prepared muffin tray.
5. Bake for 25-30 minutes.
6. Serve and enjoy.

Nutritional Value (Amount per Serving):
Calories 63; Fat 4.2 g; Carbohydrates 3.6 g; Sugar 1.8 g; Protein 3.4 g; Cholesterol 42 mg

Lemon Strawberry Granita

Preparation Time: 5 minutes; Cooking Time: 5 minutes; Serve: 8
Ingredients:
- 2 lbs strawberries, halved
- 1/2 tsp fresh lemon juice
- 1 cup of water
- 1 tsp liquid stevia
- 1/4 tsp balsamic vinegar
- Pinch of salt

Directions:
1. Add all ingredients into the blender and blend until smooth.
2. Pour blended mixture into the baking dish. Place baking dish in freezer for 45 minutes.
3. After 45 minutes lightly stir the granita mixture using a fork and again place in the freezer for 40 minutes.

4. Stir granita using a fork and serve.

Nutritional Value (Amount per Serving):
Calories 36; Fat 0.3 g; Carbohydrates 8.7 g; Sugar 5.6 g; Protein 0.8 g; Cholesterol 0 mg

Silky Chocolate Mousse

Preparation Time: 5 minutes; Cooking Time: 5 minutes; Serve: 4

Ingredients:
- 1 1/2 cups heavy whipping cream
- 1/3 cup unsweetened cocoa powder
- 2 tbsp Swerve

Directions:
1. Add heavy whipping cream in bowl and beat until thickens.
2. Add cocoa powder and swerve and beat again until stiff peaks form.
3. Pour in serving glasses and place in the refrigerator for 2 hours.
4. Serve and enjoy.

Nutritional Value (Amount per Serving):
Calories 174; Fat 17.6 g; Carbohydrates 6.2 g; Sugar 0.2 g; Protein 2.3 g; Cholesterol 62 mg

Avocado Coconut Pops

Preparation Time: 5 minutes; Cooking Time: 5 minutes; Serve: 6

Ingredients:
- 2 avocados, pitted
- 2 tbsp fresh lime juice
- 1/4 cup Swerve
- 1 1/2 cups unsweetened coconut milk

Directions:
1. Add all ingredients into the blender and blend until smooth.
2. Pour into the Popsicle molds and place them in the refrigerator until set.
3. Serve and enjoy.

Nutritional Value (Amount per Serving):
Calories 162; Fat 16 g; Carbohydrates 5.6 g; Sugar 2.3 g; Protein 1.8 g; Cholesterol 0 mg

Cinnamon Protein Bars

Preparation Time: 10 minutes; Cooking Time: 10 minutes; Serve: 8

Ingredients:
- 2 scoops vanilla protein powder
- 1/4 cup coconut oil, melted
- 1 cup almond butter
- 1/2 tsp cinnamon
- 15 drops liquid stevia
- Pinch of salt

Directions:
1. In a bowl, mix together all ingredients until well combined.
2. Transfer bar mixture into a baking dish and press down evenly. Place in refrigerator until firm.
3. Slice and serve.

Nutritional Value (Amount per Serving):
Calories 99; Fat 8 g; Carbohydrates 0.6 g; Sugar 0.2 g; Protein 7.2 g; Cholesterol 0 mg

Lemon Yogurt Muffins

Preparation Time: 10 minutes; Cooking Time: 15 minutes; Serve: 12
Ingredients:
- 2 eggs
- 1 fresh lemon juice
- 1 tbsp lemon zest
- 1 tsp baking powder, gluten-free
- 1/4 cup coconut flour
- 1 cup almond flour
- 1/3 cup swerve
- 1/3 cup butter, melted
- 1/2 cup yogurt

Directions:
1. Preheat the oven to 350 F. Spray a muffin tray with cooking spray and set aside.
2. Add all ingredients into the mixing bowl and mix until just combined.
3. Pour batter into the prepared muffin tray and bake for 12-15 minutes.
4. Serve and enjoy.

Nutritional Value (Amount per Serving):
Calories 96; Fat 8.2 g; Carbohydrates 3.4 g; Sugar 1.3 g; Protein 2.7 g; Cholesterol 41 mg

Peanut Butter Chaffle

Preparation Time: 10 minutes; Cooking Time: 8 minutes; Serve: 2
Ingredients:
- 1 egg
- 1/2 cup mozzarella cheese, shredded
- 2 tbsp peanut butter
- 3 tbsp Swerve

Directions:
1. Heat waffle iron.
2. In a small bowl, mix together egg, cheese, Swerve, and peanut butter.
3. Pour 1/2 of the batter into the waffle iron and cook for 4 minutes.
4. Serve and enjoy.

Nutritional Value (Amount per Serving):
Calories 153; Fat 11.5 g; Carbohydrates 6.6 g; Sugar 1.7 g; Protein 8.8 g; Cholesterol 86 mg

Vanilla Blackberry Yogurt

Preparation Time: 5 minutes; Cooking Time: 5 minutes; Serve: 6
Ingredients:
- 4 cups frozen unsweetened blackberries
- 1 tbsp fresh lemon juice
- 1 cup yogurt
- 1 tsp vanilla

Directions:
1. Add all ingredients into the blender and blend until smooth.
2. Pour blended mixture into the air-tight container and place in the freezer for 2 hours.
3. Serve and enjoy.

Nutritional Value (Amount per Serving):
Calories 48; Fat 0.6 g; Carbohydrates 7 g; Sugar 5.7 g; Protein 2.6 g; Cholesterol 2 mg

Vanilla Coconut Bars

Preparation Time: 10 minutes; Cooking Time: 10 minutes; Serve: 24
Ingredients:

- 1/2 cup coconut cream
- 3 cups unsweetened desiccated coconut
- 1/4 tsp vanilla
- 1/4 cup of coconut oil
- 1/2 cup erythritol

Directions:
1. Line 8*5-inch baking pan with parchment paper and set aside.
2. Add all ingredients into the blender and blend until sticky mixture form.
3. Transfer coconut mixture in prepared baking pan. Spread mixture evenly and place in refrigerator for 15 minutes.
4. Slice and serve.

Nutritional Value (Amount per Serving):
Calories 71; Fat 7.3 g; Carbohydrates 1.5 g; Sugar 0.6 g; Protein 0.5 g; Cholesterol 0 mg

Pumpkin Cheese Ice Bombs

Preparation Time: 5 minutes; Cooking Time: 5 minutes; Serve: 12
Ingredients:
- 3 eggs
- 1/2 cup pumpkin puree
- 1/2 cup cottage cheese
- 1 tsp cinnamon
- 1/4 cup Swerve
- 8 oz cream cheese

Directions:
1. Add all ingredients into the blender and blend until smooth.
2. Pour blended mixture into the small silicone muffin molds and place them in the freezer until set.
3. Serve and enjoy.

Nutritional Value (Amount per Serving):
Calories 94; Fat 7.9 g; Carbohydrates 1.9 g; Sugar 0.5 g; Protein 4.2 g; Cholesterol 62 mg

Chocolate Ice Cream

Preparation Time: 10 minutes; Cooking Time: 10 minutes; Serve: 12
Ingredients:
- 4 egg yolks
- 4 eggs
- 1/2 cup unsweetened almond milk
- 1/4 cup unsweetened cocoa powder
- 1/4 cup Swerve
- 2 tsp vanilla
- 4 tbsp MCT oil
- 3/4 cup of coconut oil
- Pinch of salt

Directions:
1. Add all ingredients into the blender and blend until smooth.
2. Pour blended mixture into the ice cream maker and churn according to machine instructions.
3. Store in an airtight container in the freezer.
4. Serve and enjoy.

Nutritional Value (Amount per Serving):
Calories 198; Fat 21.7 g; Carbohydrates 1.5 g; Sugar 0.3 g; Protein 3.1 g; Cholesterol 125 mg

Vanilla Almond Ice Bombs

Preparation Time: 5 minutes; Cooking Time: 5 minutes; Serve: 8
Ingredients:

- 1 cup unsweetened almond milk
- 1 cup heavy cream
- 1 tsp vanilla
- 1/4 cup Swerve

Directions:
1. Add all ingredients into the blender and blend until well combined.
2. Pour bended mixture into the small silicone muffins molds and place them in the freezer until set.
3. Serve and enjoy.

Nutritional Value (Amount per Serving):
Calories 58; Fat 6 g; Carbohydrates 0.8 g; Sugar 0.1 g; Protein 0.4 g; Cholesterol 21 mg

Delicious Chocolate Fudge

Preparation Time: 10 minutes; Cooking Time: 10 minutes; Serve: 10

Ingredients:
- 1/2 cup cashew butter
- 1/2 cup coconut oil
- 1/2 cup unsweetened chocolate chips

Directions:
1. Line 9*5-inch loaf pan with parchment paper and set aside.
2. Add all ingredients into the double boiler over medium heat until melted. Stir well.
3. Pour melted mixture into the prepared pan and place in refrigerator until set.
4. Cut into pieces and serve.

Nutritional Value (Amount per Serving):
Calories 249; Fat 23.6 g; Carbohydrates 6.7 g; Sugar 0.6 g; Protein 3.9 g; Cholesterol 0 mg

Choco Cheese Fat Bombs

Preparation Time: 5 minutes; Cooking Time: 5 minutes; Serve: 12

Ingredients:
- 5.5 oz mascarpone cheese
- 7 oz unsweetened chocolate, grated
- 1/4 cup Swerve

Directions:
1. Add mascarpone cheese and Swerve into the bowl and beat until fluffy.
2. Add grated chocolate and mix well.
3. Spoon mixture into the small silicone muffins molds and place in the freezer until firm.
4. Serve and enjoy.

Nutritional Value (Amount per Serving):
Calories 106; Fat 10.3 g; Carbohydrates 5.4 g; Sugar 0.2 g; Protein 3.6 g; Cholesterol 7 mg

Fudge Bars

Preparation Time: 10 minutes; Cooking Time: 10 minutes; Serve: 36

Ingredients:
- 1 cup unsweetened peanut butter
- 8 oz cream cheese
- 1 tsp vanilla
- 1 cup butter
- 1/2 cup whey protein powder
- 1 tsp stevia
- 1 cup erythritol

Directions:
1. Grease baking pan and line with parchment paper. Set aside.

2. Melt butter and cream cheese in a saucepan over medium heat. Add peanut butter and stir to combine. Remove pan from heat.
3. Add remaining ingredients and blend until just combined.
4. Pour mixture into the prepared pan and spread evenly.
5. Place in refrigerator for 1-2 hours or until set.
6. Slice and serve.

Nutritional Value (Amount per Serving):
Calories 111; Fat 11g; Carbohydrates 1.6 g; Sugar 0.3 g; Protein 2.6 g; Cholesterol 21 mg

Strawberry Ice Cream

Preparation Time: 5 minutes; Cooking Time: 5 minutes; Serve: 10
Ingredients:
- 12 oz strawberries
- 1 1/2 cups heavy cream
- 1/2 tsp vanilla
- 1 1/2 cups sour cream
- 1/2 cup Swerve

Directions:
1. Add 1/4 cup sweetener and strawberries into a blender and blend until pureed.
2. In a large bowl, whisk the strawberry mixture, vanilla, and sour cream until combined.
3. In a separate bowl, beat heavy cream with remaining Swerve until stiff peaks form.
4. Gently fold heavy cream mixture into the strawberry mixture and pour it into the air-tight container. Place in the freezer for 6-8 hours or until firm.
5. Serve and enjoy.

Nutritional Value (Amount per Serving):
Calories 148; Fat 14 g; Carbohydrates 4.7 g; Sugar 1.8 g; Protein 1.7 g; Cholesterol 40 mg

Whipped Cream & Fresh Berries

Preparation Time: 5 minutes; Cooking Time: 5 minutes; Serve: 2
Ingredients:
- 2/3 cup heavy whipping cream
- 1/4 cup fresh strawberries, sliced
- 1/2 cup fresh raspberries
- 1/4 cup fresh blueberries
- 1/4 tsp vanilla

Directions:
1. Add heavy whipping cream in a large bowl and beat until soft peaks form. Add vanilla and fold well.
2. Serve immediately with fresh berries.

Nutritional Value (Amount per Serving):
Calories 172; Fat 15.1 g; Carbohydrates 8.9 g; Sugar 4.2 g; Protein 1.5 g; Cholesterol 55 mg

Almond Peanut Butter Bars

Preparation Time: 10 minutes; Cooking Time: 30 minutes; Serve: 9
Ingredients:
- 2 eggs
- 1/2 cup erythritol
- 1/2 cup butter softened
- 1/2 cup peanut butter
- 1 tbsp coconut flour
- 1/4 cup almond flour

Directions:

1. Grease 9*9-inch baking pan with cooking spray and set aside.
2. In a bowl, beat together butter, eggs, and peanut butter until well combined.
3. Add dry ingredients and mix until a smooth batter is formed.
4. Spread batter in prepared baking pan.
5. Bake at 350 F for 30 minutes.
6. Slice and serve.

Nutritional Value (Amount per Serving):
Calories 203; Fat 17.1 g; Carbohydrates 6.8 g; Sugar 2.9 g; Protein 9.2 g; Cholesterol 36 mg

Chocolate Cake

Preparation Time: 10 minutes; Cooking Time: 30 minutes; Serve: 12
Ingredients:
- 6 eggs
- 10.5 oz butter, melted
- 10.5 oz unsweetened chocolate, melted
- 1 1/2 cup erythritol
- 1/2 cup almond flour
- Pinch of salt

Directions:
1. Preheat the oven to 350 F. Grease 8-inch spring-form cake pan with butter and set aside.
2. In a large bowl, beat eggs until foamy. Add sweetener and stir well.
3. Add melted butter, chocolate, almond flour, and salt and stir until combined.
4. Pour batter in the prepared cake pan and bake for 30 minutes.
5. Remove cake from oven and allow to cool completely.
6. Slice and serve.

Nutritional Value (Amount per Serving):
Calories 360; Fat 37.6 g; Carbohydrates 8.6 g; Sugar 0.6 g; Protein 7.2 g; Cholesterol 135 mg

Pecan Carrot Cake

Preparation Time: 10 minutes; Cooking Time: 35 minutes; Serve: 16
Ingredients:
- 2 eggs
- 1/4 cup pecans, chopped
- 6 tbsp erythritol
- 3/4 cup almond flour
- 1/2 tsp vanilla
- 2 tbsp butter, melted
- 1/2 cup carrots, grated
- 1/8 tsp ground cloves
- 1 tsp cinnamon
- 1 tsp baking powder
- 2 tbsp unsweetened shredded coconut
- Pinch of salt

Directions:
1. Preheat the oven to 325 F. Spray cake pan with cooking spray and set aside.
2. In a large bowl, whisk together almond flour, cloves, cinnamon, baking powder, shredded coconut, nuts, sweetener, and salt.
3. Stir in eggs, vanilla, butter, and shredded coconut until just combined.
4. Pour batter into the prepared cake pan and bake for 30-35 minutes.
5. Slice and serve.

Nutritional Value (Amount per Serving):
Calories 53; Fat 4.9 g; Carbohydrates 1.6 g; Sugar 0.5 g; Protein 1.3 g; Cholesterol 24 mg

Peanut Butter Chocolate Fudge

Preparation Time: 5 minutes; Cooking Time: 5 minutes; Serve: 8
Ingredients:
- 1 tbsp cocoa powder
- 4 tbsp peanut butter
- 1 tbsp cocoa nibs
- 8 drops liquid stevia
- 4 tbsp butter
- 1 tbsp coconut oil

Directions:
1. Add all ingredients in a pan except cocoa nibs and heat over the medium-low heat until melted.
2. Pour the mixture into the fudge tray and sprinkle cocoa nibs on top.
3. Place the tray in the refrigerator for 1 hour.
4. Once fudge set then cut into the pieces and serve.

Nutritional Value (Amount per Serving):
Calories 121; Fat 11.9 g; Carbohydrates 2.7 g; Sugar 1 g; Protein 2.3 g; Cholesterol 15 mg

Chocolate Frosty

Preparation Time: 5 minutes; Cooking Time: 5 minutes; Serve: 4
Ingredients:
- 1 cup heavy whipping cream
- 2 tbsp unsweetened cocoa powder
- 1 tbsp almond butter
- 1 tsp vanilla
- 8 drops liquid stevia

Directions:
1. Add all ingredients into the large bowl and beat using a hand mixer until soft peaks form.
2. Place in refrigerator for 1 hour.
3. Add frosty in piping bag and pipe into serving cups.
4. Serve and enjoy.

Nutritional Value (Amount per Serving):
Calories 137; Fat 13.7 g; Carbohydrates 3.2 g; Sugar 0.4 g; Protein 2 g; Cholesterol 41 mg

Berry Cheesecake Ice Bombs

Preparation Time: 5 minutes; Cooking Time: 5 minutes; Serve: 16
Ingredients:
- 3/4 cup of frozen mix berries
- 1 tsp vanilla
- 8 oz cream cheese, softened
- 2 tbsp Swerve
- 2 tbsp coconut oil

Directions:
1. Add all ingredients into the blender and blend until smooth.
2. Spoon blended mixture into the ice cube tray and place in the freezer until set.
3. Serve and enjoy.

Nutritional Value (Amount per Serving):
Calories 69; Fat 6.6 g; Carbohydrates 1.6 g; Sugar 0.8 g; Protein 1.1 g; Cholesterol 16 mg

Raspberry Cheese Bites

Preparation Time: 5 minutes; Cooking Time: 5 minutes; Serve: 24
Ingredients:

- 1/2 cup raspberries, halved
- 1/2 cup butter, softened
- 1/4 cup Swerve
- 1 tsp vanilla
- 1/4 cup unsweetened chocolate chips
- 8 oz cream cheese, softened

Directions:
1. Line baking sheet with parchment paper and set aside.
2. Add all ingredients into the bowl and mix until well combined. Place in refrigerator for 1 hour.
3. Once the mixture is chilled then scoop 1 tablespoon scoops and place onto the prepared baking dish. Place in the refrigerator for 1-2 hours.
4. Serve and enjoy.

Nutritional Value (Amount per Serving):
Calories 85; Fat 8.5 g; Carbohydrates 1.3 g; Sugar 0.2 g; Protein 1.1 g; Cholesterol 21 mg

Delicious Lemon Cake

Preparation Time: 10 minutes; Cooking Time: 60 minutes; Serve: 10
Ingredients:
- 4 eggs
- 1 tbsp vanilla
- 1/2 cup butter softened
- 2 tsp baking powder
- 1/4 cup coconut flour
- 2 cups almond flour
- 2 tbsp lemon zest
- 1/2 cup fresh lemon juice
- 1/4 cup erythritol

Directions:
1. Preheat the oven to 300 F. Grease 9-inch loaf pan with butter and set aside.
2. In a large bowl, whisk all ingredients until a smooth batter is formed.
3. Pour batter into the loaf pan and bake for 60 minutes.
4. Slice and serve.

Nutritional Value (Amount per Serving):
Calories 255; Fat 22.7 g; Carbohydrates 7.7 g; Sugar 1.6 g; Protein 7.6 g; Cholesterol 90 mg

Butter Cake

Preparation Time: 10 minutes; Cooking Time: 35 minutes; Serve: 9
Ingredients:
- 5 eggs
- 1 cup Swerve
- 4 oz cream cheese, softened
- 1 tsp vanilla
- 1 tsp orange extract
- 1 tsp baking powder
- 6.5 oz almond flour
- 1/2 cup butter, softened

Directions:
1. Preheat the oven to 350 F. Spray 9-inch cake pan with cooking spray and set aside.
2. Add all ingredients into the mixing bowl and whisk until batter is fluffy.
3. Pour batter into the prepared pan and bake for 35-40 minutes.
4. Remove cake from oven and set aside to cool completely.
5. Slices and serve.

Nutritional Value (Amount per Serving):
Calories 287; Fat 27.2 g; Carbohydrates 5.4 g; Sugar 1 g; Protein 8.5 g; Cholesterol 132 mg

Vanilla Custard

Preparation Time: 10 minutes; Cooking Time: 40 minutes; Serve: 6
Ingredients:
- 2 egg yolks
- 3 eggs
- 1/2 cup erythritol
- 2 cups heavy whipping cream
- 1/2 tsp vanilla
- 1 tsp nutmeg

Directions:
1. Preheat the oven to 350 F.
2. Add all ingredients into the large bowl and beat until just combined.
3. Pour custard mixture into the greased pie dish.
4. Bake in preheated oven for 40 minutes.
5. Remove from the oven and let it cool completely then place in the freezer for 2 hours.
6. Serve and enjoy.

Nutritional Value (Amount per Serving):
Calories 190; Fat 18.6 g; Carbohydrates 1.7 g; Sugar 0.4 g; Protein 4.5 g; Cholesterol 207 mg

Almond Peanut Butter Fat Bombs

Preparation Time: 5 minutes; Cooking Time: 5 minutes; Serve: 8
Ingredients:
- 3/4 cup almond flour
- 4 tbsp erythritol
- 2 tbsp peanut butter

Directions:
1. Add all ingredients into the bowl and mix until well combined.
2. Cover bowl and place in the freezer until the mixture is firm.
3. Remove from the refrigerator and make small balls from the mixture.
4. Serve and enjoy.

Nutritional Value (Amount per Serving):
Calories 39; Fat 3.3 g; Carbohydrates 1.4 g; Sugar 0.5 g; Protein 1.6 g; Cholesterol 0 mg

Smooth Peanut Butter Mousse

Preparation Time: 5 minutes; Cooking Time: 5 minutes; Serve: 5
Ingredients:
- 3/4 cup heavy cream
- 3 oz cream cheese, softened
- 1/4 cup Swerve
- 2 tbsp peanut butter powder
- 1/4 cup peanut butter

Directions:
1. Add all ingredients in a large bowl and beat using a hand mixer until thick and creamy.
2. Pipe mousse into serving cups and place in the refrigerator for 1-2 hours.
3. Serve and enjoy.

Nutritional Value (Amount per Serving):
Calories 214; Fat 19.5 g; Carbohydrates 4.8 g; Sugar 2.5 g; Protein 6.1 g; Cholesterol 43 mg

Blackberry Ice Cream

Preparation Time: 5 minutes; Cooking Time: 10 minutes; Serve: 8

Ingredients:
- 1 egg yolks
- 1 1/2 cup heavy whipping cream
- 1 cup blackberries
- 1/2 cup erythritol

Directions:
1. Add all ingredients to the bowl and blend until well combined.
2. Pour ice cream mixture into the ice cream maker and churn ice cream according to the machine instructions.
3. Serve and enjoy.

Nutritional Value (Amount per Serving):
Calories 92; Fat 9 g; Carbohydrates 2.4 g; Sugar 0.9 g; Protein 1.1 g; Cholesterol 57 mg

Vanilla Pumpkin Ice Cream

Preparation Time: 5 minutes; Cooking Time: 5 minutes; Serve: 5

Ingredients:
- 2 cups heavy whipping cream
- 1 tbsp vanilla
- 1/2 cup pumpkin puree
- 1 1/2 tsp liquid stevia
- 2 tsp pumpkin pie spice

Directions:
1. Add all ingredients into the food processor and process until fluffy.
2. Transfer ice cream mixture in air-tight container and place in the freezer for 1 hour.
3. Remove ice cream mixture from refrigerator and whisk until smooth.
4. Again place in the refrigerator for 2 hours.
5. Serve chilled and enjoy.

Nutritional Value (Amount per Serving):
Calories 184; Fat 17.9 g; Carbohydrates 4.1 g; Sugar 1.2 g; Protein 1.3 g; Cholesterol 66 mg

Coffee Fat Bombs

Preparation Time: 5 minutes; Cooking Time: 5 minutes; Serve: 10

Ingredients:
- 1 tbsp cocoa powder, unsweetened
- 2 tbsp heavy cream
- 4 tbsp butter
- 4 tbsp coconut oil
- 10 drops of liquid stevia
- 1/2 tsp coffee extract

Directions:
1. Add coconut oil and butter in microwave-safe bowl microwave for 30 seconds.
2. Add heavy cream, cocoa powder, coffee extract, and liquid stevia in coconut oil mixture. Stir well.
3. Pour mixture into the mold and place it in the refrigerator for 1 hour.
4. Serve and enjoy.

Nutritional Value (Amount per Serving):
Calories 99; Fat 11.2 g; Carbohydrates 0.4 g; Sugar 0 g; Protein 0.2 g; Cholesterol 16 mg

Berry Yogurt

Preparation Time: 10 minutes; Cooking Time: 10 minutes; Serve: 6

Ingredients:
- 1 cup mixed berries
- 1 cup coconut cream
- 2 tbsp erythritol
- 1/2 lemon juice
- 1 tsp vanilla

Directions:
1. In a bowl, whisk together coconut cream, sweetener, lemon juice, and vanilla and place in the freezer for 30 minutes.
2. Add berries and frozen coconut cream mixture into the blender and blend until smooth.
3. Transfer blended mixture in container and place in the refrigerator for 1-2 hours.
4. Serve and enjoy.

Nutritional Value (Amount per Serving):
Calories 108; Fat 9.7 g; Carbohydrates 5.2 g; Sugar 3.2 g; Protein 1.1 g; Cholesterol 0 mg

Delicious Lemon Mousse

Preparation Time: 5 minutes; Cooking Time: 5 minutes; Serve: 2
Ingredients:
- 15 oz can unsweetened coconut milk
- 1/2 tsp lemon extract
- 15 drops liquid stevia
- Pinch of turmeric

Directions:
1. Place coconut milk in the refrigerator overnight. Scoop out thick cream into a large bowl.
2. Add remaining ingredients to the bowl and beat using a hand mixer until smooth.
3. Transfer mousse mixture into a piping bag and pipe into serving cups.
4. Place in refrigerator.
5. Serve and enjoy.

Nutritional Value (Amount per Serving):
Calories 376; Fat 39.9 g; Carbohydrates 5.5 g; Sugar 5.5 g; Protein 2.7 g; Cholesterol 0 mg

Cocoa Butter Raspberry Candy

Preparation Time: 5 minutes; Cooking Time: 5 minutes; Serve: 12
Ingredients:
- 2 oz cocoa butter
- 1/2 cup dried raspberries
- 1/4 cup Swerve
- 1/2 cup coconut oil

Directions:
1. Melt cocoa butter and coconut oil in a saucepan over low heat.
2. Remove saucepan pan from heat.
3. Grind the raspberries in a blender.
4. Add swerve and ground raspberries to the saucepan and stir well.
5. Pour mixture into the silicone candy molds and place them in the freezer until set.
6. Serve and enjoy.

Nutritional Value (Amount per Serving):
Calories 101; Fat 11.5 g; Carbohydrates 0.7 g; Sugar 0.2 g; Protein 0.1 g; Cholesterol 0 mg

Coconut Butter Fat Bombs

Preparation Time: 5 minutes; Cooking Time: 5 minutes; Serve: 8
Ingredients:
- 1/4 cup unsweetened cocoa powder
- 1/2 cup coconut butter
- 1/4 cup coconut oil, melted

- 1 tbsp liquid stevia
- Pinch of salt

Directions:
1. Add all ingredients into the bowl and beat using a hand mixer until smooth.
2. Pour mixture into the silicone candy molds and place them in the freezer until set.
3. Serve and enjoy.

Nutritional Value (Amount per Serving):
Calories 85; Fat 9.1 g; Carbohydrates 2.2 g; Sugar 0.2 g; Protein 0.7 g; Cholesterol 0 mg

Coconut Butter Pops

Preparation Time: 5 minutes; Cooking Time: 5 minutes; Serve: 12
Ingredients:
- 1/2 cup peanut butter, sugar-free
- 2 cans of coconut milk
- 1 tsp liquid stevia

Directions:
1. Add all ingredients into the blender and blend until smooth.
2. Pour mixture into the popsicle molds and place in the refrigerator for 3 hours or until set.
3. Serve and enjoy.

Nutritional Value (Amount per Serving):
Calories 102; Fat 9.4 g; Carbohydrates 3 g; Sugar 1.6 g; Protein 3.1 g; Cholesterol 0 mg

Choco Peppermint Mousse

Preparation Time: 5 minutes; Cooking Time: 5 minutes; Serve: 4
Ingredients:
- 1 1/4 cup heavy cream
- 4 drop peppermint stevia
- 4 oz cream cheese
- 1/2 cup cocoa powder, unsweetened
- 1/2 tsp peppermint extract

Directions:
1. Add all ingredients into the blender and blend until smooth.
2. Pour mixture into the serving glasses and place in the refrigerator.
3. Serve and enjoy.

Nutritional Value (Amount per Serving):
Calories 254; Fat 25.2 g; Carbohydrates 7.8 g; Sugar 0.4 g; Protein 4.9 g; Cholesterol 83 mg

Almond Butter Fat Bombs

Preparation Time: 5 minutes; Cooking Time: 5 minutes; Serve: 6
Ingredients:
- 1/4 cup almond butter
- 1/4 cup Swerve
- 2 tbsp unsweetened cocoa powder
- 1/4 cup of coconut oil

Directions:
1. Add coconut oil and almond butter in a microwave-safe bowl and microwave for 30 seconds. Stir until smooth.
2. Add cocoa powder and Swerve and stir well.
3. Pour into mini silicone muffin molds and place in refrigerator until firm.
4. Serve and enjoy.

Nutritional Value (Amount per Serving):

Calories 87; Fat 9.7 g; Carbohydrates 1.2 g; Sugar 0.1 g; Protein 0.5 g; Cholesterol 0 mg

Raspberry Cheese Fat Bombs

Preparation Time: 5 minutes; Cooking Time: 5 minutes; Serve: 8
Ingredients:
- 1 cup raspberries
- 2 tbsp Swerve
- 3/4 cup cream cheese
- 1/4 cup of coconut oil
- 1 tsp vanilla

Directions:
1. Add all ingredients into the blender and blend until smooth.
2. Pour into the ice cube tray and place in the refrigerator until set.
3. Serve and enjoy.

Nutritional Value (Amount per Serving):
Calories 145; Fat 14.5g; Carbohydrates 3 g; Sugar 0.8 g; Protein 1.8 g; Cholesterol 24 mg

Chocolate Custard

Preparation Time: 10 minutes; Cooking Time: 40 minutes; Serve: 4
Ingredients:
- 2 eggs
- 2 tbsp unsweetened cocoa powder
- 1 cup heavy whipping cream
- 1 cup unsweetened almond milk
- 1/4 cup Swerve
- 1 tsp orange zest
- 1 tsp vanilla
- Pinch of salt

Directions:
1. Preheat the oven to 325 F.
2. Place ramekins in a baking dish and set aside.
3. Add all ingredients into the blender and blend until well combined.
4. Pour mixture into the ramekins.
5. Pour hot water into the baking dish up to halfway through ramekins.
6. Place baking dish in the oven and bake for 35-40 minutes.
7. Remove from oven and allow to cool completely.
8. Serve and enjoy.

Nutritional Value (Amount per Serving):
Calories 155; Fat 14.5 g; Carbohydrates 3.4 g; Sugar 0.4 g; Protein 4.2 g; Cholesterol 123 mg

Mint Ice Cream

Preparation Time: 5 minutes; Cooking Time: 5 minutes; Serve: 8
Ingredients:
- 1 egg yolk
- 1 1/2 cups heavy whipping cream
- 1/4 tsp peppermint extract
- 1/2 cup erythritol

Directions:
1. Add all ingredients to the bowl and blend until well combined.
2. Pour ice cream mixture into the ice cream maker and churn ice cream according to the machine instructions.
3. Serve and enjoy.

Nutritional Value (Amount per Serving):

Calories 85; Fat 8.9 g; Carbohydrates 0.7 g; Sugar 0.1 g; Protein 0.8 g; Cholesterol 57 mg

Berry Sorbet

Preparation Time: 5 minutes; Cooking Time: 5 minutes; Serve: 1
Ingredients:
- 1/2 cup frozen raspberries
- 1 tsp fresh lemon juice
- 1/2 tsp liquid stevia
- 1/2 cup frozen strawberries

Directions:
1. Add all ingredients into the blender and blend until smooth.
2. Pour into the container and place it in the freezer for 3 hours.
3. Serve chilled and enjoy.

Nutritional Value (Amount per Serving):
Calories 29; Fat 0 g; Carbohydrates 8.6 g; Sugar 4.1 g; Protein 1.5 g; Cholesterol 0 mg

Raspberry Coconut Pudding

Preparation Time: 5 minutes; Cooking Time: 5 minutes; Serve: 2
Ingredients:
- 1/2 cup raspberries
- 4 tbsp chia seeds
- 1 cup unsweetened coconut milk

Directions:
1. Add all ingredients into the blender and blend until smooth.
2. Pour into the glass jar and place it in the freezer for 3 hours.
3. Serve chilled and enjoy.

Nutritional Value (Amount per Serving):
Calories 160; Fat 12.9 g; Carbohydrates 11 g; Sugar 2.5 g; Protein 3.3 g; Cholesterol 0 mg

Delicious Strawberry Yogurt

Preparation Time: 5 minutes; Cooking Time: 5 minutes; Serve: 8
Ingredients:
- 4 cups frozen strawberries
- 1 tbsp fresh lemon juice
- 1/2 cup plain yogurt
- 1 tsp liquid stevia

Directions:
1. Add all ingredients into the blender and blend until yogurt is smooth.
2. Serve immediately and enjoy it.

Nutritional Value (Amount per Serving):
Calories 36; Fat 0.2 g; Carbohydrates 7.6 g; Sugar 5.6 g; Protein 0.9 g; Cholesterol 1 mg

Lemon Ricotta Cheesecake

Preparation Time: 10 minutes; Cooking Time: 55 minutes; Serve: 8
Ingredients:
- 4 eggs
- 1 fresh lemon zest
- 18 oz ricotta cheese
- 2 tbsp swerve
- 1 fresh lemon juice

Directions:
1. Preheat the oven to 350 F. Spray cake pan with cooking spray and set aside.

2. In a large bowl, beat ricotta cheese until smooth. Add egg one by one and whisk well.
3. Add lemon juice, lemon zest, and swerve and mix well.
4. Transfer mixture into the prepared cake pan and bake for 50-55 minutes.
5. Remove cake from oven and set aside to cool completely.
6. Place cake in the refrigerator for 1-2 hours.
7. Slice and serve.

Nutritional Value (Amount per Serving):
Calories 122; Fat 7.3 g; Carbohydrates 4.2 g; Sugar 0.5 g; Protein 10.1 g; Cholesterol 102 mg

Chapter 9: 21-Day Meal Plan
Week One of the keto Diet Meal plan

Monday
Breakfast: Spinach Egg Scramble
Lunch: Simple Cajun Salmon
Dinner: Creamy Garlic Butter Chicken

Tuesday
Breakfast: Cauliflower Breakfast Casserole
Lunch: Flavorful Deviled Egg Salad
Dinner: Delicious Chicken Cacciatore

Wednesday
Breakfast: Jalapeno Breakfast Casserole
Lunch: Southern Chicken Salad
Dinner: Easy Pulled Pork

Thursday
Breakfast: Sausage Ricotta Cheese Casserole
Lunch: Quick Cajun Shrimp
Dinner: Lemon Pepper Chicken

Friday
Breakfast: Easy Cheese Quiche
Lunch: Keto Italian Salad
Dinner: Flavorful Chili Lime Chicken

Saturday
Breakfast: Broccoli Egg Bake
Lunch: Classic Chicken Salad
Dinner: Keto Butter Beef

Sunday
Breakfast: Ranch Breakfast Quiche
Lunch: White Fish Fillets
Dinner: Roasted Pepper Artichoke Chicken

Week Two of the Keto Diet Meal Plan

Monday
Breakfast: Cauliflower Casserole
Lunch: Shrimp Avocado Salad

Dinner: Cajun Chicken Stew

Tuesday

Breakfast: Baked Breakfast Egg

Lunch: Flavorful Blackened Shrimp

Dinner: Pesto Chicken

Wednesday

Breakfast: Healthy Veggie Frittata

Lunch: Flavors Salmon Salad

Dinner: Cheesy Chicken Casserole

Thursday

Breakfast: Breakfast Cheese Tomato Quiche

Lunch: Balsamic Chicken

Dinner: Curried Pork Chops

Friday

Breakfast: Delicious Cheese Bacon Quiche

Lunch: Parmesan Garlic Shrimp

Dinner: Chicken with Mushrooms

Saturday

Breakfast: Cheese Ham Baked Omelet

Lunch: Easy Bacon Ranch Chicken Salad

Dinner: Lamb Chops

Sunday

Breakfast: Sausage Zucchini Casserole

Lunch: Chicken Cheese Casserole

Dinner: Lamb Roast

Week Three of the Keto Diet Meal Plan

Monday

Breakfast: Spinach Egg Scramble

Lunch: Baked Halibut

Dinner: Classic Pork Cacciatore

Tuesday

Breakfast: Spicy Scrambled Egg

Lunch: Chicken Broccoli Casserole

Dinner: Pork Roast

Wednesday

Breakfast: Mexican Frittata
Lunch: Italian Baked Pesto Chicken
Dinner: Italian Beef Chuck Roast

Thursday

Breakfast: Simple Asparagus Omelet
Lunch: Baked Swordfish Fillets
Dinner: Rosemary Lamb Roast

Friday

Breakfast: Spinach Kale Egg Bake
Lunch: Flavorful Chicken Casserole
Dinner: Chili Chuck Roast

Saturday

Breakfast: Cheesy Zucchini Quiche
Lunch: Baked Basa Fillets
Dinner: Beef Ribs

Sunday

Breakfast: Cauliflower Breakfast Casserole
Lunch: Avocado Salmon Salad
Dinner: Juicy & Tender Chuck Roast

Conclusion

When people pursue weight loss without guidance, they often end up just skipping random meals and eating unsatisfying "diet" foods to lose weight fast. Consequently their health suffers. By using these recipes and meal plans to make your own meals, you can take control of your health and weight. I want this Weight Loss Meal Prep cookbook to transcend the myths that delicious meals don't have a place in low-calorie diet, and that to lose weight, you have to give up your favorite foods and suffer through endless bland salads. I also want to provide you with valuable tips on how to make low-calorie eating a seamless habit in your lifestyle and how to keep the weight off long after you've succeeded in reaching your goals.

Thank you for buying this book. Now let's start your gourmet journey!

www.ingramcontent.com/pod-product-compliance
Lightning Source LLC
Chambersburg PA
CBHW081357070526
44583CB00020B/2582